Ecological Imperialism, Development, and the Capitalist World-System

Two major trends are currently challenging the sustainability of human civilization: extreme inequality and the ecological crisis. This book argues that these are intrinsically linked by further exploring the complex relationships between global ecological crises, neoliberal globalization, orthodox development policies, and imperialism.

Drawn from extensive theoretical, historical, policy, and empirical research, as well as fieldwork in Africa and Asia, this book examines the crucial characteristics of the capitalist world-system and how it enables and drives ecological imperialism. Neoliberal globalization has allowed for capital's unfettered access to and exploitation of Nature across the planet, and neoliberal development policies have reinforced a contemporary form of ecological imperialism where the environments of the Global South are enclosed and exploited, and local communities are dispossessed of their land and livelihoods. Simultaneously, resources from the Global South are funneled to the Global North in the form of consumer goods and ecologically unequal exchange, while the profits from those resources are siphoned away to transnational corporations, financiers, and government elites. This work traces the historical development of free market policies, while also paying special attention to the role of Northern international financial institutions, emerging economies (the semi-periphery), and the often-hidden role of international finance in ecological imperialism.

This volume will be of keen interest to scholars and students of political economy, critical development studies, environmental sociology, and political ecology.

Mariko Lin Frame is an Assistant Professor of Economics at Merrimack College, USA, where she teaches courses related to the environment, development, and the global economy. She has lived, researched, and worked extensively in East Africa and Asia.

New Political Economy
General Editor: **Richard McIntyre**, *University of Rhode Island, USA*

Seeking Sustainability
On the Prospect of an Ecological Liberalism
G.J. Paton

Class, Gender, and the American Family Farm in the 20th Century
Elizabeth Ramey

Late Neoclassical Economics
The Restoration of Theoretical Humanism in Contemporary Economic Theory
Yahya M. Madra

From Economics to Political Economy
The Problems, Promises and Solutions of Pluralist Economics
Tim B. Thornton

Cooperatives, the State, and Corporate Power in African Export Agriculture
The Case of Uganda's Coffee Sector
Karin Wedig

Ecological Imperialism, Development, and the Capitalist World-System
Cases from Africa and Asia
Mariko Lin Frame

For more information about this series, please visit: www.routledge.com/New-Political-Economy/book-series/TFSE00174

Ecological Imperialism, Development, and the Capitalist World-System

Cases from Africa and Asia

Mariko Lin Frame

Routledge
Taylor & Francis Group
LONDON AND NEW YORK

First published 2023
by Routledge
4 Park Square, Milton Park, Abingdon, Oxon OX14 4RN

and by Routledge
605 Third Avenue, New York, NY 10158

Routledge is an imprint of the Taylor & Francis Group, an informa business

British Library Cataloguing-in-Publication Data
A catalogue record for this book is available from the British Library

Library of Congress Cataloging-in-Publication Data
Names: Frame, Mariko Lin, author.
Title: Ecological imperialism, development, and the capitalist world-system : cases from Africa and Asia / Mariko Lin Frame.
Description: Abingdon, Oxon ; New York, NY : Routledge, 2023. |
Series: New political economy | Includes bibliographical references and index.
Identifiers: LCCN 2022005596 (print) | LCCN 2022005597 (ebook)
Subjects: LCSH: Economics—Asia. | Economics—Africa. |
Political ecology—Asia. | Political ecology—Africa. | Sustainable development—Asia. | Sustainable development—Africa.
Classification: LCC HC412 .F723 2023 (print) | LCC HC412 (ebook) |
DDC 338.95—dc23/eng/20220610
LC record available at https://lccn.loc.gov/2022005596
LC ebook record available at https://lccn.loc.gov/2022005597

ISBN: 978-0-367-20410-5 (hbk)
ISBN: 978-1-032-31210-1 (pbk)
ISBN: 978-0-429-26130-5 (ebk)

DOI: 10.4324/9780429261305

Typeset in Bembo
by codeMantra

To Spencer Ames

Contents

Preface

By the beginning of the 21st century, ecological crises of such formidable magnitude are threatening the very liveability of our planet for both humanity and many of the non-human species inhabiting it. Ultimately, these ecological crises are socio-ecological—that is, they are the product of a radical restructuring of human societies, economies, and relations to Nature occurring in the past several hundred years. The physical aspect of this restructuring is known as industrialization, the intensive use of machinery in the production process and the dependence on fossil fuels as the primary energy source. However, no form of production ever rises wholly independent of social relations, politics, and economics. Since the Industrial Revolution, industrialization has been thoroughly driven by and embedded in the capitalist mode of production. Beginning with the European colonial conquest that spanned from the Americas to Africa and parts of Asia, capitalism for the past several hundred years has been the dominant socio-economic system globally.

The contradictions between the capitalist mode of production and the environment, where the drive for profit dominates the logic of production, and where the manifold complexity of Nature is transformed into a mere atomized input in the production, have been written about extensively. Likewise in the rapidly burgeoning literature on environmental justice, scholars, activists, and civil society organizations have copiously documented the numerous environmental inequalities perpetuated by a system where profits accrue to a global minority but environmental destruction is shouldered by the marginalized and impoverished. The genesis of this book owes much to both sets of literature, and it attempts to contribute in several important ways.

Specifically, this book seeks to clarify the interrelationships between global ecological crises, neoliberal globalization, orthodox development policies, and imperialism. The particular form of capitalism that currently prevails globally is, to a great extent, laissez-faire or free market capitalism. It is also known, by its critics, as neoliberal capitalism. All of these terms refer to a type of capitalism premised on the removal of any barriers to capital accumulation and the promotion of market-based solutions as the most desirable answers to societal/environmental problems and challenges. Neoliberal capitalism, as this book discusses, is nothing more than the evolution of capitalism since its origins in colonialism and the Industrial Revolution. In this sense, it retains all the basic features of capitalism and is in no way a major departure from its essential workings. However, the hegemonic rise of neoliberal capitalism over the more regulated forms of capitalism of the post-WWII era coincides with the most massive use of the Earth's resources and degradation of Nature that humanity has ever witnessed. Explaining how and why this is the case is an essential aim of this book. As such, one of the major topics this book focuses on is the complex interrelationships between global ecological crises and the three fundamental political economic pillars of the neoliberal global economy—the liberalizations of international trade, international investment, and international finance. The liberalizations of these three pillars of the global economy have, this book argues, allowed for capital's unfettered access to and exploitation of Nature across the planet.

However, this book is ultimately about the Global South and ecological imperialism, not about globalization more broadly. Consequently, the second major aim of this book is to untangle the relationships between the neoliberal development policies that have dominated the development paradigm of the Global South since the developing world debt crises of the 1980s and global environmental issues. This book explores how the dependent position of the Global South was reinforced through a series of changes in neoliberal development policies regarding the aforementioned pillars of the global economy—international trade, international investment, and international finance. Such neoliberal development policies, the book argues, have reinforced the recipient position of the Global South in a global economy characterized by the dominance of large transnational corporations and transnational financial corporations. Neoliberal development policies and the workings of neoliberal globalization have enabled the enclosure, privatization, marketization, and exploitation of Nature in the Global South through such transnationals, while both profits and resources are primarily funneled to wealthier regions. Neoliberal development policies, in other words, have established the foundations for contemporary ecological imperialism.

This book places all of the above issues in historic context, tracing their origins to European colonization and then focusing on the post-WWII era. It includes a discussion of the brief but significant era of economic nationalism, when the Third World sought some form of economic independence and resource sovereignty. By providing the historical context, the book seeks to lay bare the political agenda of neoliberal capitalism and its relation to ecological imperialism. For decades neoliberal policies have been promoted on the seemingly neutral basis of efficiency and economic growth, yet a close examination of case after case of socio-ecological crises in the Global South can be attributed to development policies involving liberalized trade, investment, and finance.

On a more specific level, this book seeks to clarify some topics that are not as thoroughly explored in the extant literature on capitalism and the environment nor in the literature on environmental justice. While Chapters 3 and 4 are devoted to what is traditionally termed the periphery in world-systems theory, Chapter 5 attempts to establish a basic theoretical framework for understanding the role of the semi-periphery in ecological imperialism. With the saturation of capitalist relations of production worldwide, and the industrialization of formerly peripheral regions, emerging economies have become significant loci of accumulation and economic power in their own right. Emerging economies are now significant sources of investment flows into other countries in the Global South, especially into natural resource sectors. However, their role in imperialism is often ignored or, if addressed, is seen through the lens as a rising competition to the West. This lens has produced unfortunately one-sided analyses and Cold War-reminiscent rhetoric, while the reality of the situation is arguably more complex.

While international trade and foreign investment are the more visible forms of ecological imperialism and have been explored in some literature already, this book also seeks to further explain the role of international finance in ecological imperialism. The role of international finance in ecological imperialism is simply not as visible as, for example, the activities of multinational extractive industries in the Global South. However, the role of international finance, and the liberalization of international finance, cannot be underestimated as factors driving ecological crises and ecological imperialism.

In addition, this book seeks to ground all of these issues in case studies from Africa and Asia. The book itself is the result of over a decade of research, a substantial part of it conducted while researching or working in Africa and Asia. First-hand conversations with NGOs, activists, and ordinary citizens in Tanzania and Cambodia have contributed immensely to ideas and insights of this book. Finally, the book makes a special effort to include recent evidence, from the sustainability sciences and social sciences more generally, that empirically captures the links between environmental degradation and the workings of the global economy. Currently, there are scores of detailed, empirical studies that investigate such important topics as global commodity chains, trade, environmental degradation, and unequal consumption of the world's resources. The book also utilizes relevant socio-ecological data to provide further insight into the environmental situation of the African and Asian case studies. In doing all of this, the book hopes to provide the broader, contextual narrative behind such empirical evidence and make visible the very real, concrete relationships between the workings of the global economy and global sustainability challenges.

Acknowledgments

Over the years, numerous friends, colleagues, and mentors have helped in some way with the writing of this book. I owe many thanks to Adrienne Rosenberg for her careful and thoughtful editing, and Richard McIntyre, Felix Mantz, and Zoe Sherman for their helpful suggestions. Thank you to the supportive Association for Economic and Social Analysis (AESA), whose workshops offered a platform to present and review certain chapters of the book. Communications with NGOs such as Forests & Finance and REPOA in Tanzania were very helpful with the research of this book. George DeMartino and Haider Khan gave invaluable feedback on the early research that formed the foundation of this book. Finally, a special thanks to my husband Spencer Ames for his tireless support.

Acknowledgments

1 The Ecological Aspect of Imperialism

In 1975, gold was discovered by nomadic herders in Bulyanhulu, northwest Tanzania, and following its discovery, families from Northern Tanzania began to carry out small-scale artisanal mining. In 1994, Tanzania's Small Scale Miners' Association submitted an official request to the government to gain community title to hundreds of mine shafts constructed by the artisanal miners in Bulyanhulu. However, around the same time, the Canadian Embassy submitted a competing proposal for a mining license under the local subsidiary, Kahama Mining. The Tanzanian government, pressured by the International Monetary Fund and the World Bank to promote private foreign investment and do away with all public ownership of the mineral extractive industries, relented and gave permission for Kahama to begin its operations. Small-scale miners of the area were subsequently declared illegal intruders, and in July 1996, Kahama forcefully evicted the residents with reinforcement from the Tanzanian Field Force Unit riot police. Homes were flattened, settlers' properties were confiscated, and the entire population was forced to flee. While a number of people were working in the mine shafts, company officials ordered bulldozers to fill the mine shafts with gravel. The exact number of people who died remains unknown, but from accounts of families and eyewitnesses, over 70 people were allegedly buried alive. The police arrived a few days later, and in the end, little was done; the government closed the case despite calls for independent, comprehensive investigation backed by Amnesty International. By 1999, the Canadian mining giant Barrick Gold bought Sutton Resources and became the operator at Bulyanhulu Gold Mine under an arrangement made possible with financial backing from World Bank and the Canadian Government's Export Development Corporation (Women and Mining Network/ Red Internacional Mujeres y Mineria, 2010). Today Tanzania's gold mining sector, one of the most lucrative in sub-Saharan Africa (SSA), is almost entirely owned by foreign transnational corporations. Billions of dollars of profits bleed overseas from an impoverished country whose GDP per capita is a little over $1,100 per year.

Tanzania's gold mining conflict is only one small example of the thousands of social conflicts over resources and environmental issues recorded in recent years. And it is only one example of the numerous instances

DOI: 10.4324/9780429261305-1

where the profits of large multinational corporations have been privileged over the land, resources, and livelihoods of the native populations. The Environmental Justice Organisations, Liabilities, and Trade (EJOLT) Global Atlas of Environmental Injustice has recorded some 3,450 cases of social conflict around global environmental issues (Environmental Justice Atlas, n.d.a). EJOLT commented, "communities are struggling to defend their land, air, water, forests and their livelihoods from damaging projects and extractive activities with heavy environmental and social impacts: mining, dams, tree plantations, fracking, gas flaring, incinerators, etc." (Environmental Justice Atlas, n.d.b). Yet even this number seems too small to capture the extent of the crises. In some countries the situation is extreme, such as in Cambodia where an estimated 770,000 people—about 6% of the population—have been forcibly kicked off their land due to large-scale land investments and left in squalid conditions from the activities of elites and multinational corporations (Global Diligence, 2014). Often, the dynamics are similar—the insidious entanglement of environmental crises with the dispossession of land, resources, and livelihoods coupled with violence against indigenous peoples, small farmers, and marginalized urban poor. All of these dynamics are promulgated by an unholy alliance of corrupt state officials, domestic elites, international financial institutions, and transnational corporations that are introducing forms of extraction and production driven by profit.

The central quandary of these seemingly unremitting socio-ecological crises is that they cannot be isolated to one particular practice, one specific economic policy, or the actions of one particular country. Nor are these crises limited to the lack of ecological practices in a specific sector, such as in agriculture or energy though these sectors are often the site of the most visible conflicts and environmental destruction. Rather, this book argues that these crises are intimately entwined with the history and growth of industrial capitalism and its expansion globally. This expansion is also entangled with the history of what is commonly considered "development" but may be more appropriately described as a form of mal-development accompanied by ecocide at a planetary level.

Since the Industrial Revolution, capitalism has required the appropriation of resources globally; at first, this appropriation occurred under colonialism through direct forms of occupation and political-economic control. And yet, it is actually after the 1950s, and in particular within the past several decades, that resource use has spiked. The post-WWII era witnessed an

> extraordinary surge in global economic activity [that] produced an insatiable need for resources of all types: energy for transportation, manufacturing, and electricity production; minerals for buildings, infrastructure, and consumer products; and food and water to sustain a growing (and increasingly urbanized) global population.
>
> (Klare, 2012, pp. 23–24)

In response to the increased demand for bauxite, cobalt, copper, iron ore, fossil fuels, and other minerals, metals, and energy for industrial growth, the world's extractive industries again sought new resources overseas in the Middle East, Africa, Asia, and Latin America. Today, this global demand for resources continues relentlessly and goes far beyond strategic metals and minerals to include farm land, water sources, forests for timber, and ocean fisheries. In short, the demand includes the appropriation and exploitation of Earth's entire ecological commons. The destruction is not limited to the extraction of resources, the sink capacity of our Earth, that is, the capacity to sustainably absorb wastes and pollution, is also increasingly degraded. Sustainability scientists at the International Geosphere-Biosphere Programme (n.d.) dub our contemporary era the "The Great Acceleration," a time period over the past 60–70 years of escalating use of resources and environmental degradation. Figure 1.1, for example, shows the rapid surge in CO_2 emissions worldwide after 1950. Figure 1.2 shows that global resource extraction has more than tripled between 1970 and 2017.

Since the 1970s, contemporary capitalism has been what the economist Andrew Glyn has aptly termed "capitalism unleashed" (Glyn, 2007). Following the collapse of various forms of economic alternatives, capitalism has emerged as the dominant economic model globally. While capitalism has always been a global phenomenon, this era of capitalism is explicitly predicated on the removal of the remaining barriers to capital accumulation, the

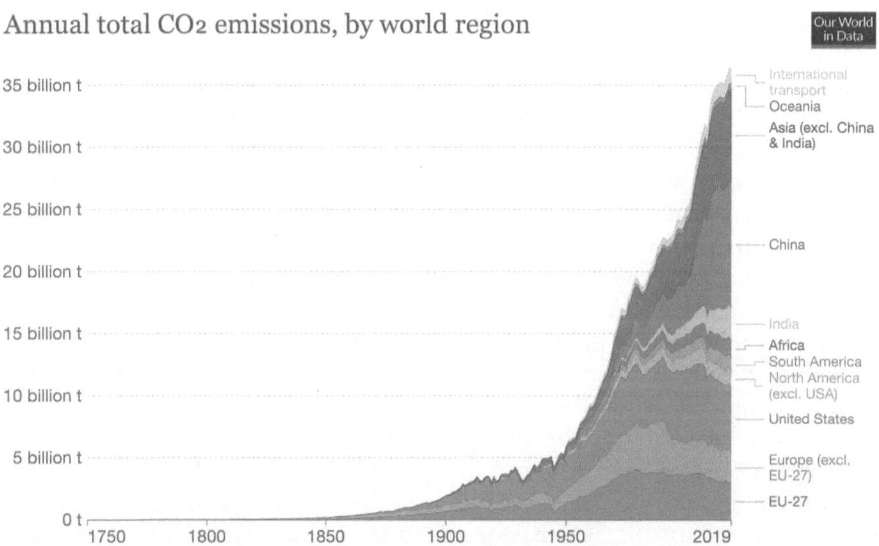

Figure 1.1 Annual Total CO_2 Emissions, by World Region

Source: Our World in Data based on the Global Carbon Project at https://ourworldindata.org/co2-and-other-greenhouse-gas-emissions

Note: This measures CO_2 emissions from fossil fuels and cement production only—land use change is not included

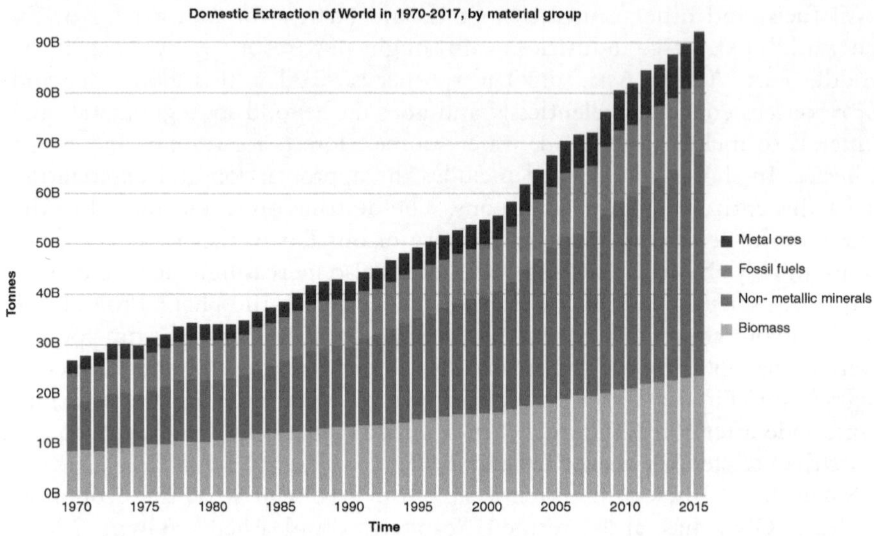

Figure 1.2 Domestic Extraction of World in 1970–2017
Source: WU Vienna (2020): Material flows by material group, 1970–2017. Visualization based upon the UN IRP Global Material Flows Database. Vienna University of Economics and Business. Online available at: materialflows.net/visualisation-centre

replacement of these barriers by free market principles, and the relative freedom for capital to scour the globe for profitable opportunities. This era of contemporary globalization is *neoliberal* globalization, marked by the liberalization of international trade, international investment, and international finance. And this globalization, that ambiguous term that describes so much while explaining so little, has at its root the concentration and internationalization of capital as large and powerful transnational corporations have outsourced their activities in search of cheaper labor and amenable environmental contexts. By the 21st century, through the outsourcing of billions of global commodity chains, capitalist relations of production have saturated the far-flung reaches of the globe while pulling into orbit economies that once sought greater independence from the world-capitalist system as well as subsuming peripheral regions once considered remote frontiers.

For the Global South, the integration into neoliberal globalization has proceeded step-by-step through development plans enacted within the past four to five decades. As the case studies of this book seek to document, the economic restructuring that has occurred in the name of development has played a key role in the depletion and degradation of Nature globally. With the withdrawal of direct colonialism, development paradigms have actively sought to replace traditional forms of livelihoods and communal property with private property and market-based relations, with an emphasis on export-led growth. At the same time, development plans that encouraged industrialization, urbanization, and industrial agriculture within developing countries have set the stage for intensified resource use and environmental degradation (Obeng-Odoom, 2021). Though one can dive endlessly into the nuances and differences at the local level, development paradigms across the globe have promoted an astonishingly one-size-fits-all blueprint with largely uniform goals and policies. Ultimately, development paradigms have aimed to integrate countries globally, promote production for the world market, and propagate economic growth as the overarching form of legitimacy (McMichael, 2017). The dilemma is that the workings of global capital, freed from burdensome environmental and social regulation and national boundaries, has catalyzed severe socio-ecological crises. At the same time, it has funneled trillions of dollars of profit into mammoth transnational corporations and international financial institutions, and away from countries mired in poverty and inequality. The central purpose of this book is to elucidate the following connections: the complex interrelationships between the expansionary dynamics of global capitalism through trade, investment, and finance, the neoliberal development paradigm adopted by the Global South in the 1980s, the global environmental crises, and what should arguably be identified as a form of contemporary imperialism.

Global Ecological Crises, Global Inequality

In 2009, a group of Earth system and environmental scientists created a classification of nine Earth system processes known as "planetary boundaries" that delineate a safe operating zone for humanity. These nine processes and systems are critical in regulating the stability and resilience of the Earth system. Once certain thresholds or tipping points are crossed by human activity, these scientists argue that there is a risk of irreversible and abrupt environmental change. That is, crossing the planetary boundaries risks the entire Earth system, as complex interactions between land, oceans, atmosphere, ice sheets, biodiversity, and humans become destabilized. Currently, four of nine planetary boundaries have been crossed as a result of human activity: climate change, loss of biosphere integrity, land-system change, and altered biogeochemical cycles (phosphorus and nitrogen). Two of these, climate change and biosphere integrity, are what the scientists call "core boundaries." Significantly altering either of these core boundaries, they assert, would drive the Earth system into a new state of high risk (Commonwealth Scientific and Industrial Research Organization et al., n.d.).

Despite the alarming levels of environmental degradation with potentially catastrophic repercussions, including increased conflict, poverty, and forced migration, there is little evidence that adequate solutions are being undertaken. Rather, in this era of globalization, global GDP has grown, and with it, the use of the world's resources has skyrocketed. As Figure 1.3 shows, world GDP (in constant prices) between 1980 and 2013 grew by almost 150%. At the same time, global material extraction[1] increased by around 130%.

The global ecological crises before us were not supposed to happen; or rather, the current paradigm of the market system, industrial development, economic growth, and technology were supposed to offer the solutions to prevent such crises (and many argue, still do). Since the 1970s, schools of thought such as "ecological modernization theory" have argued that industrial development and technological innovation offer the best solution to the environmental crises (Spaargaren et al., 2000). Ecological modernization theory identifies modern science and technology as central institutions that can help humanity avoid or mitigate ecological crises. Scientific and technological trajectories, through confrontation with ecological crises, are believed to adapt and reform reflexively. The theory also argues that market dynamics can be conducive to ecological reform. In addition to state agencies and new social movements, innovators, entrepreneurs, and other economic agents can act as social carriers of ecological restructuring. Ecological modernization theory rejects the argument that there is any fundamental opposition between the market economy and ecology. Rather, theorists argue that modern economic institutions and mechanisms can be, and are to an increasing extent, reformed according to the criteria of ecological rationality. Finally, while wary of a strong bureaucratic state, ecological modernization theory argues that the state can play a vital role in environmental management while social movements would increasingly support the ecological reconstruction of modern society (Spaargaren et al., 2000).

Along these lines, an extended argument has been proposed. Theorists from the neoclassical school of economics claimed that with industrial/technological development and economic growth, spurred by the development of market relations, nations can become "post-consumerist." That is, as people become post-consumerist in their consumption pattern, the world's wealthier nations can "dematerialize" their economies by increasingly valuing consumption of services and experiences over material products (Adriaanse et al., 1997). Because of this, wealthier nations are supposedly decoupling economic growth from the use of energy, materials, and waste flows into the environment while reducing the environmental impact of each additional monetary increment of GDP (World Bank, 1992). What is needed, according to ecological modernization theory, is not a reduction in economic growth but the acceleration toward dematerialization in order to ensure that the environment is integrated within a more knowledge driven, innovative economy. To achieve this, developing countries should focus their attention on economic growth, rising incomes, and technological advancement through laissez-faire economic policies. Technological optimists argue that economic and technological progress, spurred through market incentives, would result in more efficient use of resources and environmental protection and would create a decoupling of GDP growth and material use (World Bank, 1992; Spaargaren et al., 2000; Bhagwati, 2003). Along these lines "green growth" is currently promoted as a central strategy in policy circles (UNEP, 2011; European Commission, 2018), including by the recent United Nations Sustainable Development Goals adopted in 2015 (Hickel, 2019).

More recent empirical research has pointed out several problems with these theories. Figure 1.3 shows that between 1990 and 2009, the global GDP growth rate exceeded the material extraction rate globally. This did represent a trend of relative resource decoupling at the global level. However, from 2009 on, this trend of increasing material productivity stagnated. In other words, at a global level the amount of economic output generated, in terms of GDP, did not decouple from the per unit amount of materials consumed (Material Flow Analysis Portal, n.d.).

Other studies confirm this dilemma between economic growth and the environment. Drawing on empirical data of two key indicators, resource use and CO_2 emissions, Hickel (2019) shows that aggregate global growth of 3% per year, the amount that would be required by the United Nations Sustainable Development Goals to lift developing countries out of poverty through economic growth, renders it empirically infeasible to achieve any reductions in aggregate global resource use. Such growth would also render it empirically infeasible to achieve reductions in CO_2 emissions rapid enough to stay within the widely agreed upon carbon budget of 2°C past pre-industrial levels that is required to prevent catastrophic climate change. Significantly, according to Hickel (2019), existing empirical evidence suggests that the absolute decoupling of GDP from material footprint is not feasible on a global scale in the context of such continued economic growth, even under the best possible conditions—i.e., *even under the best possible conditions of increasing technological efficiency.*

It is also highly doubtful that wealthy societies have become post-consumerist. When analyzing with the indicator Raw Material Consumption (RMC), or "Material Footprint," that accounts for the physical quantity of materials required along the supply chains of all goods and services finally

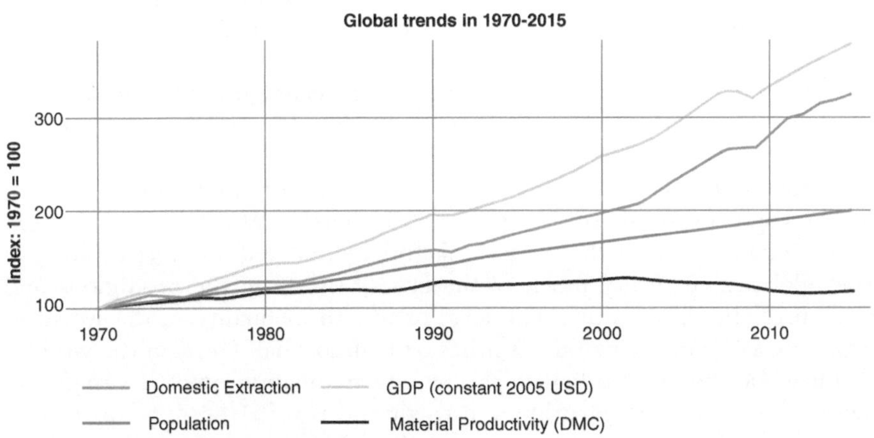

Figure 1.3 Global Trends in 1970–2015
Source: http://www.materialflows.net/decoupling-material-use-and-economic-performance/

consumed in a country, no developed country from 1990 to 2013 has achieved absolute decoupling. That is, no developed country has achieved economic growth while at the same time decreasing overall material use. Some, such as the United States and Sweden, have achieved relative decoupling, a situation when economic growth is exceeding growth in material use. However, countries are interpreted as achieving relative decoupling even if material use remains the same or even increases as long as economic growth increases at a faster rate (Material Flow Analysis Portal, n.d.). For highly wasteful and consumerist countries such as the United States, relative decoupling hardly indicates a move toward real sustainability. Other developed countries, such as Switzerland and Denmark, have experienced no decoupling at all in terms of overall material use. A report by Parique et al. (2019) that examines a wide range of indicators for evidence of decoupling states,

> The validity of the green growth discourse relies on the assumption of an absolute, permanent, global, large and fast enough decoupling of economic growth from all critical environmental pressures. The literature reviewed clearly shows that there is no empirical evidence for such a decoupling currently happening. This is the case for materials, energy, water, greenhouse gasses, land, water pollutants, and biodiversity loss for which decoupling is either only relative, and/or observed only temporarily, and/or only locally. In most cases, decoupling is relative. When absolute decoupling occurs, it is observed only during rather short periods of time, concerning only certain resources or forms of impact, for specific locations, and with very small rates of mitigation.
>
> (Parique et al., 2019, p. 4)

Considering how imminent the multiple global ecological crises are, the results of such studies severely undercut the post-consumerist argument for continued economic growth as the solution. Rather on the brink of multiple ecological crises (IPCC, 2022), spanning from climate change to a sixth mass extinction, we have entered a stage which ecological economists term "uneconomic growth" where the costs of continued economic growth are outweighing the benefits.

Equally troubling, wealthier countries continue to consume an unsustainable and disproportionate share of the world's resources. While overpopulation is often cited as one of the primary factors behind the multiple ecological crises globally, in reality much of the crises arise from the prodigious use of resources by the wealthy. The level of wealth inequality in the world is staggering as 1% of the world's families own almost half (46%) of the world's wealth while the bottom half of the world's population owns less than the richest 85 people in the world. And this trend is reflected in terms of the environment. For example, the poorest half of the global population, approximately 3.5 billion people, are responsible for only around 10% of total global emissions attributed to individual consumption (Oxfam, 2018). In contrast, around 50% of global emissions can be attributed to the richest 10% of people around the world. These wealthy individuals have carbon footprints that are on average 11 times as high as the poorest half of the population and 60 times as high as the poorest 10% (Oxfam, 2015).

Significantly, similar inequality is reflected in overall per capita consumption of resources when broken down according to region. The Raw Material Consumption per capita of a typical American was over 30 tonnes in 2013 while a typical European was over 20 tonnes. In contrast, a typical African consumer was less than 5 tonnes. In Asia and the Pacific, RMC per capita was around 12 tonnes (Material Flow Analysis Portal, n.d.).

Why would there be such stark differences in resource consumption between nations? According to some sustainability scholars the specific stage of development of a society, or its "mode of subsistence," determines the magnitude of this throughput. Primitive hunter-gatherer societies largely performed what is known as "basic metabolism," by largely remaining within their environment's carrying capacity. Over time, however, the emergence of agriculture as a new socio-ecological regime evolved whereby humans started "colonizing" Nature at the expense of other species and utilizing land solely for crops useful to humans (Weisz et al., 2001; Haberl et al., 2011). This enabled human access to surpluses, which in turn resulted in the expansion of populations as well as the increased scale of throughput and consequently greater pressure on the surrounding ecosystems. Many economies are still largely agrarian in the world-system today, especially in Africa (UNCTAD, 2012).

Industrialization, however, emerged as a qualitatively and quantitatively new socio-ecological regime. Through technological and scientific development, humans have learned how to utilize non-renewable sources of energy, in particular fossil fuels. Industrial societies are characterized by "extended metabolism" with unprecedented levels of productivity, surplus, and per capita material and energy consumption increases. However, while industrialization has solved some of the problems of previous modes of subsistence, such as periodic scarcity, it has also severely strained the Earth's ecosystems. Resource extraction has surpassed the Earth's natural regeneration rates, and the production of wastes is greater than what can be absorbed by the planet's sink mechanisms (Steffen et al., 2011). Currently, the world contains all the socio-ecological regimes with varying levels of transition between them (though very few hunter-gatherer regimes remain). The metabolic profile of the least developed countries is largely agrarian with total energy and material use per capita and per area unit being quite low. For developing and emerging economies, total energy and material use per capita is higher though on average they seem to be closer to an agrarian profile than to an industrial one. In contrast, developed nations utilize high levels of energy and resources while strongly depending on fossil fuels (Krausman et al., 2008; UNCTAD, 2012). For example, in agrarian societies, energy use per capita is estimated to be approximately 40–70 GJ/year/capita, and in industrial societies, it is estimated to be 150–400 GJ/year/capita. Material use per capita in agrarian societies is approximately 3–6 tons/year/capita while in industrial societies material use per capita runs up to 15–25 tons/year/capita (Krausman et al., 2008).

Importantly, while industrial societies may seem "post-industrial" or "dematerialized," they continue to depend on materially intensive activities, such as agriculture and mining, that are located in developing countries (Krausman et al., 2008). Concomitantly, developing countries which are resource exporters also reveal higher levels of material extraction rates and resource use. As a result, resource-exporting countries that are also least developed countries (LDCs) can experience high levels of environmental pressure coupled with low levels of per capita consumption (UNCTAD, 2012). Industrialized countries, in other words, are importing the resources needed for their unsustainable levels of consumption.

Some scholars have noted that the unequal consumption of the world's resources by wealthier regions is accomplished through international trade and have termed this trend as "ecologically unequal exchange." According to ecologically unequal exchange, trade acts as a fundamental mechanism in the redistribution of resources, which allows wealthier regions to consume and pollute more than their sustainable share. There is substantial empirical work that has corroborated many of the tenets of ecologically unequal exchange. Relatedly, other studies of environmental injustice document how environmental burdens, from vulnerability to climate change and from proximity to polluting industries, are shouldered by poorer and marginalized peoples. Chapter 2 overviews the theory of ecologically unequal exchange and the empirical studies on these topics in detail.

What is apparent from such studies on ecologically unequal exchange and other forms of ecological debt is that differences in the consumption and exploitation of the Earth's resources do not arise from merely physical processes. Instead, what we are dealing with is an imminently social phenomenon supported by a specific type of political economic regime. However useful a biophysical approach is to understanding differences in resource consumption across the globe, there is little in such explanations that shed light on how these differences are actually enabled. Why should it be that a citizen in a wealthier nation is able to consume such a disproportionate share of the world's resources? How is it that the global economy came to be structured in such a way as to allow for this? There is no reason to believe this is an inherently normal or natural state of affairs, and indeed for most of human history it was not. Further, as this book will discuss, unequal consumption of resources itself is only the tip of the environmental injustice iceberg. Nature is a contested, politicized sphere; the questions of who has access to it, who is able to exploit it and profit from it, and who shoulders the burdens are ultimately determined in the realm of political economy.

The Ecological Dimension of Imperialism

As discussed, the link between environmental impact and affluence[2] has long been acknowledged by mainstream social science; it seems little more than a simple observation that as one's wealth grows, one can consume more. For example, the IPAT equation, developed in the 1970s, equates overall environmental impact to aggregate changes in population, affluence (an indicator for consumption), and technology. Using the IPAT, sustainability scientists found that from 1900 to 1950 population, consumption, and technology had roughly equal effects. However, increases in consumption and technology from 1950 to the present have become the dominant factors driving environmental impacts (Steffen et al., 2011). Yet behind this seemingly natural trend is a multifaceted global economy that is decidedly *political economic* in Nature, a hierarchical global capitalist world-system that systematically favors the capacity of particular social groups to accumulate wealth, consume a lion's share of the Earth's resources, and pass the burden of ecological degradation onto others. Such trends are the consequence of a world-system that—through a long history of colonialism, neocolonialism, and neoliberal policies adopted under the aegis of development—has kept global resources cheap and accessible for production, consumption, and, increasingly in recent years, speculative investments. Understanding the ecological aspects of imperialism, or what I term "ecological imperialism",[3] is central to understanding these dynamics.

In its simplest definition, imperialism is the system by which a dominant power is able to control the trade, investment, labor, and natural resources of other peoples. Theories of imperialism have always acknowledged the role of natural resources in global capital accumulation, and there is no real way to separate the deep interrelations between the exploitation of labor and the exploitation of Nature in the study of imperialism. So why is a study of specifically *ecological* imperialism even necessary? Because in an era of global ecological crises, it becomes all the more important to emphasize imperialism's ecological aspect. Even as mainstream discourses on sustainability are proliferating, economic policies, environmental degradation, and global structures of inequality are continuously treated as separate and unrelated issues.[4] In actuality, sustainability itself is a contested political issue. Attempts to explain global environmental crises without explicitly acknowledging the economic system that enables the grossly unequal accumulation of capital and consumption of resources by certain groups and the impoverishment and environmental devastation shouldered by less powerful groups leads to analyses that are consistently fragmented, incomplete, and, perhaps most importantly, biased toward business-as-usual solutions. What follows is some essential characteristics of ecological imperialism.

The first and primary characteristic of ecological imperialism is that it is rooted in the endless drive for capital accumulation and capitalist relations of production. This must be pointed out because even critical perspectives sometimes fail to link issues such as ecological debt or ecologically unequal exchange explicitly with the capitalist mode of production. Capitalism is an expansionary system, and it is expansionary for many reasons. Fundamentally capitalism is expansionary because at its root is the ceaseless pursuit of capital accumulation that knows no bounds. It is also expansionary for reasons inherent to its normal operations, such as continuously seeking out new markets, new sources of resources, and new investment outlets for overaccumulated capital. And, it is expansionary in reaction to its own inner contradictions and created crises. As such, it is not just the biophysical needs of industrialization that require industrial societies to seek their resources needs elsewhere; it is impossible to disentangle the biophysical needs of industrializing countries from their socio-economic formations because industrialization has, for the most part, historically occurred through capitalist relations of production.

This fundamental expansionary drive of capitalism is highly problematic for a living, finite, and, in many ways, ecologically fragile Earth. In contrast to other modes of production, the capitalist mode of production's drive for capital, that is the advancement of value in monetary form in order to produce more value (M-C-M'),[5] dominates production. Marx had argued that capitalism as a social relation is defined by the complete social separation of the direct producers from the necessary material conditions of production starting with the appropriation of land. Separated from any way of sustaining themselves, workers become forced to sell their labor-power for wages. Marx denoted this process as "primitive accumulation," and instances of peasants being forced off land still very much occurs, only now, in an era of global ecological crises, the land has become just as important, and at times even more so, than the labor! With primitive accumulation, these "freed" material conditions and "freed" labor are recombined in the wage-labor production of commodities in pursuit of the endless accumulation of capital. From the standpoint of capital, as Marx wrote, the natural conditions of production become "free gifts" of Nature to be freely appropriated by capital providing use-values that capital needs to produce and realize surplus value (Burkett, 2006). In other words, capitalism is continuously engaged in a process to appropriate and commodify labor and Nature as inputs for production in the pursuit of endless profit.

The problem is that the conversion of labor and Nature into separate capital assets for the purpose of creation of profit is fundamentally destructive, to both Nature and human development. As Marxist ecologists like Burkett (2006) have pointed out, capitalism's reproduction requirements are autonomous from the sustainable reproduction of labor-power and natural conditions. For capitalist production, all that matters is labor-power and material conditions be separately, reliably, and widely available in forms that can be combined as commodity production by wage-labor. As such capitalist reproduction does not recognize any of the processes, complexities, and limits of the natural world. Given its drive of endless accumulation, capitalism has an inherent tendency to overextend the limits of its natural conditions (Burkett, 2006). In capitalist economies, individual capitals use profits to make more profits, which become self-expanding capital. Quantitatively, capitalist self-expansion has no strict limits per se. However, Nature, which organizes itself on very different principles, very much does (O'Connor, 1998).

Thus, on the one hand, a relatively straightforward reason for ecological imperialism is that the continued accumulation of capital is dependent upon the accessibility and affordability of "natural capital," which is obtained globally. This dynamic underpins the history of capitalism from the very beginning with the appropriation of colonial resources during the Industrial Revolution, and it continues today (Galeano, 1971; McNeil, 2000; Chew, 2001; Wolf, 2010). Magdoff and Foster (2003) also pointed out that capital, in its drive for endless accumulation, undergoes technological changes that require specific and strategic resources—many of which are largely found overseas, a process intensified by competition between capitalist powers. Such a dynamic can be witnessed in the current scramble for African resources that is not just between individual capitals from the United States and Europe but emerging "Southern" countries as well.

On the other hand, a more complex dynamic behind imperialism may also stem from spatio-temporal fixes for crises of accumulation—both under- and overaccumulation—arising from contradictions that are unresolvable within the capitalist system itself. Classical theorists of imperialism, such as Rosa Luxemburg (1964), emphasized how crises of "overaccumulation" (overaccumulation being the surplus of capital, and potentially also labor, lying idle and having no profitable outlets) necessitated global expansion for the restoration of the conditions for accumulation. More recently, Harvey (2005) links neoliberalism to an overaccumulation crisis that began in the early 1970s. He argues that accumulation by dispossession helped solve the overaccumulation problem through releasing a set of assets, including labor-power, at a very low and in some cases zero cost. Neoliberal privatization, he argues, opened up vast fields for overaccumulated capital to seize upon, releasing cheap raw materials, such as oil, into the system whereby input costs would be reduced and profits thereby enhanced.

In contrast, Moore's substantial work emphasizes how crises of "underproduction" have historically led to new spatial expansions of capitalism and new capitalist appropriation of natural wealth. This appropriation, in turn, creates new ecological and human development crises while setting the stage for future accumulation crises. Moore argues that capitalism has a tendency to undermine its conditions of production. Specifically, increasing the extraction of surplus value hinges on increasing labor productivity, which does involve technical and social innovation. But most importantly from an ecological perspective, it is the abundance of "free gifts" which has fueled capitalism's technological dynamism. Capitalism, Moore asserts, has sustained itself on the basis of cheap inputs (Moore, 2001, 2003, 2011, 2012, 2015). These dynamics necessarily push expansionary tendencies on a global scale as they typically reward the rapid exhaustion of Nature (and human Nature) and instigate ecological crises, which can act as fetters on the accumulation of capital. Thus when the exhaustion of human and biophysical Natures becomes significant enough to fetter labor productivity in a serious way, capitalists and empires begin to look for new frontiers. This dialectic of plunder and productivity, Moore (2014) insists, is at the heart of capitalism's recurrent waves of geographical expansion. He cites the examples of sugar, silver, forest products, fish, iron, and copper, all having moved with the same rhythm: occupying, producing, and exhausting the ecological formations of the North Atlantic.

Additionally, both Foster (2002) and Burkett (2006) have pointed out that environmental crises do not always create a crisis of capital accumulation and that any ecological crisis itself may be used as a new source of investment and profit (e.g., excess carbon dioxide leading to carbon trading, the melting of the Arctic from climate change causing the rush to obtain fossil fuel deposits, even biofuel production for renewable energy driving global land grabbing). I would also add that the creation of *scarcity* through ecological degradation can be a source of profit for individual capitals through rising prices and opportunities for speculation, which can incentivize the drive to appropriate peripheral resources. The global drive to privatize scarce water resources and to speculate on fuel and food, among other examples, are attempts within the system to directly expand private riches by exploiting scarcity.

At any rate, it is nearly impossible in this age of multifold ecological crises and the complex workings of the global economy to isolate one single dynamic driving every or even most forms of ecological imperialism. I would argue that for any given instance, it is more likely that several dynamics are at work and specific cases must be examined concretely rather than abstractly. For example, following the global financial crisis of 2008, multiple crises converged—a crisis of accumulation in the developed world, a glut of capital in the financial sector, and ecological crises in the form of climate change, drought. These crises created a global food supply shock, which in turn sparked a sudden rise in large-scale land investments in the Global South. In this instance, multiple global ecological crises created a circumstance that led to scarcity and rising prices of farmland, which culminated in a global land grab of arable land as a form of safe investment for over accumulated capital in the financial sector. Finally, it is worthwhile to note that environmental degradation often occurs from the expansion of capital even when the origins of that expansion are not necessarily, or at least not solely, about the extraction of natural resources. The tremendous degradation of the environment of industrializing countries such as China due to the outsourcing of manufacturing from TNCs in the Global North seeking cheap labor is an example. In short, there are a lot of reasons why capitalism is expansionary and imperialist in Nature, and interwoven with that expansionism are many ecological repercussions.

The second characteristic of ecological imperialism is obvious but complex in how it actually manifests; ecological imperialism hinges upon unequal power between countries (economic, political, military, ideological, and so on) and a hierarchical international division of labor. As capitalism must constantly and consistently obtain resources that are cheap and easily accessible, it is necessary that political economic conditions must be created, made adequate, and reinforced—just as the necessary political economic conditions for access to amenable labor must be created and reinforced. Since roughly the 1980s, the current political economic configuration is neoliberal globalization, and with it is a general and intensified trend of commodifying nearly every aspect of the environment across the globe. This can manifest as outright forms of neocolonialism, such as foreign dominance in extractive sectors in sub-Saharan Africa facilitated through binding multilateral and bilateral treaties. But it also manifests as relations of dependency within a hierarchical, international division of labor in the world-system. These relations of dependency originate from a history of colonialism and uneven development as countries are locked into the export of natural resources as their primary source of income.

The third characteristic is that ecological imperialism results in negative socio-ecological impacts for peripheral countries, which cannot be truly compensated in a monetary sense. This is a trend increasingly captured by the literature on ecologically unequal exchange and environmental injustice more broadly. Again, this third characteristic seems fairly obvious, but if this were not true, what we would be witnessing is the textbook version of international trade described in orthodox trade and investment theories, which consider all forms of trade voluntary, welfare enhancing, and Pareto optimal. Orthodox trade and investment theories have no real way to account for the socio-ecological degradation arising from neoliberal globalization aside from the limited and reductionist notion of negative externalities. As such, the study of ecological imperialism is also the study of how environmental and social burdens are displaced outside of imperial centers' borders.

A fourth characteristic is that the form that ecological imperialism takes is also an outcome of the dialectical unfolding of movements and counter-movements that arise in response to social resistances. Ecological imperialism necessitates an amenable political-economic context within the imperialized country; historically this has been met with periodic resistance at certain times. The price of Nature in the periphery depends not only on market supply and demand and ground rent but also on counter-movements such as class, anti-imperialist, and environmental struggles. The neoliberal economic policies concerning trade, foreign investment, and international finance that we see today are very much a reflection of counter-movements against such resistances.

The fifth characteristic of ecological imperialism is the outcome of all of the above—the continued accumulation of capital for imperial countries. For imperial countries, ecological imperialism ensures the capture of profits associated with environmentally degrading activities and the unequal access to the Earth's resources and sink. The Earth's ecological bounties, and the profits from them, flow away from the regions that are the recipients of ecological imperialism and toward the imperial countries.

Ultimately, when we discuss ecological imperialism, what we are discussing is the ecological aspect of imperialism and the global expansionary tendencies of capitalism. This expansionism has necessitated a wholesale reconfiguring of socio-ecological relations between humans and Nature globally. Nature has become, worldwide, natural capital—a mere input into the process of capital accumulation. Importantly, this expansionism has necessitated the subjugation of the economic, political, and/or social institutions throughout the Global South in order to make their Nature accessible and amenable to the needs of capital accumulation in the Global North.

Throughout this book, many different aspects of ecological imperialism are examined. In terms of political economy, the book traces the history of the subjugation of the Global South's economic, political, and/or social institutions relevant to the issue of ecological imperialism. On the environmental side, the book reviews cases of resource and land grabbing in the Global South by transnational corporations, environmental degradation associated with the relocation of manufacturing processes overseas, and patterns of ecologically unequal exchange. Finally, on the monetary side, the book examines the capture of profits by transnational corporations (TNCs) in the natural resource sectors as well as the flow of such profits into the financial sector. Through looking at the multiple aspects of ecological imperialism, we can piece together a narrative that explains the numerous instances of environmental injustice and socio-ecological crises throughout the Global South as well as some of the most important dynamics behind the broader global ecological crises.

Ecological Imperialism and the Capitalist World-System

In our globalized world, even localized ecological crises often have connections to the workings of the global economy. This is especially the case in the Global South where peripheral countries' resources are frequently geared for export, and peripheral Natures are directly exploited as part of the supply chains for transnational corporations. Why is this the case? For one, in the past four decades, the global economy has both grown and become increasingly integrated through the liberalization of foreign investment, international trade, and capital flows. Within the developing world, this was abetted by neoliberal development policies. This integration has important repercussions for the global ecology, as Chapter 2 discusses more in-depth.

The important point here is that ecological imperialism occurs within a global economy that operates as an integrated system, one that since colonialism has been structured as a hierarchical international division of labor. World-systems theory is a school of thought that analyzes the global economy as a hierarchical system composed of interlinked economies where different economic tasks are distributed geographically, and the overall hegemony of certain countries is reproduced and maintained through an international division of labor. Dependency and world-systems theories emerged as radical critiques to orthodox theories of development in the 1960s, particularly modernization theory which saw engagement with Western capitalist nations as a source of economic growth and development for poorer nations (Van Den Berg, 2017). The fundamental theoretical common ground between diverse theorists, ranging from Samir Amin, Arghiri Emmanuel, Immanuel Wallerstein, Andre Gunder Frank, Raul Prebisch, to Walter Rodney was the insistence that capitalism must be theorized as a hierarchical world-system. In the capitalist world-system, core (or metropole) regions dominate or exclude a subordinate and dependent peripheral (Kiely, 2010). Andre Gunder Frank (1967) further argued that, in direct contrast to modernization theory, the development of the core regions was predicated on the underdevelopment of peripheral regions. Others like Prebisch (1950) sought to uncover the structural inequalities in the world economy, such as deteriorating terms of trade for primary commodity producers. Wallerstein (1974, 1980), building upon such fundamental ideas, argued that the capitalist world-system contains a core, periphery, and also a semi-periphery, which he suggested had developed in southern Europe and East Asia. Semi-peripheral countries tend to contain a mixture of both core and peripheral economic activities, and while able to appropriate a relatively greater share of the global surplus than the periphery, semi-peripheral countries nonetheless appropriate less surplus than core countries (Wallerstein, 1974).

Theorists of imperialism, such as Galtung (1971) and Emmanuel (1972), have long recognized the significance of the world-system as a hierarchical international division of labor in enabling imperialism, and theorists of ecologically unequal exchange use the world-systems framework as the basis of their analysis. This book, as well, makes use of this important framework.

In the world-system schema, the first fundamental relationship upon which ecological imperialism hinges is the deep inequality perpetuated by the continued dependency and exploitation of peripheral regions by core regions (but also increasingly by emerging economies as discussed below). The origins stem from colonialism as peripheral economies throughout Africa, Latin America, and parts of Asia were re-organized to become exporters of natural resources to fuel the industrial needs of their European colonizers. This division of labor and dependent relationship that continued post-independence were described as "neocolonial" by many post-colonial leaders in order to denote the continued economic, political, and technological dependency of peripheral countries on their former colonial masters.

Though the global economy is becoming increasingly complex due to the outsourcing of manufacturing from developed countries to certain regions of the developing world, many economic tasks are still geographically distributed across a core and periphery. Core countries remain characterized by high development of forces of production, including high-paid labor, capital-intensive production, and technological advancement. In contrast, peripheral countries are characterized by low-level forces of production, including low-paid labor and labor-intensive production such as the export of raw materials. Geographically, the core is constituted by the advanced industrial countries, such as Europe, North America, and Japan. Peripheral areas are composed of regions such as most of sub-Saharan Africa as well as some countries in Latin America and in Asia.

Peripheral countries experience ecological imperialism in two primary ways: first, within the world-system international division of labor, their economies are based on export of natural resources, leading to ecologically unequal exchange and ecological debt. This structural position is a *dependent* condition. This dependent position also leaves peripheral countries vulnerable to intensified levels of ecologically unequal exchange and ecological debt through a host of contingent factors that have plagued peripheral countries since colonialism. For example, at times in history falling terms of trade for primary commodities and debt have forced them to increase their levels of natural resource exports (Muradian and Martinez-Alier, 2001b; Perez-Rincon, 2006; Shandra et al., 2008; Vallejo, 2010; Manrique et al., 2013). Second, as will be discussed in Chapter 2, in regions like sub-Saharan Africa especially, such international trade is primarily controlled by transnational corporations, particularly in the extractive and agricultural sectors, so that profit as well as resources flow overseas. Such economies are what scholars have long identified as "dis-articulated," mal-developed, and plagued by uneven development. Often these economies possess a comprador elite aligned with the interests of foreign investors and associated with the extraction of resources. Chapter 2 discusses the role of neoliberal development policies in reinforcing the dependent position of peripheral countries in ecological imperialism. Chapters 3 and 4 assess sub-Saharan Africa as a whole and Tanzania specifically as case studies for the above-mentioned issues.

However, by the 21st century, there are some important new characteristics of the capitalist world-system, some of which began decades ago but have since grown to new levels. These new characteristics and their relation to ecological imperialism form an important focus of this book. One of the most important changes in the past half-century has been the saturation of economies across the globe by capitalist relations of production, which was driven by multinational corporations that began outsourcing manufacturing tasks in roughly the 1960s. Correlated with this has been the economic growth and industrialization of emerging semi-peripheral economies as they became the recipients of the outsourced manufacturing tasks from transnationals located in the Global North. Driven by the quest for ever cheaper labor, neoliberal globalization has multinationalized the links in the chain of production and value creation across national borders, a trend which some have argued led to a new international division of labor (Frobel et al., 1979). Compared to previous eras of imperialism (classical imperialism) the world-system is now linked by billions of global commodity chains with corresponding environmental consequences across the planet. As such, the international division of labor has changed significantly. On the one hand, many formerly non-industrial economies now have substantial manufacturing sectors. On the other hand, in high-income countries, manufacturing employment has declined as a percentage of total employment while employment in services has accounted for an increasing proportion of total employment in high-income countries (Reuss, 2013).

The rise of an industrializing semi-periphery has major implications for the operations of ecological imperialism and for how ecologically unequal exchange and ecological debt are distributed throughout the world-system. World-systems theory has always had an important semi-periphery category, a category that contains both core and peripheral characteristics (Chase-Dunn, 2013). However, in the contemporary world-system this category now includes industrializing, middle-income countries also known as emerging economies that were previously considered peripheral, such as a number of East Asian and Southeast Asian countries. The semi-periphery is a complex but distinct middle position in the international division of labor whose role in discussions of environmental justice or ecologically unequal exchange is not always well understood. Often, these industrializing emerging economies of the semi-periphery are lumped together with the term Global South or "developing," which creates confusion around how the responsibilities for global environmental crises are distributed.

As Chapter 5 discusses, emerging economies such as China occupy a distinct, intermediate semi-peripheral status and, as such, face a number of complex, contradictory dynamics and pressures that drive ecological degradation both within and outside of their national borders. On the one hand, the relocation of manufacturing from the Global North has resulted in a severe degradation of emerging economies' own domestic environments. On the other hand, these economies have experienced rapid economic growth, industrialization, and increasing levels of consumption. In response to both these dynamics, emerging economies are increasingly seeking to externally secure land and resources by engaging in regional ecological imperialism. However, even as some semi-peripheral countries are engaging in forms of ecological imperialism with peripheral countries, they remain subordinate to core economies in a number of ways. In many cases, semi-peripheral economies operate as suppliers and subcontractors to corporations in the Global North, and many of their exports end up consumed in the Global North. Overall, emerging economies now occupy the ambiguous role as both the exploiter and the exploited, blurring the dichotomies of core versus periphery and Global North versus Global South that characterized earlier manifestations of the capitalist world-system. Chapter 5 discusses these issues in regard to China's increasing economic power, its sphere of influence in Southeast Asia, and the implications of the semi-periphery for the study of ecological imperialism.

Conclusion

Understanding the multiple, simultaneous ecological global crises, whether analyzed from the macro-level of the Earth's system and the crossing of planetary boundaries or experienced as a localized socio-ecological crisis like a community dispossessed from their land and livelihoods, requires a systems perspective. What we have seen from comprehensive studies and empirical data is that economic growth, growth in technology, affluence, and consumption—all things that are the very basis of modern industrial capitalism—are in an aggregate sense driving the global ecological crises. The concept of economic growth driving the ecological crises is not a new idea. Indeed, the entire subfield of ecological economics takes this fundamental contradiction as its starting point. But for obvious reasons, pointing out the contradictions between economic growth and the environment is highly politically unpalatable, and the incapacity to accept these contradictions points toward a major cognitive disconnect in our understanding of civilization, progress, development, and the mal-development and planetary ecocide underlying it.

Nonetheless, blaming economic growth, industrialization, or consumption for our current global ecological crises is incomplete. As numerous critical voices have argued, what is needed is a deep study into the growth of industrial capitalism and its expansion globally, and importantly how this expansion is entangled in the history of economic development. The chapters that follow focus on the political economy of this expansion through case studies from Africa and Asia. In particular, the book focuses on how neoliberal development policies in regard to international trade, international investment, and international finance drive, enable, and reinforce ecological imperialism. Through the lens of world-systems theory, the case studies also explore how new changes in the capitalist world-system are shaping ecological imperialism, including the rise of industrializing emerging economies, the role of global ecological crises in pushing a new scramble for resources, and the role of the increasing hegemony of the financial class and power of finance capital.

References

Adriaanse, A., Bringezu, S., Hammond, A., Moriguchi, Y., Rodenburg, E., Rogich, D., & Schütz, H. (1997). *Resource flows: The material base of industrial economies.* World Resource Institute. https://www.wri.org/research/resource-flows

Bhagwati, J. (2003). The case for free trade. *Scientific American, 269*(5), 18–23. https://doi.org/10.1038%2Fscientificamerican1193-42

Burkett, P. (2006). *Marxism and ecological economics: Toward a red and green political economy.* Leiden: Brill.

Chase-Dunn, C. (2013, February 21). *Contemporary semi-peripheral development: The regimes and the movements.* Institute for Research on World-Systems, University of California-Riverside. https://irows.ucr.edu/papers/irows78/irows78.htm

Chew, S. C. (2001). *World ecological degradation: Accumulation, urbanization, and deforestation, 3000 BC-AD 2000.* Walnut Creek: Altamira Press.

Clark, B., & Foster, J.B. (2009). Ecological imperialism and the global metabolic rift: Unequal exchange and the guano/nitrates trade. *International Journal of Comparative Sociology, 50*(3–4), 311–334. https://doi.org/10.1177/0020715209105144

Commonwealth Scientific and Industrial Research Organization (CSIRO), Globaïa, International Geosphere-Biosphere Programme (IGBP), International Human Dimensions Programme on Global Environmental Change (IHDB), & Stockholm Resilience Centre and Stockholm Environment Institute. (n.d.). *Planetary boundaries.* Welcome to the Anthropocene. https://www.anthropocene.info/planetary-boundaries.php

Environmental Justice Atlas. (n.d.a). *Global atlas of environmental justice.* Retrieved August 21, 2021, from https://ejatlas.org/

Environmental Justice Atlas. (n.d.b). *Frequently asked questions.* https://ejatlas.org/about

Emmanuel, A. (1972). *Unequal exchange: A study of the imperialism of trade.* New York: Monthly Review Press.

European Commission. (2018). *A clean planet for all: A European strategic long-term vision for a prosperous, modern, competitive and climate neutral economy.* EUR-Lex. https://eur-lex.europa.eu/legal-content/EN/TXT/PDF/?uri=CELEX:52018DC0773

Foster, J.B. (2002). *Ecology against capitalism.* New York: Monthly Review Press.

Foster, J.B., Clark, B., & York, R. (2011). *The ecological rift: Capitalism's war on the Earth.* New York: Monthly Review Press.

Frank, A.G. (1967). *Dependent accumulation and under-development.* London: Macmillan.

Frobel, F., Heinrichs, J., & Kreye, O. (1979). *The new international division of labor.* New York: Cambridge University Press.

Galeano, Eduardo. (1997). *Open veins of Latin America: Five centuries of pillage of the continent.* New York: Monthly Review Press.

Galtung, J. (1971). A structural theory of imperialism. *Journal of Peace Research, 8*(2), 81–117.

Global Diligence. (2014). Communication under Article 15 of the Rome Statute of the International Court. *The Commission of the Crimes against Humanity in Cambodia*, July 2002–Present. https://static1.squarespace.com/static/5bf447e7365f02310e09e592/t/5eb178be2da21b0620c19194/1588689097212/executive_summary-ICC.pdf

Glyn, A. (2007). *Capitalism unleashed: Finance, globalization, and welfare.* Oxford: Oxford University Press. https://doi.org/10.1093/acprof:oso/9780199226795.001.0001

Haberl, H., Fischer-Kowalski, M., Krausman, F., Martinez-Alier, J., & Winiwarter, V. (2011). A sociometabolic transition towards sustainability? Challenges for another great transformation. *Sustainable Development, 19*, 1–14.

Harvey, D. (2005). *A brief history of neoliberalism.* Oxford: Oxford University Press. https://doi.org/10.1093/oso/9780199283262.001.0001

Hickel, J. (2019). The contradiction of the sustainable development goals: Growth versus ecology on a finite planet. *Sustainable Development, 27*(5), 1–12. https://doi.org/10.1002/sd.1947

Hornborg, A. (2011). *Global ecology and unequal exchange: Fetishism in a zero-sum world.* Abingdon and Oxon: Routledge. https://doi.org/10.4324/9780203806890

International Geosphere-Biosphere Program. (n.d.). *Great Acceleration.* Global Change. http://www.igbp.net/globalchange/greatacceleration.4.1b8ae20512db692f2a680001630.html

International Women and Mining Network/ Red Internacional Mujeres y Mineria (RIMM). (2010). *Women from affected mining communities speak out: Defending land, life, & dignity.* International Women and Mining Network. https://landportal.org/node/13967

IPCC. (2022). IPCC Sixth Assessment Report Climate Change 2022: Impacts, Adaptation, and Vulnerability. IPCC. https://www.ipcc.ch/report/ar6/wg2/downloads/report/IPCC_AR6_WGII_FinalDraft_FullReport.pdf

Kiely, Ray. (2010). "Dependency and World-Systems Perspectives on Development." Oxford Research Encyclopedias. https://doi.org/10.1093/acrefore/9780190846626.013.142

Klare, M. (2012). *The race for what's left: The global scramble for the world's last resources.* New York: Picador.

Krausmann, F., Fischer-Kowalski, M., Schandl, H., & Eisenmenger, N. (2008). The Global sociometabolic transition past and present metabolic profiles and their future trajectories. *Journal of Industrial Ecology, 12*(5–6), 636–656.

Luxemburg, R. (1964). *The accumulation of capital.* New York: Monthly Review Press.

Magdoff, H., & Foster, J.B. (2003). *Imperialism without colonies.* New York: Monthly Review Press.

Manrique, Pedro Luis Perez, Julien Brun, Ana Gonzalez-Martinez, and Joan Martinez-Alier. (2013). "The biophysical performance of Argentina: 1970–2009." *Journal of Industrial Ecology, 17*(4): 590–604.

Material Flow Analysis Portal. (n.d.). *Decoupling material use and economic performance.* Materialflows.net. http://www.materialflows.net/visualisation-centre/data-visualisations/?_inputs_&sidebar=%22bar_chart_1%22

McCarthy, J. (2007). Privatizing conditions of production: Trade agreements as neoliberal environmental governance. In N. Heynen, J. McCarthy, S. Prudham, & P. Robbins (Eds.), *Neoliberal environments: False promises and unnatural consequences* (pp. 38–50). London: Routledge.

McCarthy, J., & Prudham, S. (2004). Neoliberal nature and the nature of neoliberalism. *Geoforum, 35*(3), 275–283. https://doi.org/10.1016/j.geoforum.2003.07.003

McMichael, P. (2017). *Development and social change: A global perspective.* (6th edition). Thousand Oaks, CA: Sage Publications.

Moore, J.W. (2001). Marx's ecology and the environmental history of world capitalism. *Capitalism Nature Socialism, 12*(3), 134–139. https://doi.org/10.1080/104557501101245045

Moore, J.W. (2003). 'The modern world-system' as environmental history? Ecology and the rise of capitalism. *Theory and Society, 32*(3): 307–377.

Moore, J.W. (2011). Transcending the metabolic rift: A theory of crises in the capitalist world-ecology. *The Journal of Peasant Studies, 38*(1), 1–46. https://doi.org/10.1080/03066150.2010.538579

Moore, J.W. (2012). Cheap food & bad money: Food, frontiers, and financialization in the rise and eemise of neoliberalism. *Review (Fernand Braudel Center), 33*(2/3), 225–261.

Moore, J.W. (2014). The value of everything? Work, capital, and historical nature in the capitalist world-ecology. *Review (Fernand Braudel Center): World-Ecological Imaginations*, 37(3–4), 245–292.

Moore, J.W. (2015). *Capitalism in the web of life: Ecology and the accumulation of capital.* London: Verso.

McNeil, J.R. (2000). *Something new under the Sun: An environmental history of the twentieth-century world* (The Global Century Series). New York: Norton and Company, Ltd.

Muradian, R. & Martinez-Alier, J. (2001b). "Trade and the environment: From a southern perspective." *Ecological Economics, 36*: 281-297.

Obeng-Odoom, F. (2021). *The commons in an age of uncertainty: Decolonizing nature, economy and society.* University of Toronto Press.

O'Connor, J. (1998). *Natural causes: Essays in ecological Marxism.* New York: The Guilford Press.

Oxfam. (2015, December 2). *Extreme carbon inequality: Why the Paris climate deal must put the poorest, lowest emitting and most vulnerable people first.* https://policy-practice.oxfam.org/resources/extreme-carbon-inequality-why-the-paris-climate-deal-must-put-the-poorest-lowes-582545/

Oxfam. (2018, January 22). *Reward work, not wealth*. https://www.oxfam.org/en/research/reward-work-not-wealth

Parrique, T., Barth, J., Briens, F., Kerschner, C., Kraus-Polk, A., Kuokkanen, A., & Spangenberg, J.H. (2019). *Decoupling debunked: Evidence and arguments against green growth as a sole strategy for sustainability*. European Environmental Bureau (EEB) & Make Europe Sustainable for All. https://mk0eeborgicuypctuf7e.kinstacdn.com/wp-content/uploads/2019/07/Decoupling-Debunked.pdf

Perez-Rincon, M.A. (2006). Colombian international trade from a physical perspective: Towards an ecological 'Prebisch thesis'. *Ecological Economics*, *59*(4): 519–529.

Reuss, A. (2013) *Labor and the global economy*. Boston, MA: Dollars and Sense.

Shandra, J.M., Shor, E., Maynard, G., & London, B. (2008). Debt, structural adjustment, and deforestation: A cross-national study. *Journal of World Systems Research*, *14*(1), 1–21. https://doi.org/10.5195/jwsr.2008.345

Spaargaren, G., Mol, A., & Buttel, F. (2000). *Environment and global modernity*. Thousand Oaks, CA: Sage Publications Ltd.

Steffen, W., Persson, A., Deutsch, L., Zalasiewicz, J., Williams, M., Richardson, K., Crumley, C., Crutzen, P., Folke, C., Gordon, L., Molina, M., Ramanathan, V., Rockström, J., Scheffer, M., Schellnhuber, H.J., & Svedin, U. (2011). The anthropocene: From global change to planetary. *Ambio*, *40*(7), 739–761. https://doi.org/10.1007/s13280-011-0185-x

United Nations Conference on Trade and Development (UNCTAD). (2012). *Economic development in Africa report 2012: Structural transformation and sustainable development in Africa*. New York: United Nations. https://unctad.org/system/files/official-document/aldcafrica2012_embargo_en.pdf

United Nations Environment Programme (UNEP). (2011). *Decoupling natural resource use and environmental impacts from economic growth*. Paris. https://wedocs.unep.org/handle/20.500.11822/9816

Vallejo, M.C. (2010). Biophysical structure of the Ecuadorian economy, foreign trade, and policy implications. *Ecological Economics*, *70*, 159–169.

Van Den Berg, H. (2017). *International economics: A heterodox approach* (3rd ed.). New York: Routledge.

Wallerstein, I. (1974). *The modern world-system*. New York: Academic Press.

Wallerstein, I. (1980). *The capitalist world economy*. Cambridge: Cambridge University Press.

Weisz, H., Fischer-Kowalski, M., Grunbuhel, C., Haberl, H., Krausman, F., & Winiwarter, V. (2001). Global environmental change and historical transitions. *Innovation: The European Journal of Social Science Research*, *14*(2), 117–142.

Wolf, E. (2010). *Europe and the people without history*. Berkeley and Los Angeles, CA: University of California Press.

World Bank. (1992). *World development report, 1992: Development and the environment*. Oxford: Oxford University Press for the World Bank. https://doi.org/10.1596/0-1952-0876-5

World Bank. (2011). *The changing wealth of nations: Measuring sustainable development in the new millennium*. Washington, DC: World Bank.

Notes

1 Global material extraction equals the amount of materials extracted worldwide, including biomass, fossil fuels, minerals, and metals. The indicator does not account for water or air.

2 I = P (population) × A (affluence or consumption) × T (technology) (IPAT) (Steffen et al., 2011).

3 Ecological imperialism was first used by Crosby in his study of the global transfer of organisms that accompanied European colonial endeavors. It was not a study of political economy and is quite different from how this book uses the term. Later, Clark and Foster (2009) use the term "ecological imperialism" in their work on guano trade during the colonial era and ecologically unequal exchange, but do not specifically define it. In my 2014 dissertation on FDI in Africa's natural resource sector, I use the term and attempt to give some basic definitions for it. I have also used it in subsequent publications.

4 See for example World Bank (2011).

5 M-C-M' refers to Marx's most fundamental observation about the essence of capitalism. In capitalism, money is transformed into a commodity, and the commodity is sold for M'. M' represents the original money advanced, M, (for example, invested in a factory), plus surplus value. M' = M + surplus value. This formulation is significant in that it encapsulates how in capitalism, the extraction of surplus value (profit) dominates the logic of production.

2 Neoliberal Development and Ecological Imperialism

Ecological imperialism is embedded in the fundamental structures of contemporary globalization, or more precisely "neoliberal globalization"—a specific form of economic integration built upon socio-economic structures, policies, and ideologies that at the root aim for the removal of any barriers to the accumulation of capital while promoting market-based solutions. While the Global South was initially integrated into the capitalist world-system through the violent processes of colonialism, integration into neoliberal globalization has occurred for decades under the auspices of neoliberal development. This has manifested at times through the stick of debt, structural adjustment policies, and foreign military intervention and at other times through the carrot in promises of economic growth and industrialization.

The central argument of this chapter, explored in detail through case studies from Africa and Asia in subsequent chapters, is that contemporary ecological imperialism is rooted in these neoliberal development policies. These policies are at the source of the rapid degradation of Global South Natures and hence are in large part responsible for the planetary ecological crises witnessed today. The Global South's dependent position was reinforced through a series of neoliberal development policies, including changes in the structures of international trade, international investment, and international finance. All of these policies enabled the enclosure, privatization, marketization, and exploitation of Nature in the Global South. Through neoliberal development policies, the recipient position of the Global South in a global economy dominated by large transnational corporations and transnational financial corporations has been created.

This chapter begins with a brief historical overview of the long exploitation of Global South Natures, and the various attempts of the Global South to regain resource sovereignty through resistances, movements, and countermovements. A historical perspective sheds light on the political ecological agenda of neoliberal development policies. In contrast to orthodox assertions that neoliberal policies were a logical correction to the corrupt and inefficient state-interventionist policies of economic nationalism, a historical perspective shows that, at least in part, neoliberal policies were a backlash against growing Third World economic militancy, and, importantly, against Third World attempts at resource sovereignty.

DOI: 10.4324/9780429261305-2

The chapter then highlights the essential features of neoliberal development policies in regard to the three pillars of globalization: international trade, foreign investment, and international finance. All three pillars of globalization[1] have been restructured over the last several decades along free market lines. The planetary ecological crises unfurling before us, underpinned by the dynamics of ecological imperialism, are not due to any single aspect of globalization. It is not just due to unequal patterns of resource consumption arising from international trade, nor due to the bad actions of certain unscrupulous transnational corporations; rather, ecological imperialism and planetary ecocide are arising from the totality of how all the major aspects of the global economy—trade, investment, and finance—interact and enable a system geared toward the ceaseless accumulation of capital at the expense of socio-ecological crises, dispossession, and displacement in the Global South. On the one hand, neoliberal development policies concerning trade and foreign investment have created the necessary political-economic conditions for the exploitation of the peripheral resources by foreign capital; on the other hand, financial liberalization has freed capital from its constraints to exploit such opportunities globally.

A Brief History of the Long Exploitation of Global South Natures: Resistances, Movements, and Counter-Movements

Colonialism: 1492–1960s

Ecological imperialism and the planetary ecocide that humanity faces in the 21st century have their historical roots in European colonialism that began with the exploration of the Americas by Christopher Columbus in 1492 and lasted, in varying forms, until the decolonization movements of the late 20th century. Colonialism accomplished what was to be the basis of contemporary globalization—an integrated capitalist world-system, the division of the world into a wealthy Global North and an impoverished Global South, and an international division of labor of core industrialized economies and peripheral economies that are dependent upon the extraction and export of natural resources. Colonialism was a profoundly socio-ecologically disruptive phenomenon. As parts of Asia, Africa, and the Americas fell under the control of the European capitalist countries in their competitive scramble for land, resources, and labor, colonialism simultaneously underdeveloped the societies of colonized regions while ecologically devastating their Natures. In the conquest and plundering of the colonized regions, which today constitutes nearly all of the Global South, resources were not merely looted. Rather, entire societies, economies, and indigenous relations to Nature were reconfigured to meet the needs of European colonizers with long-lasting repercussions that remain entrenched until today.

Initially under the colonialism of Spain and Portugal, resources in the Americas, such as gold and silver, were simply looted with the aid of an enslaved indigenous population without the introduction of capitalist relations of production. Spain and Portugal's colonialism led to a severe demographic crisis as up to 45–90 million of the original indigenous population died of overwork, disease, or conflict with the colonizers (Cypher, 2014). As colonialism progressed and the logic of capitalist relations of production were introduced, economies were restructured. Prior to colonialism, the majority of indigenous people depended on their local ecosystems to supply their various needs. However, with the restructuring of economies pre-colonial food systems were forcibly replaced by specialized export monocultures (McMicheal, 2017). Through appropriating the land of the colonized, colonizer nations imposed plantations, and local farmers were forced to become plantation laborers who cultivated single cash crops. For example, the British restructured Indian agriculture and forced Indians, through a combination of taxes and laws, to specialize and export the cash crops necessary for the British industrial revolution, such as indigo, cotton, and wheat. Monocrop agriculture resulted in a host of environmental repercussions. For example, the near absence of crop rotation, which, combined with overexpansion into marginal lands, set the stage for erosion, soil depletion, and eventual collapsing yields (Cypher, 2014). Through colonialism, mines were also created to extract metal and minerals for the colonizers, introducing the logic of extractivism that still characterizes the economies of the Global South today. Overall, through colonialism the initial dynamics of capitalist industrialization, whereby Nature is broken into its constitutive components and exploited as "natural capital" in the production process under the logic of profit maximization, emerged (McMichael, 2017). Colonialism introduced the logic of primitive accumulation, which meant the enclosure, privatization, and exploitation of ecological commons. For example, in order to expand their tax base, the British privatized Indian forests that were traditionally used for food, medicine, and firewood (Cypher, 2014). Colonialism also established what contemporary scholars call "ecologically unequal exchange." Ecologically unequal exchange is the asymmetrical flow of resources, with the incumbent environmental degradation, from peripheral regions to the core economies of the Global North, a pattern still occurring today.

With colonialism, resources were transformed into the privately owned assets of the colonial powers, laying the foundation for the initial accumulation of surplus in the Global North and the simultaneous underdevelopment of the Global South. The profits of colonialism resulted in a large flow of not just resources but also capital from the colonies to the colonial metropole. For example, in 1930 when coffee was the major export crop in Indonesia under Dutch rule, it is estimated that Indonesia's Net Domestic Product net drain amounted to 15.6%. Profits from Britain's colonial empire flowed into the British banking system, adding to liquidity, driving down interest rates, and releasing a flow of investment funds which could be tapped by the early British industrialists for their industrialization projects. Importantly, colonialism provided an outlet for another crucial expansionary dynamic of capitalism—external markets for the manufactured exports of the colonizers. The revenues from the export of manufactured goods such as woolens, guns, iron and steel products, and so on, all further stimulated British investment, production, and employment. In certain sectors, this resulted in the deindustrialization of the colonies whose indigenous industries could not compete with the cheaper British imports (Cypher, 2014).

Economic Nationalism and Resource Sovereignty: 1940s–Late 1970s

By the mid- to late 20th century, liberation movements throughout the colonized world brought about the final death throes of formal colonization throughout Asia and Africa; Latin America had decolonized earlier in the 19th century. Nonetheless, with decolonization, post-colonial countries globally found themselves in a common situation of being politically liberated but in a state of economic dependency and underdevelopment. In this era, many scholars and political leaders characterized this situation as a form of "neocolonialism." Colonialism, and the subsequent neocolonialism enforced by the structures of the global economy, imposed a particular global pattern of production and trade on the less developed nations. The result was an international division of labor in which less developed countries emerged as exporters of primary products to world markets and importers of manufactured goods from the more developed nations. Further, most sectors of post-colonial countries' economies still remained under the control of foreign multinational corporations (MNCs), often belonging to the country's former colonial masters.

The situation was deeply problematic for post-colonial countries. From the 1880s onward, the terms of trade moved against commodity and mineral producers, and many post-colonial countries whose economy depended upon the production and export of a limited array of primary products found themselves in precarious economic straits. Further, such extractive economies were plagued by the legacy of what development economists have called "economic dualism." Economic dualism is a form of economic disintegration, a two-sector economy where pre-capitalist, transitional forms of production are juxtaposed with modern, enclave capitalist sectors that have no linkages with the broader economy. The result is a lopsided form of mal-development geared toward the extraction of natural resources or plantation agriculture for export, while the rest of the economy experiences little to no growth or development.

Hence, despite having obtained the status of sovereign and equal states, post-colonial countries perceived the post-WWII economic order as continuing an international division of labor that disadvantaged them while largely benefiting the West (Adeniran, 1986). In pursuit of greater economic sovereignty, post-colonial countries across the world undertook the restructuring of their economies along developmentalist lines. Laissez-faire capitalism, being the ideology of the former colonial powers, was questioned or rejected and various forms of socialism or state capitalism were implemented (Thomson, 2000). State intervention was seen as integral to overcoming the structural weaknesses of the post-colonial economic position. While post-colonial economies continued their traditional roles as exporters of primary commodities, surpluses from the primary sector were channeled to meet the requirements of import substitution-driven industrialization (such as in the case of Brazil's successful, if temporary, experiment with import substitution industrialization, which served as an example for other post-colonial countries).

All in all, some form of economic nationalism characterized the development paradigm for post-independent countries. Re-examining this brief but important era from a political ecology lens is crucial to understanding the subsequent neoliberal paradigm as a *political* agenda and not merely a more efficient way to organize economies. While much radical scholarship has emphasized how neoliberalism was a backlash to the growing power of labor in the 1970s, neoliberalism was also a backlash against Third World nationalism that sought to regain sovereignty over their own resources. Third World economic nationalism was ultimately a counter-movement to the economic dependency created under colonial expansion and the expansion of the capitalist world-system. It was a counter-movement against the powerful transnational corporations (TNCs) that exerted control over the economies of the periphery post-colonialism as well as the patterns of trade and production imposed by colonialism. In the post-WWII era, transnational corporations became dominant actors in the system of production and accumulation (Girvan, 1975, 1976; Magdoff & Foster, 2003). Features of transnational capitalism included diversified, internationalized production under centralized control, the massive size and huge financial resources of the basic institutional unit, technological dynamism and vanguardism, and high and continuously growing concentration of economic power. This new system came to dominate the world economy, whether developed, underdeveloped, or socialist (Girvan, 1976). The threat to economic sovereignty posed by foreign control and decision-making in major sectors of the domestic economy contrasted with the political status of the newly independent states that were formally sovereign and equal to all other states through their admittance into the United Nations (UN) (Lozoya, 1980).

Thus began the era of Third Worldism and economic nationalism, and for post-colonial states, central to this issue of economic sovereignty was sovereignty over their own natural resources, which manifested in a series of events from the 1960s to the mid-1970s. Such events included numerous state expropriations of foreign-owned natural resource industries (and industries in the tertiary sector), the formation of primary commodity cartels such as the Organization of the Petroleum Exporting Countries (OPEC), and sets of proposals that voiced Third World grievances put forth through the United Nations platform. Despite their economic dependency, during this time period Third World states discovered that they also had powerful new sources of leverage in international economic relations. Within the changing international political climate arose the Non-Aligned Movement, a forum of 120 developing countries not formally aligned with any major power bloc. The Movement formed to keep the newly independent countries in Asia and

Africa from the superpower rivalry between the United States and the Soviet Union and to protect their newly acquired independence.

The era of economic nationalism was admittedly complicated. Economic nationalism was not an environmental movement. Like any development paradigm, economic nationalism was built upon the aims of rapid industrialization. Economic nationalism was neither fully successful since in the end the engaged countries built up considerable levels of unsustainable debt. Nor was it fully a failure as it resulted in economic growth and created the basis of industrialization for some emerging economies today. Economic nationalism was anti-imperialist in rhetoric and sometimes in policy but not necessarily anti-capitalist. Unlike the neoliberalism that would replace it, economic nationalism in theory was premised upon development for all social classes, but it was not necessarily driven as a movement from below.[2] With its complicated history, economic nationalism has been duly criticized from both the political right and the political left. Nonetheless, from the perspective of political ecology, under economic nationalism the ideological stance and political-economic policies regarding resource sovereignty represented the first coordinated attempt at the state level and international level to wrest resources since their appropriation under colonialism from the Global North. In many ways economic nationalism represented the last such coordinated attempts at the state and international level since its fall. In contrast, today many government officials throughout the Global South are actively aligned with the interests of foreign investors, particularly in natural resource sectors. The central point is that economic nationalism, in regard to natural resources, was a relatively militant Third World movement that challenged the ecological imperialism of neocolonialism.

Needless to say, these attempts at resource sovereignty represented a clear threat to the industrializing needs of the Global North and were not well received. The growth of the socialist bloc, the influence of the UN, the economic growth of Western Europe and Japan, and the emergence of the Soviet Union and China as major economic powers all resulted in increased competition among major industrial nations for the Third World's natural resources (Lozoya & Cuadra, 1980). During this time period, access to energy and raw materials became crucial to the developed world's economic machinery as well as rapid industrialization and urbanization. Despite the end of formal colonialism, the First World continued to rely on the exploitation of the Third World's resources in the post-colonial period. Neocolonialism, the era of post-colonial imperialism, was predicated on this reliance (Magdoff, 1969, 1978, Magdoff & Foster, 2003). By the end of the 19th century within each of the industrialized nations, economic power had shifted to a relatively small number of large, integrated industrial and financial firms. As mentioned in Chapter 1, the rapid economic growth of the post-WWII era and the development of new technology drove the search for new energy sources. During this time period, industry became mechanized, and technology required the investment of large amounts of capital, large production units, and large amounts of strategic metals and fossil fuels. Technological advancement in steel, electricity, industrial chemistry, and oil also allowed for large-scale production through large-scale transportation, electricity, and advances in industrial chemistry. These advances consequently allowed for large concentrations of economic power in industry and finance, accelerated monopolistic trends, and the rise of big business, which in turn further spurred the drive for raw materials. The new industries, new technology, and the rise of competition among industrialized nations all gave a renewed importance to the role of raw materials, all central dynamics of post-WWII imperialism.

The Third World began to realize that this dependency constituted a potential source of economic power and sovereignty for primary commodity exporters (Lozoya & Cuadra, 1980). In fact, the years between 1972 and 1974 witnessed a shortage of many primary commodities, especially those of strategic importance in high-growth industries such as petroleum, bauxite, and phosphates (Girvan, 1976). As the Third World controlled the supply of many important fuels and raw materials, Third World demands for a more equitable international economic system became increasingly potent (Lozoya & Cuadra, 1980). The OPEC oil embargo of 1972–1973 was a prime example of the Third World increasingly recognizing its own economic power in the face of advanced industrial countries increasing dependence on strategic resources. Arab Members of the Organization of Petroleum Exporting Countries (OPEC) placed an embargo on nations supporting Israel during the Yom Kippur War and caused the price of oil to increase by nearly 300%, sending an oil shock throughout the global economy.

Though many importers of oil in the Third World also suffered from increased oil prices due to OPEC's oil embargo, the Third World's reaction was largely supportive. OPEC represented a set of primary producers from the Third World who successfully demanded their fair share of the world's incomes by their own actions. From the OPEC experience, developing countries inferred that their primary commodity exports, which had traditionally been viewed as a sign of weakness, could be turned instead into weapons of collective action (Bhagwati, 1977). The concept behind primary commodity cartels was to allow countries in the Third World to actively control their terms of trade with the industrialized world and the returns they got from the powerful MNCs in contrast to their historical subjugation. The OPEC action inspired similar attempts from dozens of other Third World primary commodity exporters. For example, seven leading bauxite exporters formed the International Bauxite Association, and six leading phosphate producers tripled their prices (Girvan, 1976). Third World states also actively contested the power of transnational capital and neocolonialism through the expropriation of foreign-owned natural resource industries. As early as 1937–1938 in Bolivia and Mexico, conflicts around the expropriations of foreign oil companies erupted between Third World states and MNCs. Kennedy (1992) divides the relations between TNCs and the host countries' governments into three eras since 1945: TNC domination, confrontation between governments of host countries and TNCs, and negotiation between TNCs and governments of host countries. The first era lasted into the early 1960s and the second era was at its height during the 1970s. By the 1980s, the third era had begun. In the mid-1960s, the number of expropriations had begun to rise, reaching a zenith between 1970 and 1979. But by the 1980–1985 period, as experiments in economic nationalism collapsed globally and neoliberalism became hegemonic, the number of expropriation acts dropped dramatically (Kennedy, 1992).

Nationalizations and cartels were not the only ways in which the Third World sought to regain resource sovereignty and present an increasingly militant stance against First World hegemony. The Third World also realized that without major structural changes in the international economic system economic independence and development would be difficult. This realization, together with OPEC success, spurred the Third World to adopt a series of coherent demands despite the major ideological differences among individual nations. Known as the New International Economic Order (NIEO), these demands were presented on a platform to the UN. By the 1970s, demands for a New International Economic Order were vocalized when Presidents Boumediene of Algeria and Echeverria of Mexico, among others, called for structural reforms in the international economic system. Their initiatives resulted in the adoption of UN resolutions such as the "Sixth and Seventh Special Session" and the "Charter of Economic Rights and Duties of States." These were followed by a long series of declarations, resolutions, position papers, and studies of various NIEO issues by the UN and the international community at large (Lozoya, 1980). During this time period, they adopted the ideological position that the international economic system should be more equitable, and make it possible for post-colonial states to industrialize and be relieved of debt to the Western capitalist countries. The goal, ultimately, was to achieve economic independence and development (Adeniran, 1986).

The New International Economic Order was in many ways the apex of Third World collective demands for sovereignty over their resources and increased returns for their resource exports. Essentially, the NIEO demanded the sovereign equality of states and self-determination of all peoples, the non-interference in the internal affairs of states, the right of every country to adopt the economic and social system that it deems the most appropriate for its own development (and not be subjected to discrimination of any kind as a result), and full and permanent sovereignty of every state over its natural resources and all economic activities. In order to safeguard these resources, the NIEO demanded that each state is entitled to exercise effective control over its resources and the exploitation of its resources with means suitable to its own situation, including the right to nationalization or transfer of ownership to nationals. The NIEO further demanded that no state may be subjected to economic, political, or any other type of coercion that prevents the free and full exercise of this inalienable right. Further, the NIEO demanded compensation for the exploitation of natural resources that occurred under colonialism (Haight, 1975). Along these lines, the NIEO argued for the right for developing countries to regulate and supervise TNCs operating within their territories and the right to implement measures regulating TNCs that were in accordance with national development plans. The NIEO also sought to establish a more equitable relationship between the prices of raw materials and primary commodities that the Third World exported, and those of the capital goods and equipment imported from the First World (i.e., more equitable terms of trade). Importantly, it advocated for the developing world's right to utilize producers' associations (primary commodity cartels) within the framework of international cooperation (Haight, 1975).

At the heart of these stipulations lay the recognition of the inextricable relations between political and economic sovereignty and the capacity for the formerly colonized states to have full and permanent sovereignty over their resources. The rhetoric of the NIEO gave strong recognition of the injustice engendered by colonialism and the necessity of the formerly colonized states to be free from any form of neocolonialism, including the structural inequalities of the international economic order which remained deeply unequal. Not surprisingly, economic nationalism as signified by the expropriations, the growing number of primary commodity cartels, and the sets of proposals such as the NIEO was not received well by the developed countries. Even before the NIEO, Northern hostility to the increasing economic nationalism and perceived threat from the Third World was manifesting (Bergstein, 1973; Girvan, 1976). The main issue was simple to understand; at a time when the developed countries became crucially dependent on various resources from the periphery, the push for greater returns for their exports and full sovereignty over their own resources ran directly counter to the concerns of consuming countries to retain assured access to foreign supplies at reasonable prices (Bergstein, 1973).

Thus the West's reaction was a resounding rejection of the Third World's demands for an adjustment to the international economic order, heralding what Samir Amin regards as a new phase of "aggressive anti-Third Worldism" (Amin, 1990). For one, the demands were deeply at odds with the rising currents of neoliberalism and in the hegemonic powers of the US and UK and threatened a free market-based international economic system. Keynesian economics and sympathy for a more regulated capitalism with state intervention was becoming increasingly challenged within the developed countries themselves. From a neoliberal ideological standpoint, the USA argued that the principal cause of developing countries' poverty was not external but internal, in particular its incapacity to internally mobilize resources for economic development due to Third World socialism (Bhagwati, 1977). Whatever the ideological standpoint or reasoning, the NIEO and Third World economic nationalism threatened developed world interests in continuing the secure and cheap access to resources that had been established under colonialism and neocolonialism. Due to developed world rejection, the demands from the NIEO collapsed before any real implementation of the adjustments they called for were made.

By the early 1980s, the tides began to irrevocably turn against economic nationalism. In addition to the First World rejection of economic nationalist policies, the developing world was caught in a severe global debt crisis that stemmed from multiple sources. For one, the economic nationalism of the post-independence years had included the adoption of varying import substitution policies. Import substitution industrialization (ISI) is a set of strategies that promotes the substitution of (manufactured) imports through domestic production by using protectionist trade policies and other domestic policies that target selected industries. Its aim is to create a domestic manufacturing industry as a deliberate strategy to increase the economic and technological independence of Third World countries from their former colonial masters and the neocolonial First World. Yet despite the objective of self-reliance, import substitution required capital that ultimately had to be borrowed from the developed world. In the end, developing countries were unable to repay the debts for both external and internal reasons. Studies have documented the following external reasons for the debt crises: the decline of international prices paid for primary commodities in the late 1970s (Helleiner, 1983; Cheru, 1989; Thomson, 2000), the 1973 OPEC oil price hikes that strained developing economies which were oil importers (Cheru, 1989; DeLancey 1992; Thomson, 2000), the decline of the official sources of development aid (Thomson, 2000), the increase of borrowed capital costs (Helleiner, 1983), and the rise of US interest rates during the early 1980s (Satgar, 2009). Scholars often blame internal reasons such as governmental inefficiency, pervasive mismanagement, and corruption for the debt crises (Onwuka & Aluko, 1986). Other internal issues included the failure to diversify sufficiently during the 1960s and 1970s, which was a period of faster growth (UNCTAD, 2005). DeLancey (1992) also argues that the use of the loans failed to generate the foreign exchange required to service the debts. Overall, it is arguable that both internal and external factors precipitated the collapse of import substitution industrialization—and with this collapse, the end of an era of economic nationalism that sought greater autonomy for the Third World in the global economy. In addition, the Third World now found itself on the brink of a major debt crisis that would usher in the era of neoliberal ecological imperialism.

Debt, the Collapse of Economic Nationalism, and the Turn toward Neoliberal Development: Early 1980s–Current

While the 1970s witnessed the apex of Third World economic nationalism, crucial events in both the First and Third World would soon result in economic nationalism's collapse. This collapse was soon superseded by economic restructuring along free market lines, or what would come to be called "neoliberalism." With the building debt crises, many developing countries were unable to get further private loans and turned to the International Monetary Fund (IMF) and the World Bank for credit. These entities imposed a series of conditions that included domestic policies of austerity (eliminating government price controls and subsidies, cutting government spending and employment, devaluing the country's currency, among others) as well as deeper economic policy changes known as structural adjustments. In the developing world, these neoliberal policies manifested as a wholesale backlash against economic nationalism.

In the First World, neoliberalism arose from capitalist crises in the core. In the United States, the world's superpower since WWII, a series of economic crises exposed the contradictions of the so-called Golden Era of capitalism's high economic growth—relatively more equal distributions of wealth and income and low unemployment. Post-WWII, US capitalism was regulated capitalism; for the US, this meant an uneasy truce between Big Capital and Big Labor, an extended welfare state following the Great Depression of the 1930s, and, more generally, an increase of government intervention in the economy. By the 1970s, however, several factors threatened this state of affairs, primarily the competition from the exports of the newly rebuilt economies of Japan and Europe, the increasing costs of government regulations on business profits, a full-employment profit squeeze as high employment levels made workers bolder in demanding wage increases, and, discussed above, the threat of Third World militancy over resource sovereignty, in particular the OPEC oil embargo of the early 1970s (Reuss, 2013). The solution for US capitalism was two pronged. Domestically, tactics included crackdowns on unions and policies favorable to business, such as weakened regulation and tax cuts for corporations. Externally, it included the establishment of worldwide production sites in search of cheaper labor costs and international trade pacts that reflected the interests of large transnational corporations.

Due to the debt crises in the Third World and the subsequent structural adjustment policies, economic nationalism in much of the Third World had essentially collapsed by the 1980s, and their societies underwent an extended series of radical structural adjustments realigning Third World economies according to the principles of laissez-faire capitalism, comparative advantage, and increased external integration. The central features of neoliberal policy, captured in a set of economic policies known as the Washington Consensus, encouraged trade liberalization, devaluation of currencies to stimulate export growth, foreign direct investment, and the securing of property rights, among other policies. As Peet (2009) writes, such policies favored an outward-oriented, export economy that was organized through markets with minimal state regulation along with privatization, trade liberalization, and limited state budget deficits. These policies accomplished in one fell swoop two major concerns of the First World. First, these policies restructured developing countries' economies in a way that would ensure First World banks and other financial institutions would see their debts repaid. Second, under economic nationalism, sovereignty over natural resources and the capacity to regulate TNCs were perceived as central to economic independence and the end of neocolonialism. Under the neoliberal reforms, Third World ecological resources were once again made accessible to the demands of capital accumulation as lingering obstructions enacted during the developmentalist era were removed, one after the other. Within a context of economic and political crisis, the Third World counter-movement, born from the contradictions engendered by the expansion of the world-capitalist system, was replaced by the neoliberal counter revolutionary movement (Table 2.1).

Table 2.1 Essential Phases, Dates, and Characteristics of Ecological Imperialism

Phases in Ecological Imperialism	*Dates*	*Essential Characteristics*	*Characteristics Salient to Ecological Imperialism*
Colonialism (formal)	• 1492–1960	• Formal colonialism: political, economic, military control over colonies • Creation of colonial international division of labor • Integration of periphery into capitalist world-system	• Restructuring of colonized economies to become natural resource exporters • Restructuring of socio-ecologies; rupturing of indigenous and local sustainable agricultural practices • Land grabbing, dispossession, enclosure of the commons • Introduction of profit motive as dominant logic of production
Economic Nationalism	• 1940s–late 1970s	• Post-colonial era • Era of neocolonialism • Economic nationalism as response to neocolonialism • UN NIEO • Non-aligned movement • Height of nationalizations, commodity cartels • Import substitution and other state interventionist economic alternatives	• Third World militancy in regard to resource sovereignty • Greater regulation, nationalizations of TNCs • Demands for better terms of trade for primary commodities • Demand for reparations for colonialism
Neoliberal Globalization	• Early 1980s–current	• Laissez faire economics • Liberalization of international trade, investment, finance • Structural adjustment policies • Outsourcing of manufacturing to periphery	• Repealing of regulations of TNCs, nationalizations • Greater flows of international investment, profit flows restored to TNCs • Re-entrenchment of colonial division of labor in parts of periphery (ecologically unequal exchange) • Simultaneous growth of emerging economies (shifting of pollution burdens with outsourced manufacturing) • Liberalization of finance; international finance as driving force behind ecological exploitation

Neoliberal Development and Ecological Imperialism: International Trade, International Investment, and International Finance

Nature is a politicized sphere. As O'Connor (1997) recognized, neither human labor-power, nor infrastructure, nor external Nature are produced "capitalistically," although capital treats these conditions of production as if they are commodities or commodity capital. Because neither labor-power nor external Nature are produced and reproduced in ways governed by the law of value, their price cannot be explained strictly in terms of exchange value. Further, there is no guarantee that either labor-power or Nature will be available in the form of what O'Connor, following Polanyi, termed "fictitious commodities"—commodities not produced capitalistically but still sold on the market as commodities. Much less is it guaranteed that labor-power and Nature will be reproduced under conditions that permit or favor capitalist production and accumulation (O'Connor, 1997). Rather, Nature, like labor, must be made available to capital in requisite quantities, and qualities, at the right place and time (O'Connor, 1997). And it is because of these reasons, as O'Connor (1997) pointed out, that the conditions of supply must be regulated by the state or capitals. Whether or not these conditions of production are available to capital depends on the political power of a constellation of actors; the political power of capital (and the relative power of factions of capital); the power of counter-movements such as environmentalism, unions, indigenous movements, and so on.

On the one hand, the neoliberal turn can be interpreted as a counter-counter-movement, that is, a backlash against the protective Polanyian counter-movement measures post-independence countries constructed during economic nationalism in regard to their natural resources. In other words, neoliberalism can be seen as a backlash against the measures adopted by the Third World to protect themselves against the vicissitudes of the international market and ensure their quest for national sovereignty. However, by the late 1970s, in the name of such goals as stabilization, efficiency, productivity, and competitiveness, the developmental state was replaced by market-oriented principles. This restored once again the unfettered expansionary tendencies of the market, which today is known by the more ambiguous term "globalization." Through export-led development policies and the push for trade, investment, and financial liberalization, neoliberal policies concretely and very specifically repealed the nationalist policies that had been put in place by formerly colonized states. Subsequently, the adoption of neoliberal reforms has had clear repercussions for peripheral ecologies by removing obstructions to peripheral resources' accessibility for foreign capital and the international market.

On the other hand, the neoliberal turn has created the political-economic context for opening up *new* environmental vistas of previously uncapitalized Nature for integration and regulation by the market. This trend is captured in the neoliberalization of the environment literature (Heynen, 2007). Central to the neoliberal project is privatization, a process that encloses land/resources that were previously "uncapitalized." Privatization can also manifest as privatization by capital that subsumes commons that were previously regulated or protected by the state. Harvey (2005) describes privatization as "the cutting edge of accumulation by dispossession" by citing how assets held by the state or in common were released into the market where overaccumulated capital could invest, upgrade, and speculate on them. Privatization is also pivotal in rendering other neoliberal policies, and ecological imperialism in general, possible. In foreign direct investment, for example, local governments have allowed MNCs to take over resources, water, forests, land for mining operations, and even ownership of food by privatizing its genetic codes, all of which hinge on the reformulation of property relations. A number of case studies have been conducted describing this process of intensified enclosures and privatization throughout both the developed and developing world (Robbins & Luginbuhl, 2007). Due to acquisition of privatized state-owned enterprises (SOEs), major sectors such as mining and manufacturing have come under direct control of foreign investors (Haque, 1999; Bridge, 2007). In addition to the reformulation of property relations in the favor of private capital, a number of scholars have documented the scaling back of environmental protections by the state (McCarthy, 2007). Assaults on Keynesian era environmental regulation, McCarthy contends, is as central to neoliberalism as are assaults on labor and social entitlement programs. The American Lands Alliance conducted a case study of 15 countries in Asia, Africa, and Latin America and found that due to austerity requirements under neoliberal structural adjustment programs countries were pressured to reduce government spending on environmental programs. The study concludes that such structural adjustments hampered enforcement capabilities, weakened protections for forests, thwarted efforts to prevent illegal logging of protected areas, instigated the poaching of endangered species, bred corruption, and curtailed the demarcation of indigenous lands (Tockman, 2001).

All these phenomena have been described with a variety of terms—"enclosures," "continuous primitive accumulation," "accumulation by dispossession," among others. Marx, in his concept of primitive accumulation, had argued that the establishment of capitalist relations, and the subsequent potential for capital accumulation, necessitates an initial separation of laborers from the means of production. In this process of separation, the social means of subsistence and production transform into capital, and the immediate producers transform into wage-laborers (Baird, n.d.). Modern interpretations not only contend that primitive accumulation is on-going but that it is an elementary, extra-economic prerequisite to capitalist production (Angelis, 2001). Similarly, Harvey (2005) encapsulates continuous primitive accumulation in his concept of "accumulation by dispossession." Like other theorists of imperialism, Harvey insists that capitalism must perpetually have something outside of itself in order to stabilize itself. The "primitive" or original accumulation under neoliberal capitalism constitutes an important and continuing force in the historical geography of capital accumulation through imperialism and includes all transformations from state (or other forms of commons) regulation into the hands of private capital (Harvey, 2005). The next several sections look more specifically at how these dynamics, as critical aspects of ecological imperialism, manifest within neoliberal development policies in regard to international trade, international investment, and international finance.

Ecological Imperialism, Neoliberal Development, and International Trade

The first pillar of neoliberal development is the restructuring of developing countries' economies in order to liberalize trade and support export-led development. In the neoliberal development paradigm that began in the 1980s, trade liberalization (removal of barriers to trade such as tariff and non-tariff measures), specialization according to one's comparative advantage, and export-led growth policies all replaced the inward-oriented ISI experiments of economic nationalism with the assumption that such policies would increase efficiency and growth in the economy. Ideologically, trade liberalization and specialization hails from the 19th-century English political economist David Ricardo's theory of comparative advantage. Essentially, the theory of comparative advantage holds that a country should specialize in the activities in which the economy's opportunity costs are lowest. Through specializing in one's comparative advantage and trading with other countries which in turn specialize in their comparative advantage, a country makes use of its resources most efficiently, and both that country as well as the world experiences gains from increased economic growth. The other main orthodox trade model, the Hecksher-Ohlin (H-O) model, also asserts that international trade results in an increase in aggregate national welfare as a result of trade and specialization. The H-O model stipulates that the total value of output, and thus total income, increases in all countries that engage in balanced international free trade. The H-O model also predicts an increase in consumption possibilities for countries that engage in international trade.

Following the debt crises of the 1980s, the International Financial Institutions (IFIs) such as the IMF and the World Bank encouraged a large number of developing countries to expand primary production, liberalize their trade policies, and devalue their currencies.[3] By emphasizing specialization and restructuring their economies in order to encourage export-led growth, developing countries would experience economic growth that would also help them repay their debts. For peripheral economies throughout Africa, Latin America, and parts of Asia, however, these policies largely replicated a neocolonial international division of labor and deepened the patterns of ecologically unequal exchange. During the era of economic nationalism, the developmentalist states of developing countries perceived the patterns of primary commodity production inherited from colonialism as a structural weakness to be overcome by import-substitution policies; the IFIs saw primary commodity production as their comparative advantage to be exploited. For peripheral countries in Latin America and Africa, comparative advantage meant—in the eyes of the Western-dominated institutions of the IMF, the World Trade Organization, and the World Bank—specializing in the export of natural resources. Chief among the sectors that were targeted for export-promotion included (and continue to include) mining, agriculture, and forest products. But the promotion of exports in absence of real improvements in countries' environmental safeguards has been a recipe for environmental destruction, including increased deforestation rate (Tockman, 2001). Other scholars have linked trade liberalization with monocropping and its harmful effects on ecosystems (Haque, 1999).

In Africa, for example, cash crop production was encouraged with the argument that the foreign exchange from cash crops could then be used to purchase development inputs. Increased food production was not considered essential where cash crop earnings could be used to purchase imported foods. In effect, the World Bank had used financial muscle to pressure governments to give up food self-sufficiency and promote export-oriented agriculture (Cheru, 1989). The IFIs also encouraged African countries to privatize agriculture and abandon their development strategies of "inefficient" state enterprises, which were portrayed as parasitic. State restrictions on imports and exports, considered a hindrance to the economic growth that would follow free market policies, were to be lifted. Overall, the ideological approach promoted export-oriented growth strategies with reliance upon market mechanisms and the promotion of the private sector (Campbell & Loxley, 1989).

The dismal failure of the structural adjustments to promote economic growth and alleviate poverty has been well-documented, and a number of critics argue such neoliberal policies have in fact only worsened these issues (Cheru, 1989; Mkandawire, 2005). The emphasis on export-led development through comparative advantage also reproduced other disadvantages of primary commodity production experienced during colonialism and neocolonialism. For example, because the IFIs had encouraged a large number of developing countries worldwide to expand primary production, devalue their currencies, and increase production, the net outcome was that international markets reacted to the increased availability of primary goods by lowering commodity prices (Campbell & Loxley, 1989).

International Trade and Ecologically Unequal Exchange

A central dynamic of ecological imperialism is ecologically unequal exchange (EUE). Hornborg (2011) argues that the industrial metabolism of core centers necessitates the appropriation of peripheral hinterlands' resources and the usurpation of peripheral sink capacity. Ecologically unequal exchange therefore posits an asymmetrical transfer of resources between core and peripheral economies (Hornborg, 1998, 2001, 2011). As Bunker (1985), one of the original theorists of ecological unequal exchange, had written decades ago, such an exchange leads to a systematic deterioration in the ecological situation of peripheral economies (with associated social and economic losses) to the benefit of core economies (with the associated gains in high levels of resource consumption, capital accumulation, and technological advance). The perpetuation of these uneven ecological burdens is predicated on the capacity of core industrial nations to engage in trade, or other forms of exchange, with peripheral nations that are fundamentally "ecologically unequal" though nominally fair. While ecologically unequal exchange originated from the international division of labor created during colonialism, it appears that neoliberal trade policies have reinforced peripheral economies' traditional colonial role as exporters of raw materials (Giljum & Eisenmenger, 2004). Although the case is more complicated for semi-peripheral industrializing developing countries (as Chapter 5 will show), neoliberalism seems to have deepened ecologically unequal exchange in peripheral regions such as Africa (as Chapter 3 will show).

The key contention of EUE—the pattern of core regions appropriating a net asymmetrical transfer of resources from peripheral hinterlands through the mechanism of international trade and/or offshouldering environmental burdens—has generated scores of empirical studies over the period of neoliberal development, particularly in the last decade or so as socio-ecological data have become increasingly comprehensive and refined.[4] This research strongly contests ecological modernization's essential stipulation that as countries develop they become less, not more, environmentally degrading; rather it seems that developed countries have lessened their domestic environmental degradation by offshoring it onto others. Some studies specifically use the term ecologically unequal exchange and others do not, but nonetheless such studies investigate the displacement of environmental burdens through trade.

Currently, there is substantial evidence that international trade does serve as a mechanism through which developed countries are able to maintain high levels of unsustainable consumption through offshoring their environmental burdens onto developing countries. For example, a study using the comprehensive material footprint indicator[5] found that developed countries' achievements in decoupling are small or even nonexistent (Wiedman et al., 2013). Rather, the authors found that as wealth grows, countries tend to reduce their *domestic* portion of material extraction through international trade while simultaneously allowing for the overall mass of material consumption to generally increase. Due to the increasing spatial separation of production and consumption in global supply chains, this has led to a shift in resource use and environmental pressures among countries. Wiedman et al. also note that unequal consumption of global resources by developed countries through the mechanism of trade has been well-documented for the cases of greenhouse gas emissions (Hertwich & Peters, 2009; Davis & Caldeira, 2010; Wiedmann et al., 2013), land use (Weinzettel et al., 2013; Yu et al., 2013), and water use

(Feng et al., 2011; Galli et al., 2012; Steen-Olsen et al., 2012; Lenzen et al., 2013). Threats to species through consumption of specific commodities are also disproportionately caused by richer nations (Lenzen et al., 2012).

There are a host of additional empirical studies on trade and the offshoring of environmental pressures. I roughly classify current works as the following: (a) studies concerning the overall patterns of asymmetrical transfers underlying exchanges between core and peripheral economies, and (b) studies of specific politico-economic factors and their connections to EUE. Concerning asymmetrical transfer of resources, scholars at the Institute of Social Ecology in Vienna who are researching societal metabolism have noted that globally certain regions tend to be net importers of resources while other regions tend to be net exporters. Some have contended that the study of societal metabolism can be utilized for the study of EUE and synthesized with world-systems theory (Eisenmenger & Giljum, 2004; Singh & Eisenmenger, 2010). Empirical works using national material flow accounting (MFA) at both the regional and national levels have generally corroborated the central tenet of EUE theory that peripheral countries act as the "source" for the metabolic needs of core industrialized countries (Roberts & Parks, 2007b). For example, a comprehensive study that employed an MFA to examine the EU-15 region concluded that although the EU maintains a balanced external trade relation in monetary terms it also runs a substantial trade deficit in physical terms (PTB). Primarily owing to the import of fossil fuels, semi-manufactured products, and abiotic materials, the EU imports in physical terms more than four times what it exports. Yet, the EU-15 exports have a monetary value of four times that of what it imports. Further, in regard to trade relations with Southern regions such as Africa and Latin America, one ton of EU exports embody a money value ten times higher than one ton of EU imports (Giljum & Eisenmenger, 2004). Overall, researchers who employ an MFA methodology have consistently illustrated that bulk natural resource exports predominantly move from the periphery to industrialized countries.[6] Some argue that this movement provides empirical evidence of the periphery generally serving as a resource tap for more dominant industrialized countries (Hornborg, 2011). Also utilizing indicators from MFA, a United Nations Environment Programme (UNEP) report on decoupling (UNEP, 2011) reiterated the significance of international trade in redistributing resources across the globe in a manner that allows some countries to export resources and other countries to be supplied with primary products for manufacture and consumption (both domestic and abroad). The report looked at a wide variety of countries globally and found that industrialized countries tend to be net material importers, while developing countries serve as net exporters. European countries, the US, and Japan are the most important net importers of resources in the world economy. In recent years, however, a new pattern is also becoming apparent—several emerging economies, particularly Asia (such as China, India, and South Korea), have now also become net importers, augmenting domestic resource use with resources imported from abroad.

This seems to corroborate the theory that as countries transition to industrialization, resources from within national boundaries become insufficient for production and consumption demands. In contrast, the important net exporters of material resources in 2005 were Russia, Kazakhstan, Indonesia, Saudi Arabia, Iran, Brazil, Argentina, and Venezuela. In some countries that specialized in natural resource exports, such as Peru and Chile, domestic material extraction grew faster than GDP, which resulted in a rising material intensity of these economies. However, the UN study does find some industrial countries are among the group of net exporting countries, in particular Australia and Canada (though more recent calculations show this may not be the case for Canada).[7] However, it is important to note that other researchers have found that other important intervening variables, such as population size in large countries like China, can mitigate the standard core/periphery trend, which suggests a need for a more nuanced model of EUE (Singh & Eisenmenger, 2010). Chapter 6 investigates in depth the more complex position of semi-peripheral emerging economies.

A number of studies have examined specific politico-economic issues within the ecologically unequal exchange theory, such as deteriorating terms of trade for primary commodities and the impact of foreign debt on the environment. Concerning deteriorating terms of trade for primary commodities, Muradian and Martinez-Alier (2001b) find that falling prices correlate with large export drives for primary products. Of the 18 natural resource exports from developing countries, all but two had their prices fall between the 1970s and the 1990s, yet 14 exports increased dramatically in the physical terms of volume over the same period. From a monetary perspective, the movement of natural resources from the periphery to the industrialized countries frequently appears to be decreasing, but in physical terms there is often evidence of an increasing volume of trade. Case studies have also found that the physical trade balance (imports minus exports) deficit of individual countries has increased as terms of trade for primary commodities has deteriorated.

Vallego (2010) finds that in the Ecuadorian economy there is a structural trend toward decreasing terms of trade, which is verified by the increasing gap observed between import and export prices from 1970 to 2007. This increasing gap has been accompanied by an increasing PTB deficit. Such trends, Vallego finds, push countries like Ecuador toward irreversible environmental exhaustion while even renewable resources are exploited at excessive rates. Ecuador's deforestation rate, for example, is one of the highest in Latin America (Vallejo, 2010). A study on the Colombian economy by Perez-Rincon (2006) found, again, a growing deficit in Colombia's PTB accompanied by a deterioration of terms of trade. Like other Latin American countries, this trend has been accompanied by large-scale environmental loss that is precipitated through mining activities, oil extraction, and cash crops agricultural production. Tellingly, 85% of the total tonnage exported by Colombia is directed at satisfying the material and energy needs of high-income Northern countries (Perez-Rincon, 2006).

A study using an MFA on the Argentinean economy from 1970 to 2009 showed that Argentina follows a resource-intensive and export-oriented development model with a persistent physical trade deficit. Also, Argentina's terms of trade (the average weight in tons of imports that can be purchased through the sale of one ton of exports) shows a declining trend in the period of study. The authors compare Argentina's metabolic profile and the metabolic profile of other countries in Latin America, as well as Australia and Spain, and argue that the Argentinean economy presents the same pattern as other Latin American exporting economies, while its terms of trade are opposite to those of industrialized economies (Manrique et al., 2013). This trend, also corroborated by Vallejo (2010), is not necessarily surprising. As terms of trade decrease, more resources have to be exported as imports become relatively more expensive.

Aside from the factor of falling prices of primary commodities, the impact of foreign debt has also been examined. Using a cross-national model for 62 poor nations from 1990 to 2005, Shandra et al. (2008) find that foreign debt and structural adjustment increase deforestation. Both factors seem to push peripheral nations to increase export earnings in order to finance interest and principal payments (Shandra et al., 2008). The above are some examples of empirical research concerning EUE or ecological distributional issues. While far from an exhaustive empirical literature review, such studies underscore the disparities in resource use across global regions, the transfer of resources from periphery to core in terms of weight, and the ecological losses associated with economic policies that are unaccounted for when exchange is measured solely in monetary terms. Further relevant studies on ecologically unequal exchange are discussed throughout this book.

Neoliberal Development, Foreign Investment, and Ecological Imperialism

The second pillar of neoliberal development has been the restructuring of developing countries' economies to attract foreign investment. Ultimately, transnational corporations are the capitalist organizational structure around which imperialism of any sort pivots; when we discuss ecological imperialism what we are really discussing is the ecological repercussions of transnational corporate activities and their supply chains as well as the political economy of how these transnationals capture the majority of profit. Most international trade is, in fact, intra-industry trade that occurs within vertically organized transnational corporations. As the excellent work by Smith (2016) on imperialism and labor discusses, developing countries' share of imperialist nations' manufactured imports have rocketed since 1980. Smith quotes a study by UNCTAD in 2013 that found that about 80% of global trade is linked to the international production networks of TNCs, while 67% of the total value-added generated in global value chains is captured by firms based in rich nations.

In terms of ecological imperialism, the restructuring of developing countries' economies to attract foreign investment has resulted in foreign capital's exploitation of resources throughout the Global South. This restructuring has occurred through two primary channels—first, cracking open the periphery and, in many cases, semi-peripheral resources to foreign direct investment for the extraction of resources, and second, offshoring production and the exploitation of sink capacity in industrializing developing countries through various forms of pollution and environmental degradation associated with manufacturing processes.[8] While TNCs were challenged in the brief era of economic nationalism, these efforts quickly collapsed with the developing world debt crises of the 1980s. After the debt crises, neoliberal structural adjustment programs (SAPs) sought to create favorable conditions for multinational corporations by opening up developing countries through privatization and various incentives. As Chapter 3 on Africa reviews in detail, the policies used to attract foreign investment are a wholesale repeal of the policies enacted under economic nationalism for development purposes, including bans on nationalization, reduction of taxes on foreign investors, and removal of barriers to profit repatriation, among many others. The IMF, World Bank, and the Organization for Economic Cooperation and Development (OECD) have for decades argued that foreign direct investment (FDI) is central to increasing the foreign exchange of low-income countries and to avoiding further build-up of debt (Organization for Economic Development and Cooperation, 2002). The result, as Chapter 3 discusses, is a new scramble for African resources and the capture of Africa's extractive sectors by foreign control.

Multilateral trade agreements, in particular, are one of the primary channels that encourage foreign investment through providing sweeping protections for investors. Looking at multilateral trade agreements, McCarthy (2007) notes that the North American Free Trade Agreement (NAFTA) and other recent trade agreements all share the primary goals of increasing FDI and shifting important state functions to the private sector or NGOs. Bilateral trade treaties, as Chapter 3 will overview, contain even more stringent provisions that bind the hands of the developing countries governments and shift power to foreign investors. In addition, trade treaties include substantial investor protections in the form of the investor-state dispute settlement (ISDS) mechanism. ISDS is a type of arbitration procedure that decides whether shifts in government policies have harmed an investor, and if so, it forces the government to pay investors for the financial losses caused. It is, in other words, a channel for transnational corporations to sue governments for policies harmful to their bottom line. Both the Trans-Pacific Partnership and the Transatlantic Trade and Investment Partnership, as well as NAFTA and CAFTA, contain provisions for independent ISDS mechanisms. Investor-state disputes are often resolved under private dispute settlement tribunals such as the London Court of International Arbitration or the International Chamber of Commerce, which are both aligned with private industrial and financial interests (Van Den Berg, 2017). ISDS tribunals have been known to award private foreign investors for damages in order to compensate them for new environmental taxes or for imposing new regulations to protect the safety and health of workers (Van Den Berg, 2017). For example, a multiple organizational report, which included the Sierra Club, exposed that since 1994 corporations have been using the ISDS mechanism to challenge restrictions on land use, mining, and energy as well as other socially beneficial laws that have been passed by all three NAFTA countries. By 2012, Mexico and Canada paid more than $350 million to investors through a series of investor-state cases under NAFTA alone, and there are billions more in pending claims. In addition, a disproportionate number of legal challenges are related to the extractive industry (Karpilow et al., 2014). Further, as the report states, the fear of even attracting a lawsuit has a "chilling effect" on government policy and legislation. Investor protections similar to the ones in NAFTA have been replicated in hundreds of free trade agreements and bilateral investment treaties since NAFTA. According to the report, by the end of 2012, corporations launched 514 known cases against 95 governments—61 of the 95 countries facing investor-state disputes are from developing countries (Karpilow et al., 2014).

Not all structural reforms have been through trade treaties. Some have centered on domestic reforms. As Chapters 3 and 4 discuss in depth, investor protections in multilateral and bilateral trade treaties have been accompanied by a host of domestic reforms in sectors such as mining and land. In the ten-year period from 1985 to 1995, for example, over 90 countries globally adopted new mining laws or revised existing legal codes in an effort to promote foreign investment in their mining sector. As discussed extensively throughout this book, the rewriting of laws and regulations regarding large-scale investment in land in order to attract foreign investors is fundamental to understanding the global land grab. Overall, critics argue that attracting foreign investors aimed at stimulating growth in developing countries is prioritized above other important social and environmental objectives (Tockman, 2001; UNCTAD, 2005).

There are a number of empirical studies linking foreign investment with environmental degradation and also the exploitation of sink capacity through offshoring of production, notably the work of the sociologist Andrew Jorgenson. For example, a study by Jorgenson (2010) finds that deforestation in less developed countries is positively associated with both the vertical flow of primary sector exports to developed countries and the dependence on primary sector foreign direct investment. Jorgenson (2010) further notes that as agricultural and livestock enterprises are integrated into the world economy, especially those owned by transnational firms, the intensity and scale of their production tend to increase substantially, which results in forests being cleared and soils depleted for large-scale operations. Jorgenson continues to cite other studies (Grimes & Kentor, 2003; Shandra et al., 2004; Kentor & Grimes, 2006; Jorgenson, 2007; York, 2008) that connect foreign investment and environmental degradation. While Jorgenson (2009) shows that secondary sector foreign investment contributes to higher levels of carbon dioxide emissions per unit of production, these studies listed above found that secondary sector foreign investment and total foreign investment contribute to growth in total anthropogenic carbon dioxide emissions. Jorgenson (2006b) and Jorgenson et al. (2009) find that growth in the per capita emissions of various air pollutants and greenhouse gases is tied to the transnational organization of production in the context of foreign investment dependence. In other words, transnationally controlled manufacturing firms appear to be relatively highly polluting in scale and intensity and are relatively less "eco-efficient." Similarly, increasing levels of industrial organic water pollutants are at least partly a function of foreign investment in manufacturing (Jorgenson, 2007).

Neoliberal Development, Financial Liberalization, and Ecological Imperialism

The third pillar of neoliberal globalization has been the liberalization of financial markets and the unleashing of financial capital globally, marked by the rise of a hegemonic financial class and an overaccumulation of capital in the financial sector. While trade and investment policies created the necessary conditions for the enclosure, privatization, and continuing primitive accumulation of peripheral resources, financial liberalization has freed financial capital from its national restrictions. Now, global capital, whether in the form of international investment (the acquisition of real assets located in one country by citizens, firms, or governments of another country) or international finance (international borrowing or lending), has relatively free access to peripheral resources cracked-open by decades of structural adjustments. Beginning in the early 1970s, market economies around the world started removing government regulations of their financial sectors. Most market economies had largely deregulated their financial sectors by the mid-1990s. The liberalization of the financial sector included the liberalization of capital accounts, allowing banks and corporations to freely borrow money abroad, and the removal of restrictions on capital outflows or repatriation of profits. It also included the liberalization of domestic financial sectors and markets in stocks and other securities. This liberalization allowed foreigners to freely invest and repatriate profits with few restrictions on the types of financial instruments that could be bought and sold while also applying minimal controls on leverage (Daly & Farley, 2011).

Like international investment flows, international financial flows have grown rapidly in recent decades. As Chapter 6 will discuss, the combination of the super-exploitation of workers through neoliberal labor policies and the funneling of this mass of exploited surplus value into the financial sector, instead of reinvesting into productive activities and workers' wages, has resulted in a glut of capital flowing into a highly liberalized, increasingly hegemonic financial sector. As such, the past several decades have seen a rapid proliferation of what Marx termed "interest-bearing capital," signifying a systemic shift in capitalism with the emergence of the hegemony of the financial class and the increasing control of the economy by the finance sector. No discussion of ecological imperialism, or of the global environmental crises more generally, is complete without an acknowledgment of the role of globalized financial capital.

Chapters 6 and 7 dive more deeply into the specifics, but it is worth summarizing the main points here in order to tie the connections between international trade, foreign investment, international finance, and ecological imperialism. First, quite simply, the link between international trade, international investment, international finance, and ecological imperialism is that financial capital is what funds nearly all economic activity in the capitalist mode of production. While this may seem obvious, it was not the case for pre-capitalist modes of production and marks something unique about the expansionary capacities of capitalists in the capitalist mode of production. As Marx had noted in *Capital Volume III*, what is unique in capitalism is that a large number of loans are used as *capital*—that is, they are used as credit for capitalist enterprises. In other words, money used to create more money. As the expansion of individual capitalist enterprises need not be limited to the reinvestment of their retained earnings, the system of credit accelerates the expansion of the scale of production, development of technology, and creation of the world market (Vasudevan, 2017). Concomitantly, the financial system acts as a mechanism concentrating multiple streams of revenues, from non-reinvested industrial profits (previously exploited surplus value) to the savings of workers, essentially centralizing the revenues of various social classes. Through this process the multiple scattered, small funds that are unable to act on their own accord become a concentration of what Marx called a "money power" at the disposal of the financial class (Vasudevan, 2017). What Marx termed "interest-bearing capital" is the lifeblood that enables the global economy. Financial capital ultimately intensifies the global ecological crises. It is a system built on debt, and the repayment of that debt with interest is a system locked into endless growth.

Second, since the integration of the capitalist world-system and the creation of the hierarchical international division of labor of the capitalist world-system, this concentrated and internationalized money power, the locus of which is in the developed countries and economically powerful emerging economies such as China, has acted and continues to act as a carrot and stick in the shaping of peripheral countries' economies. As discussed above, from colonialism onward through the structural adjustments of the 1980s and 1990s, Third World loans and debts have been instrumental in shaping the economic policies of developing countries that are conducive to ecological imperialism and ecologically unequal exchange. Peet (2009), for example, traces the substantial influence that the financial sector played in creating the neoliberal structural adjustment policies by arguing that the structural adjustment policies of the Washington Consensus, through creating export-oriented economies with minimal state spending and private properties rights, maximized the loan capacity of developing countries and ensured the ability of such countries to repay principal and interest.

Third, the super-exploitation of workers under neoliberalism and the funneling of overaccumulated capital into the financial sector combined with financial deregulation, the growth of the international capital market, and the push to diversify portfolios have created a mammoth source of funding that is available globally. This combination has meant that behind virtually every environmentally damaging extractive industry—even the direct speculation and enclosure of resources, land, and water—stands a diverse array of international financial actors who are as equally responsible as the multinational corporations and corrupt governments involved. As long as extractive, environmentally damaging industries remain profitable, the financial sector follows. As Chapter 7 discusses, the Global South's natural resource sectors have become a site for accumulation for global capital through the entanglement of banks, institutional investors, and private investors with extractive and agricultural corporations. The portion of the profits from investments in these sectors, funneling into the global financial sector in the form of interest and dividends, represents, from a Marxian perspective, the appropriated surplus value of Global South workers within the natural resource sectors. Simultaneously, from a broader ecological perspective, they also represent the enclosure and exploitation of the Global South's ecological commons.

There is also an important relation between crises in the financial sector and the expansionary dynamics of ecological imperialism. Financial crises can create the lack of safe and profitable investment opportunities for the financial class, while simultaneously global ecological crises can create lucrative opportunities for investment in natural resource sectors as resources become more valuable as their sources dwindle. For example, Klare (2012) documented the link between large-scale land investment and the financial crisis of 2008, whereby financial capital, failing to find suitable investment opportunities in the Global North, engaged in the grabbing up of land through large-scale land investments in the Global South. As another example, a recent report by Environmental Justice Organizations, Liabilities and Trade (EJOLT, 2015) documents that following the 2008 financial crisis Northern investment funds invested in lands managed by ecologically problematic industrial tree plantation companies.

Finally, Marx's other relevant insight was into the extreme fetishism characteristic of interest-bearing capital (Chesnais, 2017). With interest-bearing capital, capital appears to multiply of its own accord while its origination in the appropriation of surplus value is completely obscured. In an era of global ecological crises, the extreme fetishism of globally mobile, interest-bearing capital is now playing out at international level. Lack of regulation, the distancing of accountability, and opaqueness in the value chain all obscure the underlying appropriation and material basis of surplus value. Furthermore, there is no international regulation of financial flows in regard to the environment. As developing countries have liberalized and developed their own financial sectors, this problem is multiplied as countries, particularly in Asia, have even less environmental regulations.

Conclusion

The exploitation of Global South Natures and dynamics of primitive accumulation have been fundamental to capitalism since colonialism. However, capitalism's global expansion has proceeded in waves, and at times such expansionism has been actively contested by social and environmental movements, and even states and international solidarity, such as during the period of economic nationalism. What marks neoliberalism as an arguably distinct period in the unfolding of ecological imperialism is its defeat of the anti-neocolonial features of economic nationalism. The neoliberal era is the era of capitalism unleashed, with capitalism as the dominant mode of production and the intensification of capitalist relations of production globally. Under neoliberal globalization, the systematic removal of barriers to capital accumulation has proceeded step-by-step through trade, investment, and financial liberalization and free market development policies in the Global South. All of these trends have resulted in the repealing of important environmental protections and the enclosure of even more of the Earth's ecological commons. Over the past four decades, neoliberal capitalism has resulted in fierce competition for resources by dominant powers and near global ecological collapse.

References

Adeniran, T. (1986). Africa, the United Nations, and the NIEO. In R. Onwuka & O. Aluko (Eds.), *The future of Africa and the New International Economic Order* (pp. 115–132). New York: St. Martin's Press.

Amin, S. (1990). *Maldevelopment: Anatomy of a global failure.* Tokyo: United Nations University Press.

Angelis, M.D. (2001). Marx's theory of primitive accumulation: The continuous character of capitalism's enclosures. *The Commoner.* https://thecommoner.org/wp-content/uploads/2019/10/Marx-and-primitive-accumulation-deAngelis.pdf

Baird, S. (n.d.). Economic manuscripts: Capital Vol. I - Chapter Twenty-Six. https://www.marxists.org/archive/marx/works/1867-c1/ch26.htm

Behrens, A., Giljum, S., Kovanda, J., & Niza, S. (2007). The material basis of the global economy: Worldwide patterns of natural resource extraction and their implications for sustainable resource use policies. *Ecological Economics*, *64*(2), 444–458. https://doi.org/10.1016/j.ecolecon.2007.02.034

Bergstein, F., (1973). The threat from the third world. *Foreign Policy*, 11, 102–124. https://doi.org/10.2307/1148041

Bhagwati, J.N. (1977). *The new international economic order: The north-south debate.* Cambridge, MA: MIT Press.

Bridge, G. (2007). Acts of enclosure: Claim staking and land conversion in Guyana's gold fields. In N. Heynen, J. McCarthy, S. Prudham, & P. Robbins (Eds.), *Neoliberal environments: False promises and unnatural consequences* (pp. 74–88). London: Routledge.

Bunker, S.G. (1985). *Underdeveloping the Amazon: Extraction, unequal exchange, and the failure of the modern state.* Chicago, IL: University of Illinois Press.

Bunker, S.G. (2005). How ecologically uneven developments put the spin on the treadmill of production. *Organization and Environment*, *18*(1), 38–54. https://doi.org/10.1177/1086026604270434

Campbell, B. (2003). Factoring in governance is not enough. Mining codes in Africa, policy reform and corporate responsibility. *Minerals & Energy - Raw Materials Report, 18*(3), 2–13. https://doi.org/10.1080/14041040310019129

Campbell, B., & Loxley, J. (Eds.). (1989). *Structural adjustment in Africa.* New York: St. Martin's Press.

Castree, N. (2008). Neoliberalising nature: The logics of deregulation and regulation. *Environment and Planning A, 40*(1), 131–152. https://doi.org/10.1068/a3999

Cheru, F. (1989). *The silent revolution in Africa: Debt, development, and democracy.* Harare: Anvil.

Cheru, F., & Obi, C. (Eds.). (2010). *The rise of China and India in Africa: Challenges, opportunities and critical interventions.* London: Zed Books. http://nai.diva-portal.org/smash/get/diva2:285922/FULLTEXT01.pdf

Chesnais, F. (2017). *Finance capital today: Corporations and banks in the lasting global slump.* Chicago, IL: Haymarket Books. https://doi.org/10.1163/9789004255487

Cypher, J.M. (2014). *The process of economic development.* (4th edition). London and New York: Routledge.

Daly, H.E., & Farley, J. (2011). *Ecological economics: Principles and applications.* Washington, DC: Island Press.

Davis, S.J., & Caldeira, K. (2010). Consumption-based accounting of CO_2 emissions. *Proceedings of the National Academy of Sciences of the United States of America, 107*(12), 5687–5692. https://doi.org/10.1073/pnas.0906974107

DeLancey, V. (1992). *The economies of Africa, in understanding tropical Africa* (pp. 94–95). Boulder, CO: Lynne Rienner Publishers.

EJOLT. (2015). *Patterns of biomass global trade: Implications for food sovereignty and socio-environmental conflicts.* http://www.ejolt.org/2015/03/patterns-global-biomass-trade/

Feng, K., Chapagain, A., Suh, S., Pfister, S., & Hubacek, K. (2011). Comparison of bottom-up and top-down approaches to calculating the water footprints of nations. *Economic Systems Research, 23*(4), 371–385. https://doi.org/10.1080/09535314.2011.638276

Frame, M. (2019). The role of the semi-periphery in ecologically unequal exchange: A case study of land investments in Cambodia. In R. Scott Frey, P. K. Gellert, & H. F. Dahms (Eds.), *Ecologically unequal exchange: Environmental injustice in comparative and historical perspective* (pp. 75–106). Cham: Palgrave Macmillan. https://doi.org/10.1007/978-3-319-89740-0_4

Frey, R.S. (2003). The transfer of core-based hazardous production processes to the export processing zones of the periphery: The Maquiladora Centers of Northern Mexico. *Journal of World-Systems Research, IX*(2), 317–354. https://doi.org/10.5195/jwsr.2003.236

Galli, A., Wiedmann, T., Ercin, E., Knoblauch, D., Ewing, B., & Giljum, S. (2012). Integrating ecological, carbon and water footprint into a "footprint family" of indicators: Definition and role in tracking human pressure on the planet. *Ecological Indicators, 16*, 100–112. https://doi.org/10.1016/j.ecolind.2011.06.017

Giljum, S., & Eisenmenger, N. (2004). North-South trade and the distribution of environmental goods and burdens: A biophysical perspective. *Journal of Environment and Development, 13*(1), 73–100. https://doi.org/10.1177/1070496503260974

Girvan, N. (1975). Economic nationalists vs. multinational corporations: Revolutionary or evolutionary change. In C. Widstrand (Ed.), *Multinational firms in Africa.* (pp. 25–68). Dakar: African Institute for Economic Development and Planning.

Girvan, N. (1976). *Corporate imperialism: Conflict and expropriation: Transnational corporations and economic nationalism in the Third World.* New York: M.E. Sharpe. https://doi.org/10.4324/9781315178875

Grimes, P., & Kentor, J. (2003). Exporting the greenhouse: Foreign capital penetration and CO? Emissions 1980–1996. *Journal of World-Systems Research, 9*(2), 261–275.

Haight, G.W. (1975). The new international order and the charter of economic rights and duties of states. *The International Lawyer, 9*(4), 591–604. https://www.jstor.org/stable/40704962

Haque, M.S. (1999). The fate of sustainable development under neo-liberal regimes in developing countries. *International Political Science Review, 20*(2), 197–218. https://doi.org/10.1177/0192512199202005

Haque, S.M. (2008). Global rise of neoliberal state and its impact on citizenship: Experiences in developing nations. *Asian Journal of Social Science, 36*(1), 11–35. 10.1163/156853108X267558

Harvey, D. (2003). *The new imperialism.* Oxford: Oxford University Press.

Harvey, D. (2005). *A brief history of neoliberalism.* Oxford: Oxford University Press. 10.1093/oso/9780199283262.001.0001. https://doi.org/10.5195/jwsr.2003.244

Helleiner, G.K. (1983). *The IMF and Africa in the 1980s.* Princeton, NJ: International Finance Section, Dept. of Economics, Princeton University.

Hertwich, E.G., & Peters, G.P. (2009). Carbon footprint of nations: A global, trade-linked analysis. *Environmental Science & Technology, 43*(16), 6414–6420. https://doi.org/10.1021/es803496a

Heynen, N. (2007). *Neoliberal environments: false promises and unnatural consequences.* London: Routledge.

Hornborg, A. (1998). Ecosystems and world systems: Accumulation as an ecological process. *Journal of World-Systems Research, 4*(2),169–177. https://doi.org/10.5195/jwsr.1998.156

Hornborg, A. (2001). *The power of the machine: Global inequalities of economy, technology, and environment.* Walnut Creek, CA: AltaMira Press.

Hornborg, A. (2009). Zero-sum world: Challenges in conceptualizing environmental load displacement and ecologically unequal exchange in the world-system. *International Journal of Comparative Sociology, 50*(3–4), 237–262. https://doi.org/10.1177/0020715209105141

Hornborg, A. (2011). *Global ecology and unequal exchange: Fetishism in a zero-sum world.* Abingdon and Oxon: Routledge. https://doi.org/10.4324/9780203806890

Hornborg, A., McNeill, J.R., & Alier, J. (Eds.). (2007). *Rethinking environmental history: World-system history and global environmental change.* Lanham, MD: AltaMira Press.

Jorgenson, A.K. (2006a). Unequal ecological exchange and environmental degradation: A theoretical proposition and cross-national study of deforestation, 1990–2000. *Rural Sociology, 71*(4): 685–712. https://doi.org/10.1526/003601106781262016

Jorgenson, A.K. (2006b). Global warming and the neglected greenhouse gas: A cross-national study of the social causes of methane emissions intensity, 1995. *Social Forces, 84*(3): 1777–1796. https://doi.org/10.1353/sof.2006.0050

Jorgenson, A.K. (2007). Does foreign investment harm the air we breathe and the water we drink? A cross-national study of carbon dioxide emissions and organic water pollution in less developed countries, 1975–2000. *Organization & Environment, 20*(2), 137–156. https://doi.org/10.1177/1086026607302153

Jorgenson, A.K. (2009). The transnational organization of production, the scale of degradation, and ecoefficiency: A study of carbon dioxide emissions in less developed countries. *Human Ecology Review, 16*(1): 64–74.

Jorgenson, A.K. (2010). World-economic integration, supply depots, and environmental degradation: A study of ecologically unequal exchange, foreign investment dependence, and deforestation in less developed countries. *Critical Sociology, 36*(3), 453–477. https://doi.org/10.1177/0896920510365204

Jorgenson, A.K. (2012). The sociology of ecologically unequal exchange and carbon dioxide emissions, 1960-2005. *Social Science Research, 41*(2), 242–252. https://doi.org/10.1016/j.ssresearch.2011.11.011

Jorgenson, A.K., Austin, K., & Dick, C. (2009). Ecologically unequal exchange and the resource consumption/environmental degradation paradox: A panel study of less-developed countries, 1970-2000. *International Journal of Comparative Sociology, 50*(3–4), 263–284. https://doi.org/10.1177/0020715209105142

Jorgenson, A.K., & Birkholz, R. (2010). Assessing the causes of anthropogenic methane emissions in comparative perspective, 1990-2005. *Ecological Economics, 69*, 2634–2643.

Jorgenson, A.K., & Clark, B. (2009). Ecologically unequal exchange in comparative perspective: A brief introduction. *International Journal of Comparative Sociology, 50*(3–4), 211–214. https://doi.org/10.1177/0020715209105139

Jorgenson, A.K., & Clark, B. (2011). Societies consuming nature: A panel study of the ecological footprints of nations, 1960-2003. *Social Science Research, 40*(1), 226–244. https://doi.org/10.1016/j.ssresearch.2010.09.004

Karpilow, Q., Solomon, I., Calderón, A.V., Pérez-Rocha, M., & Trew, S. (2014). *NAFTA: 20 years of costs to communities and the environment*. The Sierra Club, Sierra Club Canada, The Mexican Action Network on Free Trade (RMALC), The Institute for Policy Studies, and The Council of Canadians. https://content.sierraclub.org/creative-archive/sites/content.sierraclub.org.creative-archive/files/pdfs/0642-NAFTA%20Report_05_low.pdf

Kennedy, C.R. (1992). Relations between transnational corporations and Governments of host countries: A look to the future. In *Transnational corporations* (Vol.1, No.1). United Nations Department of Economic and Social Development, Transnational Corporations and Management Division. https://unctad.org/webflyer/transnational-corporations-vol1-no1

Kentor, J., & Grimes, P. (2006). Foreign investment dependence and the environment: A global perspective. In A.K. Jorgenson & E. Kick (Eds), *Globalization and the environment* (pp. 61–78). Leiden: Brill Academic Press.

Lenzen, M., Moran, D., Bhaduri, A., Kanemoto, K., Bekchanov, M., Geschke, A., & Foran, B. (2013). International trade of scarce water. *Ecological Economics, 94*, 78–85. https://doi.org/10.1016/j.ecolecon.2013.06.018

Lenzen, M., Moran, D., Kanemoto, K., Foran, B., Lobefaro, L., & Geschke, A. (2012). International trade drives biodiversity threats in developing nations. *Nature, 486*(7401), 109–112. https://doi.org/10.1038/nature11145

Lozoya, J.A., & Cuadra, H. (Eds.). (1980). *Africa, the Middle East, and the new international economic order.* New York: Pergamon Press.

Magdoff, H. (1969). *The age of imperialism: The economics of U.S. foreign policy.* New York: Monthly Review Press.

Magdoff, H. (1978). *Imperialism: from the colonial age to the present: Essays.* New York: Monthly Review Press.

Magdoff, H., & Foster, J.B. (2003). *Imperialism without colonies.* New York: Monthly Review Press.

Manrique, P., Brun, J., Gonzalez-Martinez, A., & Martinez-Alier, J. (2013). The biophysical performance of Argentina: 1970-2009. *Journal of Industrial Ecology, 17*(4), 590–604. https://doi.org/10.1111/jiec.12027

Material Flow Analysis Portal. (n.d.). *Country profiles.* Materialflows.net. http://www.materialflows.net/visualisation-centre/data-visualisations/?_inputs_&sidebar=%22bar_chart_1%22

McCarthy, J. (2004). Neoliberal nature and the nature of neoliberalism. *Geoforum, 35*(3), 275–283. https://doi.org/10.1016/j.geoforum.2003.07.003

McCarthy, J. (2007). Privatizing conditions of production: Trade agreements as neoliberal environmental governance. In N. Heynen, J. McCarthy, S. Prudham, & P. Robbins (Eds.), *Neoliberal environments: False promises and unnatural consequences* (pp. 38–50). London: Routledge.

McMichael, P. (2017). *Development and social change: A global perspective.* (6th edition). Thousand Oaks, CA: Sage Publications.

Mkandawire, T. (2005). Maladjusted African economies and globalization. *Africa Development, XXX*(1 and 2), 1–33.

Muradian, R., & Martinez-Alier, J. (2001a). South-North materials flow: History and environmental repercussions. *Innovation: European Journal of Social Sciences, 14*(2), 171–187. https://doi.org/10.1080/13511610120062344

Muradian, R., & Martinez-Alier, J. (2001b). Trade and the environment: From a Southern perspective. *Ecological Economics, 36*, 281–297. https://doi.org/10.1016/S0921-8009(00)00229-9

Muradian, R., O'Connor, M., & Martinez-Alier, J. (2002). Embodied pollution in trade: Estimating the environmental load displacement of industrialised countries. *Ecological Economics, 41*, 51–67. https://doi.org/10.1016/S0921-8009(01)00281-6

O'Connor, J. (1997). *Natural causes: Essays in ecological Marxism.* New York: The Guilford Press.

Onwuka, R.I., & Aluko, O. (1986). *The future of Africa and the new international economic order.* New York: St. Martin's Press.

Organization for Economic Development and Cooperation. (OECD). (2002). *Foreign direct investment for development: Maximising benefits, minimising costs.* OECD. https://www.oecd.org/investment/investmentfordevelopment/foreigndirectinvestmentfordevelopmentmaximisingbenefitsminimisingcosts.htm

Peet, R. (2009). *Unholy trinity: The IMF, World Bank, and WTO.* (2nd edition). New York: Zed Books.

Perez-Rincon, M.A. (2006). Colombian international trade from a physical perspective: Towards an ecological 'Prebisch thesis'. *Ecological Economics, 59*(4), 519–529. https://doi.org/10.1016/j.ecolecon.2005.11.013

Reuss, A. (2013). *Labor and the global economy.* Boston, MA: Dollars and Sense.

Robbins, P., & Luginbuhl, A. (2007). The last enclosure: Resisting privatization of wildlife in the western United States. In N. Heynen, J. McCarthy, S. Prudham, & P. Robbins (Eds.), *Neoliberal environments: False promises and unnatural consequences* (pp. 25–37). London: Routledge.

Roberts, J.T., & Parks, B.C. (2007a). *A climate of injustice: Global inequality, North-South politics, and climate policy.* Cambridge, MA: MIT Press.

Roberts, J.T., & Parks, B.C. (2007b). Fueling injustice: Globalization, ecologically unequal exchange, and climate change. *Globalizations, 4*(2), 193–210. https://doi.org/10.1080/14747730701345218

Satgar, V. (2009). Global capitalism and the neoliberalization of Africa. In R. Southall & H. Melber (Eds.), *A new scramble for Africa? Imperialism, investment and development* (pp. 35–55). Scottsville, VA: University of KwaZulu-Natal Press.

Shandra, J.M., London, B., Whooley, O., & Williamson, J. (2004). International nongovernmental organizations and carbon dioxide emissions in the developing world: A quantitative, cross national analysis. *Sociological Inquiry, 74*(4), 520–545. https://doi.org/10.1111/j.1475-682X.2004.00103.x

Shandra, J.M., Shor, E., Maynard, G., & London, B. (2008). Debt, structural adjustment, and deforestation: A cross-national study. *Journal of World Systems Research, 14*(1), 1–21. https://doi.org/10.5195/jwsr.2008.345

Singh, S.J. (2003). *In the sea of influence: A world system perspective of the Nicobar Islands.* Lund: Lund University.

Singh, S.J., & Eisenmenger, N. (2010). How unequal is international trade? An ecological perspective using material flow accounting. *Journal fur Entwicklungspolitik, XXVI*, 57–88. https://doi.org/10.20446/JEP-2414-3197-26-4-57

Smith, J. (2016). *Imperialism in the* 21st *century: Globalization, super-exploitation, and capitalism's final crisis.* New York: Monthly Review Press.

Steen-Olsen, K., Weinzettel, J., Cranston, G., Ercin, A.E., & Hertwich, E.G. (2012). Carbon, land, and water footprint accounts for the European Union: Consumption, production, and displacements through international trade. *Environmental Science & Technology, 46*(20), 10883–10891. http://dx.doi.org/10.1021/es301949t

Thomson, A. (2000). *An introduction to African politics.* London: Routledge.

Tockman, J. (2001). *The IMF funding deforestation: How International Monetary Fund loans are responsible for global forest loss.* ELDIS. http://www.eldis.org/go/home&id=27219&type=Document

United Nations Conference on Trade and Development (UNCTAD). (2005). *Economic development in Africa: Rethinking the role of foreign direct investment.* New York: United Nations. https://unctad.org/system/files/official-document/gdsafrica20051_en.pdf

United Nations Conference on Trade and Development (UNCTAD). (2012). *Economic development in Africa report 2012: Structural transformation and sustainable development in Africa.* New York: United Nations. https://unctad.org/system/files/official-document/aldcafrica2012_embargo_en.pdf

United Nations Environment Programme (UNEP). (2011). *Decoupling natural resource use and environmental impacts from economic growth.* Paris. https://wedocs.unep.org/handle/20.500.11822/9816

Vallejo, M.C. (2010). Biophysical structure of the Ecuadorian economy, foreign trade, and policy implications. *Ecological Economics, 70*, 159–169.

Van Den Berg, H. (2017) *International economics: A heterodox approach.* (3rd edition). New York: Routledge.

Vasudevan, R. (2017, September 18). *The significance of Marx's theory on money: Marx's analysis of monetary phenomena has remarkable resonance in today's world.* Monthly Review Online. https://mronline.org/2017/09/18/the-significance-of-marxs-theory-on-money/

Weinzettel, J., Hertwich, E.G., Peters, G.P., Steen-Olsen, K., & Galli, A. (2013). Affluence drives the global displacement of land use. *Global Environmental Change, 23*(2), 433–438. https://doi.org/10.1016/j.gloenvcha.2012.12.010

Wiedman, T.O., Schandl, H., Lenzen, M., Moral, D., Suh, S., West, J., & Kanemoto, K. (2013). The material footprint of nations. *Proceedings of the National Academy of Sciences of the United States of America, 112*(20), 6271–6276. https://doi.org/10.1073/pnas.1220362110

York, R. (2008). De-carbonization in the Former Soviet Republics, 1992–2000: The ecological consequences of de-modernization. *Social Problems*, *55*(3), 370–90. https://doi.org/10.1525/sp.2008.55.3.370

Yu, Y., Feng, K., & Hubacek, K. (2013). Tele-connecting local consumption to global land use. *Global Environmental Change*, *23*(5), 1178–1186. http://dx.doi.org/10.1016/j.gloenvcha.2013.04.006

Notes

1 International migration is generally considered the fourth pillar of globalization. And indeed, one can argue that ecological imperialism is an important driver of international migration. However, despite its importance in globalization studies, it was beyond the capacity of the book to properly address this complex issue.

2 At the level of class analysis, Girvan (1976) argues that economic nationalism was actually a conflict wrought by the contradiction between international capitalism and particular social classes in the Third World. Imperialism, he argues, led to the continuous impoverishment of the mass population in the periphery. But it also created a dependent comprador bourgeoisie, which was dependent upon international capital and was engaged in activities as commerce, real estate, light manufacturing, and so on. Normally, Girvan states, this class allies itself with foreign capital. But if the nation-state possesses sources of leverage over international capital and core countries, such as the supply of vital products and a viable set of domestic class alliances, the comprador class can assert its independence. The result, Girvan argues, is economic nationalism. Hence, radical scholars such as Girvan and Amin sometimes critically refer to the economic nationalist movement as "bourgeois nationalism" (Girvan, 1976; Amin, 1990). Radical scholars such as Girvan and Amin criticize that these efforts only sought modifications in the relative power structures of the international capitalist order, rather than fundamental changes in the power of transnational capital (Girvan, 1976; Amin, 1990).

3 Devaluation of currencies was encouraged on the basis of making imports more expensive, but exports cheaper. This also accomplished the aim of encouraging less spending and more saving enabling developing countries to pay off their debts.

4 In a previous paper, *The Role of the Semiperiphery in Ecologically Unequal Exchange: A Case Study of Land Investments in Cambodia*, I had argued that ecological imperialism and EUE may be related, but they should be kept analytically distinct (Frame, 2019). EUE mainly refers to unequal flows of resources from one region or country to another; ecological imperialism refers to a political-economic arrangement that enforces identifiable structures of domination and socio-ecological degradation. Care must be taken not to reduce ecological exploitation to the unequal flows of resources as unequal biophysical flows do not always capture unequal dynamics of power *prima facie*. In order to obtain the full picture concerning ecological exploitation, we must also look at the politico-economic and social context of such flows, including flows of profit and ownership of resources, the socio-ecological impact of resource appropriation (rather than just the *quantitative* amount), and the history of power struggles over resources. There are cases when resources flow from core to periphery, for example food staples from the United States to certain African countries. This flow of resources does not indicate a dominance of Africa countries over the US! It actually indicates the power of large US agribusiness and their capacity to influence trade pacts as well as the vulnerability and lack of food sovereignty facing a number of peripheral countries. Nonetheless, many of the empirical patterns of EUE can

be interpreted as an important consequence of ecological imperialism, and the research of EUE paint a crucial component of the overall picture of imperialism and exploitation.

5 Material footprint is an indicator which measures the global allocation of used raw material extraction to the final demand of an economy. Essentially, it captures how much resources a national economy uses for purposes of final demand.

6 See also Behrens et al. (2007) Also, Muradian and Martinze-Alier (2001a). Also, Muradian, R. and Martinez-Alier. (2001b).

7 A methodological note. The study quoted here used the physical trade balance (PTB), which measures the physical trade surplus or physical trade deficit of a country using physical imports and exports, which is the measurement of the physical weight of an import or export as it crosses the national border. PTB is calculated as imports minus exports. However, since this study, new calculations have been made for all countries using the Raw Material Trade Balance (RTB), which measures the physical trade surplus or physical trade deficit of a country but also includes all domestic and foreign material extraction needed along all supply chains to produce the imports and exports. It should be noted that in this UN study Canada held a net physical trade deficit (exporting more resources than importing). This was calculated using the RTB, which shows Canada has as a net importer due to the high import of non-metallic minerals (Material Flow Analysis Portal, n.d.).

8 As Chapter 5 will explain, not all offshoring of production followed neoliberal policies domestically per se, such as in the case of China's more state-oriented capitalism that opened to foreign investment but maintained substantial regulation.

3 Africa in the Global Ecology

The Eco-Neocolonial Relations of Trade and Foreign Investment

The foundation of ecological imperialism is the deep inequality perpetuated by the continued dependency and exploitation of peripheral regions in the capitalist world-system. Few places reflect this as clearly as Africa,[1] and much of the literature and media on the endless wars, corruption, and authoritarianism in the continent miss a fundamental point—peripheral nations are characterized by socio-ecologies structured not for the sake of their own populations but for the needs and functioning of the capitalist world-system. From the forcible restructuring of peripheral socio-ecologies under colonialism to the economic pressures of neoliberal globalization, peripheral economies are largely characterized by extractivism. For the rest of the world-system, this has enabled access to a manifold variety of resources. While monetary measurements of international trade and foreign investment flows underestimate the importance of peripheral economies in the world-system, trade and investment nonetheless play a crucial role in providing the raw materials necessary for the workings of the global economy. But for peripheral regions, their integration into the capitalist world-system has led to ecological and monetary debt, environmental degradation, and what scholars have long identified as dis-articulated economies and mal-development.

Africa, with perhaps some exception in regard to South Africa, exhibits some of the clearest signs of ecological imperialism in the capitalist world-system, and imperialism, as the African scholar Obeng-Odoom points out, represents one of the greatest threats to African ecological commons. In a time of global ecological crises, Africa plays an increasingly important role as a final frontier of raw materials, land, and water. Africa is also an important destination for the waste of wealthier countries (Obeng-Odoom, 2021). Neocolonialism and neoliberal reforms have made it difficult for Africa to break out of the pattern of resource dependent economies, despite efforts made during the era of economic nationalism. As a result, Africa, in the era of neoliberal globalization, is increasingly a net exporter of resources even as most of the profits from those resources are captured by transnational corporations. While Africa increasingly exports net resources, empirical evidence shows that its own people consume even less resources than they did following independence. Africa is also a region most likely to suffer the greatest

DOI: 10.4324/9780429261305-3

from climate change while being the least responsible for it. The following chapter traces the evolution of ecological imperialism in Africa, and how neoliberal trade and foreign investment development policies form the basis of the eco-neocolonial political economy that continues to bind the continent.

Africa in the Global Ecology: The New Scramble for Africa

Between 1881 and 1914, the European powers occupied, divided, and colonized Africa, a conquest known as the Scramble for Africa. With the rise of global ecological crises, the 21st century is witnessing a renewed scramble for Africa. In the first decade of the 21st century, FDI inflows began to increase rapidly in African primary sectors. This "new scramble for Africa" is heavily concentrated in minerals and fossil fuels, but also includes land, forests, fisheries, and water. In a world-capitalist system characterized by the tension between a growing global economy and dwindling sources and sinks, Africa has emerged as a last frontier for resources. Africa accounts for 41% of world reserves of cobalt, 56% of diamonds, 34% of gold, 10% of oil, 12% of chromites, 53% of phosphate rock, and a number of other important resources (UNCTAD, 2012).

Africa's minerals are of enormous economic and strategic importance. To begin with, Africa holds about 18% of the world's recoverable uranium resources, and the demand for uranium has increased dramatically in recent years as it is the key raw material in nuclear energy production. While Western companies remain predominant, China is becoming an increasingly significant actor and is competing, especially with Russia, for deals in Namibia and Niger (Southall & Melber, 2009). Coltan, from which the metals columbium and tantalum are extracted, is another key strategic resource, vital for electronic equipment such as mobile phones. Of known global tantalite resources, 80% are found in the Democratic Republic of the Congo (DRC). As with oil, both uranium and coltan have been associated with conflict and environmental degradation. For example, a regional scramble for coltan helped fuel civil war in the DRC from 1998 to 2003 and involved eight African militaries at its height. Uranium mining also has been associated with pollution and violent conflict in Niger over the distribution of rents (Southall & Melber, 2009).

With the projected massive increase in global demand, coupled with dwindling supplies, fossil fuels are also central to the new scramble for Africa. Both core and emerging economies alike are competing to secure their access to oil, and Africa has attracted investments from virtually all the major oil companies in Europe and the US. While Middle Eastern oil reserves are substantially greater than African reserves (Africa contains about 7% of known global oil reserves), interest in African oil has been catalyzed by the desire to reduce energy dependency on the volatile Middle East. Consequently, the US and other Western powers are seeking to decrease their dependence upon the Middle East and turning to Africa, especially North Africa, West Africa, and the Gulf of Guinea. The demand for oil is also rising dramatically in emerging economies such as China and India as both have become net importers of oil. In the past decade and a half, China has been increasingly engaged with African states in its quest for oil and other commodities. India's growth rate, like China's, has led to growing oil imports, and Indian state-owned enterprises have also intensified their quest for access to African oil (Obi, 2010). The developmental repercussions of such a massive inflow of foreign interest and investment in Africa's petrostates have been far from laudable. Africa's petrostates have suffered from corruption and lack of democracy, the dispossession of local communities in oil-producing areas, and environmental despoliation. Further, the determination of the US to secure its access to African oil, gas, minerals, and other energy sources has led to the build-up of a formidable apparatus of political military alliances with strategically placed countries in Africa, often justified by reference to the war on terror (Southall & Melber, 2009).

Aside from strategic metals and fossil fuels, Africa is also at the heart of the global land grabbing trend. Land and water for agriculture are increasingly becoming commodified and accessible to the global market. Despite the orthodox contention that land is plentiful and underutilized in Africa, "land grabbing," as dubbed by its critics, has become an area of special concern, as it is often associated with the dispossession of land from local communities and the deprivation of their current and future livelihoods. There are a number of factors driving the land grabbing in Africa and elsewhere in the periphery. Primarily developed and emerging economies, in a global context of shrinking resources, are trying to achieve food, water, and energy security outside of their national boundaries (Smaller & Mann, 2009). Concerning energy security, with high oil prices and depleting supplies, developed country and emerging country governments and their private sectors are acquiring land for energy crops. As such, biofuel production has become a major driver of land grabbing in Africa.

Due to the current frameworks of domestic and international law for foreign investment, the legalities surrounding foreign investment in land and water often shift rights from domestic to foreign actors. In many of the host states, for example, domestic laws concerning land rights, water rights, or pollution controls for intensive agriculture are either insufficient or lacking. However, the international law framework often provides numerous hard rights for foreign investors (Smaller & Mann, 2009). GRAIN, an international non-profit organization working to support small farmers and social movements in their struggles for community-controlled and biodiversity-based food systems, argues that behind the scramble for land in Africa is a global struggle for water. In general, land deals in Africa involve large-scale, industrial agricultural operations that consume, or plan to consume, large amounts of water. Hence, land grabbing in Africa concentrates around the continent's largest river and lake systems. The dispossession of African water supplies reflects the larger global ecological crisis involving water shortages; in the near future, it is predicted that water will become the single most important physical commodity-based asset class. In this context, many corporations are rushing to sign land deals that give them wide-ranging control over African water, especially when African governments are almost giving it away (GRAIN, 2012). However, a third of Africans already live in water-scarce environments, and climate change is likely to increase these numbers significantly. According to GRAIN, the massive land deals could rob millions of people of their access to water and deplete much of the continent's most precious fresh water sources. Ecologically, nearly all land deals are located in major river basins with access to irrigation and often occupy fertile and fragile wetland, or in more arid areas that can draw water from major rivers. In some cases, farms directly access groundwater by pumping it up. These water resources are lifelines for local farmers, pastoralists, and other rural communities. Countries that the Nile River passes through, including Egypt, South Sudan, Sudan, and Uganda, have received special attention. Ethiopia, South Sudan, and Sudan have leased out millions of hectares (ha) and will continue to lease out more. To bring such land into production, it will need to be irrigated, and GRAIN argues that such irrigation will severely deplete the water resources.

Another part of Africa targeted by agribusiness are lands along the Niger River, which millions rely on for agriculture, fishing, trade, and a primary water source. Mali, Niger, and Nigeria are most dependent on the river, but seven other countries share its water (GRAIN, 2012). The legalities surrounding the scramble for African water also tend to work in the favor of investors. Contracts are rarely made public, and from contracts that have been leaked, it has become apparent that these contracts tend not to contain any specific mention of water rights. This generally leaves companies free to build dams and irrigation canals at their discretion. Further, even in instances where governments may have the political will to protect local communities and environment, existing international trade and investment treaties generally give foreign investors strong rights (GRAIN, 2012). Figure 3.1 shows a map of the Niger River.

African forests have long been targeted for foreign harvesting, and deforestation remains a serious problem today. It is estimated that 4 million hectares of forest are lost each year, twice the world average rate of deforestation. The Worldwide Fund for Nature estimates, for example, that at current rates Congo-Brazzaville's forests will be deforested by two-thirds by 2050 (Carmody, 2011). European companies, under generous concessions granted by African governments, dominate the logging sector though much of the logging is done illegally. Exports primarily flow to Southern Europe although China is rapidly becoming a major destination for timber (Southall & Melber, 2009). Overall, it is largely Euro-American consumption that is driving the demand for tropical timber, and often European and American companies are involved in deforestation. This recurring dynamic means that while European and American consumers benefit from deforestation in Africa, local forest dwelling communities suffer the losses.

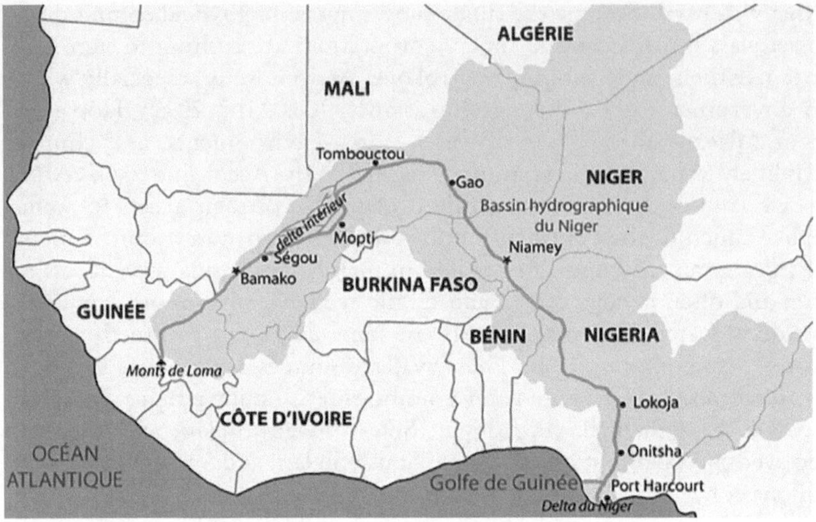

Figure 3.1 Niger River
Source: No machine-readable author provided. Kimdime assumed (based on copyright claims)

Over the past 25 years, the global trade in fish and fish products has sharply increased, and around 50% of world's fish exports come from developing countries (Carmody, 2011). For Africa, the growth of industrial fishing by foreign fleets has contributed greatly to the depletion of local fish stocks along the continent's coastlines. With external demand for fish, the continent exports around $2.7 billion worth of fish annually. Western Africa in particular is increasingly supplying fish for Western Europe, Russia, and China (Carmody, 2011). However, while foreign interests and consumers benefit from the exploitation of Africa's fisheries, the local people suffer. Historically, local fishing populations have depended upon Africa's rivers, lakes, and coastlines as important supplies of food. While population expansion and urbanization have taxed fish stocks, the industrial fishing by foreign fleets in particular has contributed to the over-exploitation of Africa's fisheries. As a result, many fishermen are becoming poorer as some fishing sectors decline while the bulk of profits flow to foreign interests. Further, while some fleet owners have negotiated agreements with coastal states that provide for the payment of a license fee or a share of income to the host nation, many fleet owners have not. Illegal, unregulated, and unreported (IUU) fleets, mainly from Europe and the Far East, fish within African territorial limits. Such fleets operate with de facto impunity since few coastal states have the capacity to prevent such intruders (Southall & Melber, 2009). In addition, foreign fleets have often manipulated access agreements in order to overfish (Carmody, 2011).

The Fall of Economic Nationalism and the Reestablishment of Neocolonialism in Africa

Like the rest of the global periphery, the new scramble for Africa has its roots in a history of exploitation and subjugation that originated in colonialism, neocolonialism, and the structural adjustment policies of neoliberalism. Colonialism looted Africa in terms of both labor and resources and radically restructured state borders and political, social, and economic systems to meet the needs of the colonizing countries. The repercussions last until today. Control over raw materials, copper, cotton, rubber, palm oil, cocoa, diamonds, tea, and tin was at the heart of colonial domination. Between 1600 and 1900, approximately 12 million Africans were sold into slavery and brought to the Western hemisphere. Some 36 million Africans died as a result of the warfare associated with colonialism and the brutality of being transported as slaves. With the slave trade and constant wars encouraged by slave traders, authoritarianism in the continent was strengthened. Native manufactures were undermined, inter-regional trade patterns disrupted, and the dependency on European manufactured products encouraged. Vertical trading patterns between Africa and Europe, still persisting today, were substituted in lieu of inter-regional trade (Cypher, 2014). The infrastructure of the continent, often built by forced labor, served to convert resources into plantation crops and mines. Overall, Africa's resources were transformed into privately owned assets generating income and wealth for the colonists rather than serving the developmental needs of the populace. Under colonization, the means of production, whether in natural resource industries or the tertiary sector, were controlled entirely by the colonists.

Yet like many post-colonial nations, independence did not bring an end to the foreign domination of African economies. The writings of post-colonial African leaders, activists, and intellectuals, such as Julius Nyerere (1971), Kwame Nkrumah (1966), and Walter Rodney (1981), reflected a lucid grasp of the dynamics and dangers of neocolonialism—the vulnerable state of dependency on primary commodities and the continued multinational control over key sectors of Africa's economies. As Chapter 2 discussed, some form of economic nationalism in much of the Third World characterized the post-colonial development paradigm in response to neocolonialism. This was true for African nations as well, yet it was a relatively brief period, lasting roughly only from the 1960s to the mid-1970s. Although African economies mainly continued their traditional roles as exporters of primary commodities, surpluses from the primary sector were channeled to meet the requirements of import substitution-driven industrialization through the developmental state (Saul & Leys, 1999).

African states, in conjunction with other states of the South, were also among the most vocal supporters of the United Nations New International Economic Order (NIEO) agenda. The NIEO, discussed in Chapter 2, called for a more equitable international economic system, the relief of debt to

Western capitalist countries, and the need for African states to industrialize (Adeniran, 1986). In addition, African countries created a number of other development plans that emphasized forms of self-reliance, yet these were ultimately rejected by countries in the Global North. For example, the Lagos Plan of Action (LPA) for the Economic Development of Africa (1980–2000) and the Final Act of Lagos of 1980 sought to encourage an inward-oriented development strategy rather than the externally oriented pattern inherited from colonialism. It emphasized domestic market development in Africa rather than reliance on external markets. Further, it focused on the importance of domestic factor inputs in development, the imperative of self-sufficiency in food production, the development of human capital, and provision of social infrastructure for the African people (Adejumobi, 2003). Like the NIEO, the LPA was essentially rejected (Amin, 1990), falling victim to international economic politics and the hostility of Western nations and their agencies, especially the World Bank (Adejumobi, 2003). Barely a year after the LPA was adopted, the World Bank launched its counter to the LPA, known as the Berg Report. The Berg Report presented a scathing criticism of the LPA by emphasizing the central role of the market and external trade in economic development and by attacking the role of the African state. Essentially, the Berg Report, which would become the foundational blueprint for the neoliberal policies enacted throughout the 1980s and beyond, argued that for Africa to develop economically it must liberalize its economy, cut back on the role of state, and privatize public enterprises. It targeted the policies of economic nationalism explicitly, arguing that the four major factors causing the African economic and agricultural crisis included overvalued national currencies, neglect of peasant agriculture, heavily protected manufacturing sectors, and excessive state intervention in the economy. Again with rejection of the LPA, other development strategies were proposed—all of which were met with either opposition or a cold reception (Adejumobi, 2003).

African governments rejected the Berg Report, arguing that such a development plan would leave their countries in a permanent state of poverty, and create dependency upon the developed world for food supplies, capital goods, and many manufactured consumer goods (DeLancey, 1992). Critics argue that behind the pro-peasant rhetoric, the Berg report hid the more essential commitment to intensive application of export-led agriculture. The report encouraged African countries to expand cash crop production in which they had a comparative advantage, increase privatization of agriculture, and use the foreign exchange from cash crops to purchase development inputs. Increased food production was not considered essential whereas cash crop earnings could be used to purchase imported foods. In other words, the Bank was using financial muscle to pressure governments to give up food self-sufficiency and promote export-oriented agriculture (Cheru, 1989). Further, the Organization of African Unity rejected the Bank's analysis of the economic situation, arguing that the Bank failed to recognize external causes to the continent's economic problems (Cheru, 1989).

African governments rejected such development plans out of fears of renewed neocolonialism, but by the late 1970s, African countries were caught in various stages of economic crises that were plagued by debt burdens, serious trade deficits, rising unemployment, industrial collapse, and social upheavals. The debt crisis had devastating effects on African economies. In particular, the capacity to pay for crucial imports for important capital stock had been severely compromised, and as a result, the development project itself was interrupted (Cheru, 1989). Overall, the debt overhang undermined domestic capital formation, frustrating public investment in physical and social infrastructure and deterring private investment (Thompson, 2000). By the 1980s, economic nationalism in Africa and elsewhere had collapsed, and neoliberal development policies were adopted in its place.

Consequently, in the1980s, African governments began turning to the IMF for balance of payment support and the World Bank for structural adjustment loans (Campbell & Loxley, 1989). In some cases, governments such as in Uganda, Tanzania, Ghana, and Mozambique turned to the IFIs in hopes of promoting short-term recovery that would eventually return to the ideals of economic nationalism or some form of socialism. In other countries, sections of the dominant ruling groups favored the longer-term strategies of the IMF and World Bank. Nonetheless, the principal reason why African governments accepted the policies of the IMF or the Bank was the opportunity to borrow loans necessary for reducing the import constraint (Campbell & Loxley, 1989).

At this point, IFIs introduced structural adjustment loans that required African countries to liberalize their economies and open them to international and domestic private capital while reducing the role of the state in economic governance. Kenya, Malawi, and Mauritius were the first states to introduce structural adjustment policy (SAP) reforms at the start of the 1980s, but by the mid-1990s, almost all other African countries had followed suit. Despite the variation of African economies and governments, the policies of structural adjustment were broadly the same. Essentially, structural adjustment sought to restore growth and stability by recasting relative prices, reducing domestic expenditures and state intervention in the economy, and introducing the discipline of the free market to African economies (Campbell & Loxley, 1989). The IFIs argued that the continent's development policies prior to the 1980s had resulted in urban bias that largely benefitted the urban districts and stifled productivity in the countryside (World Bank, 1994). Ultimately, like proposals from the Berg Report, the overall ideological approach promoted export-oriented growth strategies, with reliance upon market mechanisms and the promotion of the private sector (Campbell & Loxley, 1989).

For Africa this meant the rejection of any vestiges of the developmental state. The state was required to withdraw from economic intervention, which included the removal of all barriers, including exchange controls, protection tariffs, and public ownership. Massive cutbacks in social services were also advocated. Export-based agriculture became central to the neoliberal agenda

(Campbell & Loxley, 1989). SAPs also required major institutional reforms (including changes in fiscal policy, such as budgetary and debt management, export incentives and subsidies to importers, and public investment priorities). Importantly, SAPs promoted the creation of more "favorable investment climates" for foreign investors through a number of reforms (Cheru, 1989).

Once again Western financial institutions were dictating the continent's economic policy (Campbell & Loxley, 1989). As the brief historical overview above shows, the turn toward neoliberalism in the African continent was neither inevitable nor uncontested—it was a direct outcome of crises of debt, the financial muscle of IFIs, and the rejection of alternative development plans put forth by African leaders themselves. Importantly, it laid both the foundational economic and legal structures that underpin the increase of ecologically unequal exchange and patterns of dispossession of African resources occurring today.

Ecologically Unequal Exchange in Africa: Asymmetrical Flows of Resources and Dis-articulated Economies during the Neoliberal Era

The following is a biophysical overview of how neoliberal policies in Africa reinforced some of the most salient features of neocolonialism, which, with the environmental awareness of today, can more accurately be termed "eco-neocolonialism." Of all the peripheral regions, African countries exhibit some of the most unambiguous features of ecologically unequal exchange, and ecologically unequal exchange has deepened throughout the neoliberal years. As Chapter 2 discussed, the theory of ecologically unequal exchange holds that through international trade countries in the periphery of the capitalist world-system are exploited ecologically. In addition, peripheral countries consistently export a net asymmetrical amount of resources. However, this is obscured by trade that seems nominally neutral, fair, and equitable in monetary terms as monetary measurements do not account for environmental degradation and loss. As a consequence, peripheral regions like Africa experience high levels of environmental pressures coupled with domestically low levels of per capita consumption.

After the fall of economic nationalism and during the years of structural adjustment, the IFIs promoted an export-led development strategy in Africa based upon principles of comparative advantage (Cheru, 1989). Free trade with export specialization was touted as being economically preferable to diversification; for African countries, this meant specialization in the export of primary commodities while importing more sophisticated, value-added machinery and technology. African countries like other developing countries worldwide were encouraged to expand primary production, devalue their currencies, and increase production. The IFIs argued that expanded opportunities for trade and trade gains would increase individual countries' traditional exports while enabling them to diversify with the limited manufactured goods assigned to them by the law of comparative advantage. For African economies with limited domestic markets, trade would offer outlets for their exports and increase the foreign exchange needed to import goods such as investment goods like plants and equipment (Mkandawire, 2005).

However, the emphasis on export-led development through comparative advantage merely reproduced the disadvantages of unequal exchange experienced during colonialism (Campbell & Loxley, 1989). Consequently, the net outcome was that international markets reacted to the increased availability of primary goods by lowering commodity prices. Africa gained little relative advantage. Commodities such as cocoa, coffee, and cotton—of which make up the bulk of export earnings for several countries—led to an expansion of world supply and a corresponding decline in world prices. By the end of the 1990s, little had changed in terms of development goals despite major trade reforms. No major expansion occurred in the diversity of products exported by most sub-Saharan African countries, although there are one or two exceptions like Madagascar and Kenya (Campbell & Loxley, 1989). Indeed, the product composition of some African countries' exports may have become more concentrated.

Following the neoliberal policies, the share of manufacturing in GDP output dropped sharply in sub-Saharan Africa between 1980 and 1990. In the 1990s, it eventually stalled at a level below what it reached in 1960 (UNCTAD, 2005). Various cross-country studies have traced this trend to the sharp slowdown of output growth under adjustment programs, signifying a growth of the informal economy and a general "deindustrialization trend" across much of the region. Countries remained exposed to high price volatility, mainly from supply shocks, even as real prices continued their secular decline, exacting heavy costs in terms of incomes, indebtedness, investment, development, and diversification. In other words, problems that African countries sought to overcome with the policies of the post-independence era were merely reproduced with the neoliberal SAPs. Overall, the adjustment programs did little to alter the region's pattern of integration into the global economy, and worse, they had a regressive effect as in the case of manufacturing (UNCTAD, 2005). The share of manufacturing in Africa's gross domestic product fell from 15% in 1990 to 10% in 2009, with some variation among countries but substantial decline in most regions nonetheless. As such, the structural changes that African countries have witnessed over the last 30 years have not been productivity enhancing structural changes but rather the results of an increasing importance of the commodity economy and the rising importance of low-productivity informal economic activities in the service sector (UNCTAD, 2012).

Extractivism remains the most dominant feature of African economies today (Greco, 2021). More recent estimates show that in 2015 exports in SSA countries still had the highest levels of dependence on a few primary agricultural or mineral exports of any developing region. It has been estimated that unprocessed minerals and energy accounted for 80%, on average, of African exports. Agriculture employs between 65% and 80% of the workforce in the region. The evidence on export concentration reveals a substantially lower level of export diversification in Africa compared with other developing regions of Asia and the Americas. Furthermore, while in these regions diversification levels have remained similar since the mid-1990s, diversification in Africa has undergone a downward trend (UNCTAD, 2018b). Most African economies remain heavily dependent on the export of primary commodities (46 out of 54 are commodity dependent). Eighteen countries are dependent on minerals, ores, and metals exports while 17 countries are dependent on agricultural product exports and 11 countries on fuel exports (UNCTAD, 2020).

This is obviously problematic from an ecological perspective. The most important resources driving Africa's growth dynamic in the 21st century are fossil fuels and metallic and non-metallic minerals, all of which are non-renewable, being depleted at a very rapid rate, and subject to highly volatile commodity prices and global demand. Largely this depletion is occurring due to international trade, though domestic use of resources due to population growth and urbanization also contribute. In addition, Africa is suffering from land degradation, deforestation, and loss of biodiversity. Sixty-five percent of Africa's agricultural land, 31% of its pasture lands, and 19% of its forests and woodlands have been degraded. Such trends have been caused mainly through deforestation, desertification, and erosion (UNCTAD, 2012).

Figure 3.2 shows the aggregate levels of biophysical resources by material group that are being exported out of Africa (based on the available data): metal ores, fossil fuels, non-metallic minerals, and biomass from 1970 to 2017. Figure 3.2 thus covers almost the entire time period of neoliberal policies except the last few years. All material groups have shown a steady increase since the 1990s, with metal ores in particular being increasingly exported. Commodity prices boomed from 2003 to 2011, which helped to fuel the demand for African resources. However, by 2011 prices declined as global demand for commodities across all categories softened, with the exception of cocoa beans. While some may argue that this decrease in demand marks the end of the new scramble for African resources, it is significant to note that Africa continued to experience a steady increase in the overall export of natural resources through 2017, largely driven by an increase in metal ores.

Perhaps even more revealing, Figure 3.3 shows Africa's Raw Material Trade Balance from 1990 to 2013.[2] Since the 1990s, Africa has shown a steady increase in a deficit, meaning it increasingly exports more resources across all material categories than it imports. *In other words, in physical terms, Africa is a net supplier of resources to the rest of the world.* As noted in Chapter 1, physical trade balances (of which Raw Material Trade Balances are the most comprehensive) are, in the literature, widely used as a measure of ecologically unequal exchange. It appears that during the neoliberal years, ecologically unequal exchange has deepened in Africa.

In contrast to the fact that Africa is increasingly exporting resources, Africa's Raw Material Consumption per capita (approximate tonnes per

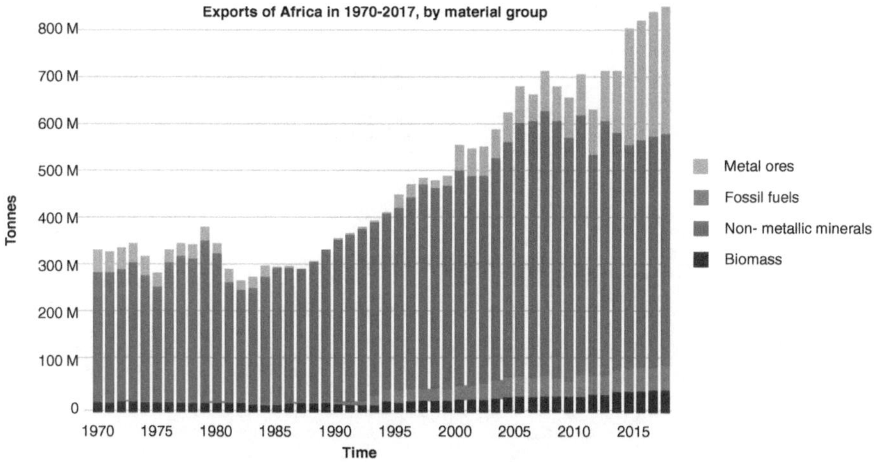

Figure 3.2 Exports of Africa in 1970–2017, by Material Group
Source: WU Vienna (2020): Material flows by material group, 1970–2017. Visualization based upon the UN IRP Global Material Flows Database. Vienna University of Economics and Business. Online available at: materialflows.net/visualisation-centre

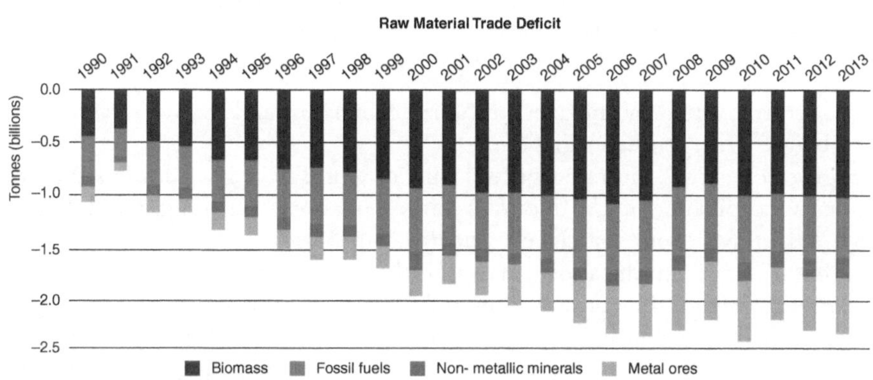

Figure 3.3 Physical Trade Balance of Africa, 1990–2013, in Raw Material Equivalents
Source: Graph compiled by author from data obtained from the materialflows.net website

capita) remains the lowest of all the regions in the world. Raw Material Consumption captures the amount of domestic and foreign extraction of materials needed along all supply chains to produce the final products consumed *within* a country. RMC equals the sum of Domestic Extraction (DE) plus Imports in Raw Material Equivalents (RME_{im}) minus exports in Raw Material Equivalents (RME_{ex}). As Figure 3.4 shows, an average African on a per capita basis will use only around 3 tonnes of material resources per year compared to the

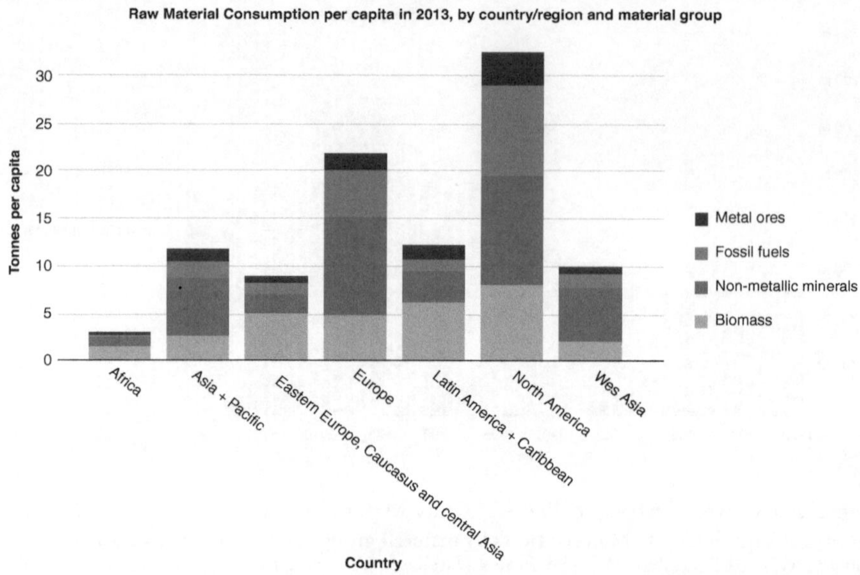

Figure 3.4 Raw Material Consumption per Capita According to Region, 2013
Source: WU Vienna (2020): Material flows by material group, 1970–2017. Visualization based upon the UN IRP Global Material Flows Database. Vienna University of Economics and Business. Online available at: materialflows.net/visualisation-centre

over 30 tonnes used by the average North American and the over 20 tonnes used by the average European.

Figure 3.5 shows the rapid growth in the world's RMC from less than 8 tonnes per capita per year to about 12 tonnes; in contrast, from the mid-1990s until 2013 RMC per capita levels *actually fell* in Africa.

What is clear from the above analysis is that the rest of the world is primarily benefiting from the consumption of Africa's natural resources, not its own people. Africa, as a continent, exports more resources than it imports. Simultaneously, the African people use far less resources than the global average, suffer greatly from the effects of climate change, and are subject to dispossession in the scramble for African land and resources.

While much ecologically unequal exchange research focuses on the empirical study of the asymmetrical transfer of resources, the work of Stephen Bunker linking the dynamics of underdevelopment and dis-articulation to ecologically unequal exchange is also equally important to the issue of eco-neocolonialism. Overlapping with the concept of economic dualism in economics,[3] Bunker (1985) argues that the socio-economic structural differences between core "productive" economies and peripheral "extractive" economies, combined with more or less intractable ecological factors, systematically lead to the increased development of one and the impoverishment

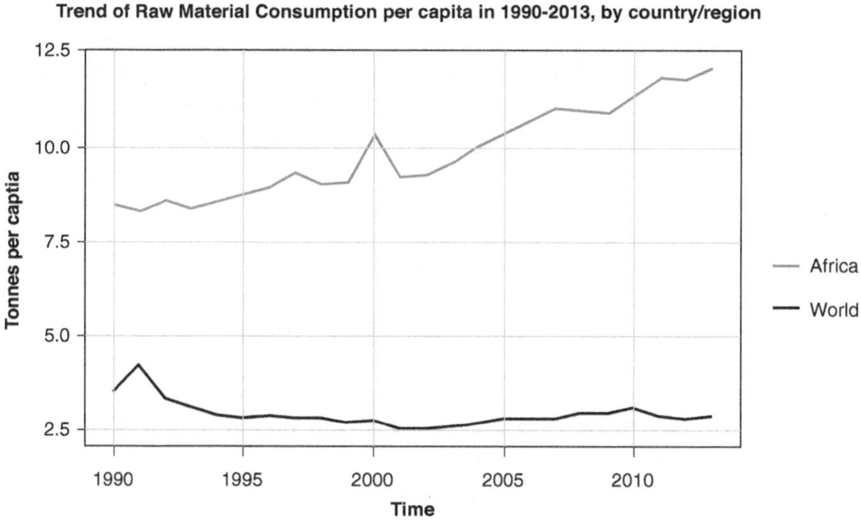

Figure 3.5 Africa and World Raw Material Consumption per Capita, 1990–2013
Source: WU Vienna (2020): Material flows by material group, 1970–2017. Visualization based upon the UN IRP Global Material Flows Database. Vienna University of Economics and Business. Online available at: materialflows.net/visualisation-centre

and underdevelopment of the other. In extractive economies, matter and energy flow to productive economies (core), which reduces the complexity and power in the former but increases complexity and power in the latter. Extractive exports are associated with the loss of "ecological values" as local environments are destroyed and the extractive commodities themselves are eventually depleted. Such economies are associated with booms and busts, initial rises in regional incomes (followed by rapid collapses with depletion of easily accessible resources and demographic and infrastructural dislocations), and consequently economic disruptions. The changes brought about by extractive activities, whether to labor or infrastructure, serve little purpose when specific resources are depleted or no longer in demand. Further, there are low levels of linkages to other economic activities and social organization in the same region. Because extractive economies tend to export extractive resources that are raw or unfinished, the majority of value creation that occurs in the processing and industrialization stages happens in other economies. These dis-articulated economies inhibit development along the lines of a diversified and integrated economy. Biophysical resources are simply transferred to core articulated economies whose multiple internal linkages enable them utilize such resources for their technological and economic growth. In other words, *extractive economies are characterized by socio-ecologies structured not for the sake of their own populations but for the needs and functioning of the capitalist world-system.*

Dis-articulation is evident in African extractive economies. The *Africa Progress Report 2013* found that even with the growth of natural resource exports in the 2000s Africa remains crippled with underlying structural weaknesses in terms of value added. Africa remains an exporter of unprocessed or lightly processed commodities, and consequently, African exporters continue to capture only a small share of the final value of mineral exports. The DRC, for example, is the world's largest exporter of cobalt, but the mineral remains mostly in the form of unprocessed ore. Meanwhile, value is added outside the country, such as by the smelting industry in China and other importing countries. Likewise, Guinea exports bauxite, but it too is processed into aluminum overseas. Angola and Nigeria continue to export low value-added crude oil, and, in a classical dependency syndrome, import high value-added petroleum and petroleum-based plastics and fertilizers. Further, the report states that studies conducted on the value chain for a range of African minerals have found that the value of processed products was typically 400 times greater than the equivalent raw material's unit value by weight. The report concludes that without processing industries that add value, mining creates fewer jobs, produces less revenue, contributes less to GDP, and creates an economy vulnerable to extreme price fluctuations on world markets. Without the capacity to derive maximum benefits, such as aiming to maximize the value of locally retained earnings, create linkages, transfer technology, or mitigate environmental and social impacts, African economies based on mineral extraction remain plagued by export enclaves (Africa Progress Panel, 2013).

Ecological Imperialism and Foreign Investment Policies in Africa

By the second half of the 1990s, Africa had undergone more far-reaching structural adjustments than any other region, yet for decades these adjustments did little to alleviate poverty or encourage development. At times, the orthodox response was to blame African governments for not carrying out reforms far enough or to insist that not enough time had elapsed to reap the gains of adjustment and globalization. At other times, the orthodox response was to blame government corruption and the lack of rule of law (World Bank, 1994; Collier & Patillo, 2000; OECD, 2002). The problem with these assessments is that Africa complied extensively with the reforms. Indeed, Africa underwent the greatest number of neoliberal programs compared to other world regions with more devaluations, lowering of tariffs and privatizations, and so on, imposed in Africa than anywhere else (UNCTAD, 2005). During the 1980s and 1990s, 35 SSA countries implemented 162 SAPs with the World Bank or the IMF in comparison to the 126 SAPs introduced throughout the rest of the world.

The problem is not that Africa is insufficiently integrated; rather, the problem stems from *how* Africa is integrated. Africa, particularly sub-Saharan Africa, is integrated into the global economy as a dis-articulated, extractive periphery where foreign companies take most of the profits generated by Africa's natural wealth. As Ferguson (2005) notes,

> capital hops over unusable Africa, alighting only in mineral rich enclaves that are starkly disconnected from their national societies. The result is not the formation of standardized national grids, but the emergence of huge areas of the continent that are effectively off the grid. These areas are in many ways excluded from the global economy, but Africa is not a "black hole" in the information society; rather, specific forms of global integration on the continent co-exist with specific and equally global forms of exclusion and marginalization.
>
> (p. 380)

Africa, and particularly sub-Saharan Africa, is not integrated deeply into global value chains in terms of higher value-added activities. A large part of FDI in Africa remains resource seeking, with 40% of all greenfield project announcements in 2019 targeting industries directly linked to natural resources (UNCTAD, 2020). Of the top 25 mining companies listed on Mining Africa (n.d.) website, 16 were Canadian, Australian, and European while the rest were primarily South African, a trend some have referred to as "regional sub-imperialism." African governments have a shareholding in only a minority of foreign investments, and even if they do, shareholding tends to be small, usually around 5–20%. A recent report by War on Want (2016) found that 101 companies listed on the London Stock Exchange control an identified $1.05 trillion worth of resources in Africa in just five commodities—oil, gold, diamonds, coal, and platinum. These 101 companies have mineral operations in 37 African countries and are mainly British, with 59 incorporated in the UK.

The continued foreign domination of African resources is not accidental; it is a direct outcome of the neoliberal SAPs foisted upon the continent in order to create favorable conditions for foreign capital through privatization and various incentives to attract multinational corporations. According to orthodox theory, foreign investment is a key component of development as it brings capital, jobs, and technology transfers. *Yet, as will be discussed, neoliberal foreign investment policies, while promising these benefits, paradoxically contain the policies that prevent these very benefits from occurring.* To attract a larger share of global FDI, African countries have introduced changes in policy through both multilateral and bilateral agreements as well as changes in domestic mining and land laws. By the early 2000s, most African countries had concluded bilateral treaties and signed multilateral agreements with international organizations in the effort to create more "favorable investment climates." The World Bank has hailed the participation of African countries in international, regional, and bilateral FDI agreements as important steps in signaling to investors that a favorable policy environment is being created. However, a number of scholars have argued that the proliferation of regulations formulated in such treaties places serious constraints on developing countries' national development strategies (Shadlen, 1999; Adejumobi, 2003; Wade, 2003; Kragelund, 2009; Gallagher & Ghosh, 2010). Ultimately, these regulations limit the capacity of developing country governments to constrain TNCs as they allow developed country firms to enter and exit markets more easily and operate with fewer restrictions and obligations (Wade, 2003). Such a level of intrusion, through the mechanism of international agreements, represents what Wade characterizes as a "shrinking of autonomous development space," whereby the development space for diversification and upgrading policies in developing countries is being shrunk behind a rhetoric of universal liberalization, privatization, and economic growth (Wade, 2003).

Multilateral and Bilateral Investment Treaties

The major multilateral institution in the post-WWII era governing international trade was GATT, which would later become the World Trade Organization (WTO). While the WTO is a trade organization, it has also promulgated important provisions concerning the governance of foreign investment. The Uruguay Round from 1986 to 1993 (dominated by the US in the negotiation process) contained several controversial propositions in the area of foreign investment in the form of Trade-Related Investment Measures (TRIMs) (Adejumobi, 2003). TRIMs cover a broad variety of developing countries' economic activities, and countries that are WTO members must satisfy the performance requirements of TRIMs (Wade, 2003). The central aim of TRIMs is to provide a safe haven for Western investments with favorable domestic conditions. TRIMs ban or aspire to ban most performance requirements on foreign firms. For example, TRIMs ban performance requirements related to local content (which require that locally produced goods be purchased or used), trade balancing, and export requirements (which require the export of a specified percentage of production volume). They also ban requirements on public agencies to procure goods from local suppliers. A country that tries to impose such requirements can be taken to the Dispute Settlement Mechanism, where it will most likely lose (Wade, 2003). Moreover, the US and EU want to modify the current TRIMs agreement so as to ban all performance requirements, including joint venturing, technology transfer, and research and design (R&D). Further, Wade argues that the language in the relevant parts of TRIMs is not legally clear, and many developing countries fear that if they do use such non-banned performance requirements they will face punitive repercussions (Adejumobi, 2003; Wade, 2003).

These types of bans are important because they severely constrain developing countries' capacity to regulate the behavior of foreign firms for the purpose of development objectives, for example through implementing policies that require technology transfer from foreign firms. A country that implements such policies can now be legally handicapped in accessing developed country markets (Shadlen, 1999; Correa & Kuman, 2003; Green & Chang, 2003). Shadlen

(1999) contends, "The bottom line is that the TRIMs agreement takes away developing countries' ability to use important policy instruments to increase local value-added, employment, and industrial upgrading" (p. 759).

Even more stringent are bilateral investment treaties (BITs) that have been proliferating throughout the developing world since the early 1990s. Compared to BITs, the obligations from TRIMs are rudimentary and are not nearly as comprehensive. Bilateral investment treaties require the host government to lift even more restrictions on foreign firms and to give even more concessions in return for better access to the US or other powerful party markets. BITs establish firm-state arbitration boards dominated by private-sector adjudicators. Such boards, Wade (2003) argues, are naturally sympathetic to the needs of firms and use private contract law rather than public law. Further concerning disputes, only countries can bring cases against other countries under the WTO. However, regional-bilateral treaties with the US allow firms to bring cases to arbitration (Shadlen, 1999). BITs clearly focus on foreign investment protection, and developing countries sign these treaties in order to signal to investors and attract more FDI. In recent decades, BITs have become the most important international legal mechanism for FDI encouragement and governance.

Prior to the advent of BITs, the protection afforded to foreign investors was minimal under the so-called Hull Rule. The Hull Rule was the customary international legal rule of minimum standard of treatment that was the only protection for foreign investors. The Hull Rule dealt exclusively with cases of expropriation and offered no general protection against discriminatory treatment (Neumayer & Spess, 2005). During the era of economic nationalism, developing countries had challenged the Hull Rule's validity as part of their demands for the NIEO as the UN General Assembly's Resolution 1803 merely requires "appropriate compensation" for expropriation. Furthermore, considering the large number of expropriations in the 1960s and 1970s, it is likely that the Hull Rule was never strongly enforced (Neumayer & Spess, 2005).

The basic provisions of most bilateral investment treaties guarantee certain standards of treatment for foreign investors that contrast strongly with the era of economic nationalism. By entering into a BIT, signatories agree to grant certain relative standards of treatment, such as "national treatment" (foreign investors may not be treated worse than domestic investors) and "most favored nation treatment" (privileges granted to one foreign investor must be granted to all foreign investors). They also agree to guarantee certain absolute standards of treatment after the investment has taken place, such as fair and equitable treatment for foreign investors in accordance with international standards. BITs typically ban discriminatory treatment against foreign investors and include guarantees of appropriate compensation for expropriated property or funds. They also usually allow for free transfer and repatriation of capital and profits. Furthermore, the BIT parties agree to submit to a binding dispute settlement should conflict concerning these provisions arise (Neumayer & Spess, 2005).

The extent of interference with domestic regulatory sovereignty when developing countries sign BITs is therefore enormous. Virtually any public policy regulation can be challenged through the dispute settlement mechanism as long as it affects foreign investors. Hence, the signing of BITs is specifically meant to signal that the developing country is serious about the protection of foreign investment (Neumayer & Spess, 2005). Shadlen (1999) argues that regional-bilateral agreements move far beyond the WTO in a way that "may have serious implications for developing countries' capacities for achieving upward mobility in the international economy," and in particular bilateral agreements with the US (p. 752). Regional-bilateral accords, he contends, "encourage specialization and pursuit of competitiveness via exploitation of existing comparative advantages" (p. 752). In fact, if we look at the countries that have successfully industrialized and sustained economic growth over the past several decades (such as Taiwan, South Korea, and China), regulation of TNCs for development purposes has been central to their economic strategies for technological upgrading, job creation, and furthering linkages within their economies.

Domestic Reforms in the Extractive Sector

While multilateral and bilateral agreements may bind developing countries' capacity to regulate foreign investment, these agreements have also been accompanied by extensive domestic reforms in the extractive sector. A large proportion of FDI in Africa goes into the mining sector, and mineral export economies are among the highest recipients of inflows. For much of the 1980s and 1990s, the investment climate in mining remained poor, at least partially due to uncertainty generated by the backlash against foreign-owned operations in the 1970s (UNCTAD, 2005). In recent years, however, major changes in mining codes have helped orchestrate a state withdrawal from the sector, expand opportunities for the private sector, and increased incentives to attract FDI. In total, African economies have witnessed an influx of FDI into the mining sector (UNCTAD, 2005). The IFIs argued that the incapacity of African state-owned enterprises (SOEs) to efficiently generate sufficient revenues hindered the wider development process, and it was proposed that such measures as privatization and investor protections would alleviate the underperformance of the mining sector in Africa (UNCTAD, 2005).

Since the 1980s, the World Bank has promoted a process of liberalization, deregulation, and privatization under the auspices of economic growth, which has resulted in the creation of new regulatory frameworks for mining in Africa. The reforms have certainly created a more favorable environment for foreign investors. However, these reforms have potentially undermined norms and standards in areas of crucial importance for social and economic development and environmental protection (Akabzaa, 2001; Campbell, 2003; Lissu & Curtis, 2008). Overall, reforms have emphasized creating a stable legal and fiscal framework, including mining codes, contractual stability, a guaranteed stable fiscal regime, and channels for profit repatriation. In return governments are expected to receive increased rents generated from the mining sector (UNCTAD, 2005).

Like multilateral and bilateral treaties, however, African mining codes illustrate a significant shift to foreign capital control over African resources at the expense of development objectives and with attendant social and environmental costs. One example is the mining sector in Ghana, which received priority attention under the country's Economic Recovery Program (ERP). The ERP initiated a generous provision of tax incentives to foreign investors. Corporate income tax, which stood at 50–55% in 1975, was reduced to 45% in 1986 and further scaled down to 35% in 1994. The initial capital allowance to enable investors to recoup their capital expenditure was increased from 20% in the first year of production and 15% for subsequent annual allowances in 1975 to 75% in the first year of operation and 50% for subsequent annual allowances in 1986. Royalty rates, which stood at 6% of total value of minerals in 1975, were reduced to 3.7% in 1987. Other duties such as the mineral duty (5%), import duty (5–35%), and foreign exchange tax (33–75%) that had contributed significantly to government revenue were abolished. In addition, exemption from the payment of customs import duties in respect of plants as well as equipment and accessories imported for mining was established. The personal remittance quota for expatriate personnel was freed from any tax imposed on the transfer of external currency out of the country (Campbell, 2003).

As Campbell (2003) argues, ultimately the role of the African state was redefined to create a favorable environment for investment and for the free play of market forces. This redefinition is such a key defining feature of neoliberal globalization and a central factor of ecological imperialism that it cannot be overstated. Developmental objectives that hampered these goals, such as redistributive measures that sought to retain greater earnings within the host country, or regulatory measures to monitor the use of non-renewables and protect the environment, were at best placed in a secondary position behind the policies to attract foreign investment and promote exports. For example, Campbell noted that the World Bank's 1992 Strategy for African Mining—the first systematic presentation of reforms considered necessary by the Bank—was based upon a survey that was sent to 80 mining companies. As per the insistence of investors, rather than the goals of sustainable, integrated development, the report recommended a stable legal and fiscal framework, which included the need for mining codes, contractual stability, a guaranteed fiscal regime, profit repatriation, rule of law, etc. The report, however, did not articulate how the mining sector would contribute to broader developmental objectives of great importance, such as the building of backward and forward linkages or the possibility of value-added processing of minerals. Rather, the primary focus was how to attract investment and reduce investment risk for private mining companies.

Overall, in terms of achieving developmental objectives, the African states face a decreased ability to ensure a sustainable flow of net returns from mining activities and political sovereignty (Campbell, 2003). As Africa's investment regime liberalized in areas of taxation, currency exchange, banking, trade, and labor, and opened all sectors to foreign investors previously reserved to the state, efforts to escape neocolonialism and promote sovereignty were abandoned. Reductions in levels of ad valorem royalties, corporate income tax rates as well as customs duties on imported capital goods all reduced the capacity for African states to retain earnings. For example, the Tanzanian mineral code was introduced in 1998 as a result of a five-year World Bank financed sector reform project. The code allows for 100% foreign ownership; provides guarantees against nationalization and expropriation; offers unrestricted repatriation of profits and capital; pegs the royalty rate at maximum of 3%; provides waivers in respect of import duties; allows tax exemptions on imported machinery, equipment, and other inputs; and waives requirements for the local procurement of goods and services. This is indeed a significant policy reversal from a country that once sought to build development based on African socialism and to institute indigenous control over their means of production.

After the commodity boom in the first decade of the 2000s that resulted in robust world market prices for African metals, the extent of revenue loss due to the tax regimes of mineral rich countries became apparent. The *Africa Progress Report 2013*, written by the Africa Progress Panel and chaired by Kofi Annan, criticized the African tax regimes as putting a drain on the public purse (Africa Progress Panel, 2013). The report acknowledges that in the 1990s many governments may have mistakenly provided excessive tax concessions to attract foreign investors (though it doesn't acknowledge the reason for the tax concessions, i.e., the structural adjustments). What the report finds especially problematic is that many such policies have continued, even despite the commodity boom of the 2000s and the increased profit margins of mining and petroleum companies. For example, the report finds that in Sierra Leone generous concessions were made to foreign investors that included royalty rates as low as 0.5% on mining exports. Also, only one of five major mining companies operating in Sierra Leone paid corporation tax in 2011. Zambia entered the copper boom with one of lowest royalty rates in the African mining sector. It was not until 2013 that tax concessions for the copper industry increased somewhat in light of the increase in world market prices. The report writes that until 2010 the average royalty payment on gold exports in sub-Saharan Africa was only 3%, one of lowest in the world. However, world prices of gold increased from $300 to $1,600 per ounce between 2000 and 2011 while investor profits increased at four times rate of government revenues (Africa Progress Panel, 2013).

Further, the Africa Progress Panel (2013) states that revenues secured by many resource-rich countries appear to be very low in relation to the value of exports and especially when compared with international standards. For example, the IMF estimates that globally the effective tax rate in mining is typically 45–65% (and is higher in petroleum). But while Zambia's copper exports generated $10 billion in 2011, government revenues from copper were only $240 million, or 2.4% of export value. In the same year, mining product exports from Guinea reached $1.4 billion, representing 12% of GDP, but government mining revenues were just $48 million, or 0.4% of GDP. Further, the report asserts, tax reform has proven difficult in many resource-rich countries due to opposition from major companies. For example, the report points out that when Zambia sought to renegotiate its royalty rate on copper export, major investors opposed the measure despite a fourfold increase in the price of copper between 2000 and 2011. Likewise in Nigeria, royalty rates were negotiated during the 1990s when oil prices were one-fifth of post-2000 prices, but major companies still strongly opposed reforms. Only in 2013 had the government raised taxes from the nominal level of 63% to 71% (still at the lower end of the tax range identified by the IMF) (Africa Progress Panel, 2013).

Another report, written by the German Development Institute (Sturmer, 2010), similarly finds that sub-Saharan Africa failed to benefit from the high prices of mineral and energy commodities from 2003 to 2008. While the extractive sector experienced strong sales revenues and high inflows of direct investments, the three case study countries of Zambia, Namibia, and Ghana indicate that they only profited "more than moderately" from tax revenues. For example, the report finds that the Zambian copper and cobalt industries sold minerals to the value of over $13 billion and benefited from nearly $4 billion FDIs in the period from 2003 to 2008. However, the average implicit tax rate[4] for the extractive sector in Zambia from 2003 to 2008 was below 2%, and consequently, the government only raised tax revenues of about $393 million. In Namibia from 2003 to 2008, sales of minerals were worth $9.4 billion and FDI totaled to $2.6 billion. In contrast, tax revenues only totaled about $893 million. Likewise, Ghana exported minerals and fuels worth $7.7 billion and attracted over $4 billion of FDI inflows from 2003 to 2008. In contrast, tax revenues totaled only $426 million from 2003 to 2008 when the average implicit tax rate in that period was 5%. Further, the report engages in a hypothetical experiment by applying Australia's implicit tax rate to the case studies. It finds that Ghana, if it had the same implicit tax rate of Australia, could have collected tax revenues of $735 million during 2003–2008, rather than $426 million. Namibia could have also raised government revenues an additional $870 million, and Zambia could have raised nearly $1.4 billion (Sturmer, 2010).

The Comprador Elite

Unfortunately, while these numbers may provide an approximation of the monetary losses that Africa suffers from low taxation rates, they fail to capture the real extent to which dis-articulated peripheral economies suffer the social losses and political conflict of economies based on resource extraction, nor do they capture even the monetary losses from illicit financial flows (IFFs). Within the enduring African legacy of colonialism and neocolonialism is the formation of a comprador elite, the elite class within the periphery whose interests coincide with foreign interests and often conflict with the interests of their own citizens. Extractive industries are notoriously plagued by corruption. Corruption and patronage are central in the granting of concessions and low implicit tax rates (Sturmer, 2010). According to the *Africa Progress Report 2013*, the privatization of the Democratic Republic of the Congo's (DRC) minerals sector has been plagued by a culture of secrecy, informal deals, and allegations of corruption—despite calls (and promises of) change toward transparency. Further, with some of the world's richest mineral resources, DRC state companies are granting concessions to foreign investors, most registered offshore, that systematically undervalue natural resources. An analysis of five deals done during years 2010–2012 found that between 2010 and 2012 the DRC lost at least $1.36 billion in revenues from the underpricing of mining assets sold to offshore companies. These total losses from just the five deals reviewed were equivalent to almost double the DRC's combined annual budget for health and education in 2012. Across the five deals, assets were sold on average at only one-sixth of their estimated commercial market value. Hence, assets valued at $1.63 billion in total were sold to offshore companies for a mere $275 million. The report also cites a pervasive problem of tax evasion by offshore companies—firms that shift profits to lower tax jurisdictions cost Africa a whooping $38 billion a year (Africa Progress Panel, 2013).[5]

UNCTAD's recent *Economic development in Africa report 2020* finds that every year an estimated $88.6 billion, equivalent to 3.7% of Africa's GDP, leaves the continent as illicit capital flight (UNCTAD, 2020). Illicit financial flows are trans-border movements of money and assets, which are illegal in source, transfer, or use. These outflows include illicit capital flight; tax and commercial practices like misinvoicing of trade shipments; and criminal activities such as illegal markets, corruption, or theft. IFFs related to the export of extractive commodities are the largest component of illicit capital flight from Africa. Of the estimated $40 billion of IFFs derived from extractive commodities in 2015, 77% were concentrated in the gold supply chain, followed by diamonds (12%) and platinum (6%). Another report estimates the capital flight from 30 African countries over the period 1970–2018 to be a combined $2 trillion (in 2018 dollars) through capital flight, of which net misinvoicing of exports and imports contributed $588 billion to total capital flight (Ndikumana and Boyce, 2021).

Conclusion

Africa exhibits some of the clearest signs of ecological imperialism in the capitalist world-system. From colonialism to neoliberal eco-neocolonialism, what characterizes peripheral regions like Africa are societies and ecologies structured not for the sake of their own populations but for the needs and functioning of the capitalist world-system. Under neoliberal trade policies that favor export-led growth based on specialization in comparative advantage, ecologically unequal exchange has deepened. Neoliberal foreign investment—promising to bring growth, jobs, and technology transfer—is built on policies that obstruct these very promises. Instead, neoliberal foreign investment policies have reinforced dis-articulated economies and enclavism while ensuring that transnational corporations can operate freely and capture the majority of profits associated with lucrative extractive sectors. For the rest of the world-system, this enables access to Africa's rich resources for unsustainable levels of growth, industrialization, and consumption. In a time of global ecological crises, Africa resources have been cracked open for decades, and the continent is now the final frontier for resources and land.

References

Adejumobi, S. (2003). Globalization and Africa's development agenda: From the WTO to NEPAD. Addis Ababa: Development Policy Management Forum.

Adeniran, T. (1986). Africa, the United Nations, and the NIEO. In R. Onwuka & O. Aluko (Eds.), The future of Africa and the new international economic order (pp. 115–132). New York: St. Martin's Press.

Africa Progress Panel. (2013). Africa progress report 2013: Equity in extractives, stewarding Africa's natural resources for all. Africa Progress Panel - Home. https://static1.squarespace.com/static/5728c7b18259b5e0087689a6/t/57ab29519de4bb-90f53f9fff/1470835029000/2013_African+Progress+Panel+APR_Equity_in_Extractives_25062013_ENG_HR.pdf

Akabzaa, T. (2001). Boom and dislocation: The environmental and social impacts of mining in the Wassa West District of Ghana. Accra: Third World Network Africa.

Amin, S. (1990). Maldevelopment: Anatomy of a global failure. Tokyo: United Nations University Press.

Bond, P. (2006). Looting Africa: The economics of exploitation. Scottsville: University of KwaZulu-Natal Press. https://doi.org/10.5040/9781350221185

Bunker, S.G. (1985). Underdeveloping the Amazon: Extraction, unequal exchange, and the failure of the modern state. Chicago, IL: University of Illinois Press.

Bunker, S.G. (2005). How ecologically uneven developments put the spin on the treadmill of production. Organization and Environment, 18(1), 38–54. https://doi.org/10.1177/1086026604270434

Bunker, S.G., & Ciccantell, P.S. (2005). Globalization and the race for resources. Baltimore, MD: Johns Hopkins University Press.

Campbell, B. (2003). Factoring in governance is not enough. Mining codes in Africa, policy reform and corporate responsibility. Minerals & Energy - Raw Materials Report, 18(3), 2–13. https://doi.org/10.1080/14041040310019129

Campbell, B., & Loxley, J. (Eds.). (1989). Structural adjustment in Africa. New York: St. Martin's Press.

Carmody, P.R. (2011). The new scramble for Africa. Cambridge: Polity Press. https://doi.org/10.1177/1464993412466509

Cheru, F. (1989). The silent revolution in Africa: Debt, development, and democracy. Harare: Anvil.

Cheru, F., & Obi, C. (Eds.). (2010). The rise of China and India in Africa: Challenges, opportunities and critical interventions. London: Zed Books. http://nai.diva-portal.org/smash/get/diva2:285922/FULLTEXT01.pdf

Collier, P., & Pattillo, C.A. (Eds.). (2000). Investment and risk in Africa. New York: St. Martin's Press. https://doi.org/10.1007/978-1-349–15068-7

Correa, C.M., & Kumar, N. (2003). Protecting foreign investment: Implications of a WTO regime and policy options. London: Zed Books.

Curtis, M., & Lissu, T. (2008). A golden opportunity? How Tanzania is failing to benefit from gold mining. Dodoma: Christian Council of Tanzania (CCT).

Cypher, J.M. (2014). The process of economic development. (4th edition). London and New York: Routledge.

DeLancey, V. (1992). The economies of Africa, in understanding tropical Africa (pp. 94–95). Boulder, CO: Lynne Rienner Publishers.

Ferguson, J. (2005). Seeing like an oil company: Space, security, and global capital in neoliberal Africa. American Anthropologist, 107(3), 377–382. https://doi.org/10.1525/aa.2005.107.3.377

Gallagher, K., & Ghosh, J. (2010). Dangers of unrestrained commerce. Livemint.com. http://www.livemint.com/Opinion/dRO2FaREGhHslMhuy3cZ3M/Dangers-ofunrestrained-commerce.html

GRAIN. (2012, June 11). Squeezing Africa dry: Behind every land grab is a water grab. GRAIN. http://www.grain.org/article/entries/4516-squeezing-africa-dry-behind-every-land-grab-is-a-water-grab

Greco, E. (2021). Africa, extractivism, and the crises of this time. Review of African Political Economy. https://roape.net/2021/02/02/africa-extractivism-and-the-crisis-this-time/

Green, D., & Chang, H. (n.d.). The Northern WTO agenda on investment: Do as we say, not as we did. Institute of Development Studies. https://www.ecolomics-international.org/n_sd_south_center_doaswesay_notaswedid_03.pdf

Kragelund, P. (2009). Knocking on a wide-open door: Chinese investments in Africa. Review of African Political Economy: Against One-Dimensional Africa, 36(122), 479–497. https://doi.org/10.1080/03056240903346111

Mining Africa. (n.d.). Mining in Africa. https://www.miningafrica.net/

Mkandawire, T. (2005). Maladjusted African economies and globalization. Africa Development, XXX(1 and 2), 1–33.

Ndikumana, L., & Boyce, J.K. (2021). Capital Flight from Africa 1970–2018. Political Economy Research Institute. https://peri.umass.edu/images/CapFlight Africa-5-28-21.pdf

Neumayer, E., & Spess, L. (2005). Do bilateral investment treaties increase foreign direct investment to developing countries? World Development, 33(10), 1567–1585. https://doi.org/10.1016/j.worlddev.2005.07.001

Nkrumah, K. (1966). Neo-colonialism: The last stage of imperialism. New York: International Publishers.

Nyerere, J.K. (1971). Ujamaa: Essays on socialism. London: Oxford University Press.

Obeng-Odoom, F. (2021). The Commons in an Age of Uncertainty: Decolonizing Nature, Economy and Society. University of Toronto Press.

Obi, C. (2010). African oil in the energy security calculations of China and India. In F. Cheru & C. Obi (Eds.), The rise of China and India in Africa: Challenges, opportunities and critical interventions (pp. 181–192). London: Zed Books. http://nai.diva-portal.org/smash/get/diva2:285922/FULLTEXT01.pdf

Organization for Economic Development and Cooperation (OECD). (2002). Foreign direct investment for development: Maximising benefits, minimising costs. OECD. https://www.oecd.org/investment/investmentfordevelopment/foreigndirectinvestmentfordevelopmentmaximisingbenefitsminimisingcosts.htm

Rodney, W. (1981). How Europe underdeveloped Africa. Washington, DC: Howard University Press.

Saul, J., & Leys, C. (1999). Sub-Saharan Africa in global capitalism. Monthly Review. http://monthlyreview.org/1999/07/01/sub-saharan-africa-in-global-capitalism

Shadlen, K. (1999). Exchanging development for market access? Deep integration and industrial policy under multilateral and regional-bilateral agreements. Review of International Political Economy, 12(5), 750–775. https://doi.org/10.1080/09692290500339685

Smaller, C., & Mann, H. (2009). A thirst for distant lands: Foreign investment in agricultural land and water. International Institute for Sustainable Development (IISD). http://www.iisd.org/publications/pub.aspx?id=1122

Southall, R., & Melber, H. (Eds.). (2009). A new scramble for Africa? Imperialism, investment and development. Scottsville: University of KwaZulu-Natal Press.

Stürmer, M. (2010). Let the good times roll? Raising tax revenues from the extractive sector in Sub-Saharan Africa during the commodity price boom. German Development Institute/Deutsches Institut für Entwicklungspolitik (DIE). https://www.die-gdi.de/en/discussion-paper/article/let-the-good-times-roll-raising-tax-revenues-from-the-extractive-sector-in-sub-saharan-africa-during-the-commodity-price-boom/

Thomson, A. (2000). An introduction to African politics. London: Routledge.

United Nations Conference on Trade and Development (UNCTAD). (2005). Economic development in Africa: Rethinking the role of foreign direct investment. New York: United Nations. https://unctad.org/system/files/official-document/gdsafrica20051_en.pdf

United Nations Conference on Trade and Development (UNCTAD). (2007). World investment report 2007 transnational corporations, extractive industries and development. Geneva: United Nations. https://unctad.org/system/files/official-document/wir2007_en.pdf

United Nations Conference on Trade and Development (UNCTAD). (2012). Economic development in Africa report 2012: Structural transformation and sustainable development in Africa. New York: United Nations. https://unctad.org/system/files/official-document/aldcafrica2012_embargo_en.pdf

United Nations Conference on Trade and Development (UNCTAD). (2018a). Economic development in Africa report 2018. https://unctad.org/webflyer/economic-development-africa-report-2018

United Nations Conference on Trade and Development (UNCTAD). (2018b). Export diversification and employment. https://unctad.org/system/files/official-document/aldc2018d3_en.pdf

United Nations Conference on Trade and Development (UNCTAD). (2020). Economic development in Africa report 2020. https://unctad.org/webflyer/economic-development-africa-report-2020

Wade, R.H. (2003). What strategies are viable for developing countries today? The WTO and the shrinking of development space. Review of International Political Economy, 10(4), 621–644. https://doi.org/10.1080/09692290310001601902

War on Want. (2016). The new colonialism: Britain's scramble for Africa's energy and mining resources. https://waronwant.org/resources/new-colonialism-britains-scramble-africas-energy-and-mineral-resources

World Bank. (1994). Adjustment in Africa reforms, results, and the road ahead. New York: Oxford University Press.

Notes

1 Throughout this chapter, Africa as a whole is discussed as well as sub-Saharan Africa specifically, depending on the particular study or report being cited. While one may argue against addressing Africa as a whole given its size and diversity, as studies in this chapter discuss, ecological imperialism appears pervasive throughout the continent, in terms of the scramble for African resources. Where points specific to Sub-Saharan Africa are being made, the term is used instead of Africa.

2 The Raw Material Trade Balance (RTB) measures the physical trade surplus or physical trade deficit of a country, including domestic and foreign extraction of materials needed along all supply chains to produce the imports and exports. RTB equals imports in Raw Material Equivalents (IMP–RME) minus exports in Raw Material Equivalents (EXP–RME).

3 In economics, economic dualism is a form of disintegration. The term "dualism" refers to economies characterized by two sectors—a pre-capitalist, traditional form of production juxtaposed with a modern, enclave capitalist sector. These two sectors exist side by side with few linkages between them. The modern capitalist sector remains an enclave—economically or socially isolated from the traditional society in which it is embedded. In other words, resources and profits are simply extracted without inducing development in the rest of the country.

4 The author defines implicit tax rates as ratios that measure aggregate revenue from one or more taxes (meaning corporate income taxes paid by the extractive sector and royalties) as a percentage of some aggregate tax base (meaning in the report sales revenues from minerals and fuels). Implicit tax rates are sometimes referred to as an average or effective tax rate.

5 Likewise, the report, reflecting the non-inclusive Nature of economic growth under the current commodity boom, finds disparities in resource-rich countries are rising with economic growth and dampening the potential for poverty reduction. The report analyzed the relationship between growth, inequality, and poverty reduction in four countries: Ghana, Nigeria, Tanzania, and Zambia. In each of the four countries, there was a significant gap between the anticipated poverty reduction effects of growth and the actual outcomes. Further, the wealthiest 10% in each of the four countries captured a disproportionately large part of the overall consumption increase generated by growth. In each case, the poorest 40% saw their income share decline. This increasingly unequal pattern of wealth distribution was already superimposed on highly unequal patterns of wealth distribution. The report also discusses the "hidden wealth of the elites." For example, in 2009, it was found under a lawsuit brought by Transparency International that Presidents Omar Bongo Ondimba of Gabon, Denis Sassou Nguesso of the Republic of Congo, and Teodoro Obiang Nguema of Equatorial Guinea each bought luxury homes with state funds. Sassou Nguesso allegedly owned 24 estates and operated 112 bank accounts in France while Bong and his relatives allegedly owned about 30 luxury estates on the French Riviera, Paris, and Parisian suburbs (Africa Progress Panel, 2013).

4 Tanzania

The Role of the State from African Socialism to Eco-Neocolonialism

Like other African countries, Tanzania has undergone periods of colonial subjugation, anti-imperialist resistance, and contemporary forms of ecological imperialism renewed and reinforced through neoliberal development policies. Tanzania is a resource-rich country that is endowed with valuable minerals, vast tracts of arable land and abundant water resources, and an extensive coastal region. Like other African countries, its resources are attracting global attention, evident through increased FDI inflows into its extractive and land sector in the past several decades. After years of heavy state intervention and control, neoliberal policies have opened Tanzanian resources to foreign investment as a key strategy for economic growth and development.

This chapter takes a closer look through the case study of Tanzania at the political economy of ecological imperialism in two of the most important resource sectors in Africa—land and mining. It also focuses on the essential role of the state as an intermediate actor in ecological imperialism. In Tanzania, mining is the most lucrative sector in terms of export earnings, and both mining and land are associated with some of the most troubling forms of accumulation by dispossession and social and political conflict. In both sectors, accumulation by dispossession is ultimately accomplished by the state—the extra-economic actor that ensures Nature is accessible and amenable to the needs of capital accumulation. The centralized power of the state over resources, originating from its colonial origins as well as its reformulation during the era of African socialism, is a crucial component of ecological imperialism in Tanzania. *While a persistent myth is that laissez-faire economics requires the removal of the state to ensure the efficiency of the market, in reality the state has far from disappeared. Rather in the neoliberal era, the centralized power of the extractive peripheral state has been reconfigured to meet the needs of foreign capital accumulation.* In other words, the rules and regulation of the government as well as the apparatus of force have been restructured to ensure the accessibility and cheapness of peripheral resources for transnational corporations. The developmental state of the economic nationalist era has been transformed into an extra-economic actor, which guarantees the property rights of foreign investors and local elites. While the exact form may manifest differently, the power of the state and the willingness of local elites to act on behalf of

DOI: 10.4324/9780429261305-4

foreign interests is a pattern repeated throughout the Global South and one of the primary sources of continued socio-ecological crisis globally.

Tanzania's mining sector attracts the largest inflows of foreign investment in gold, diamonds, tanzanite, ruby, tin, copper, nickel, iron, soda phosphate, gypsum, kaolite, coal, natural gas, and uranium. In terms of its share of exports, mining is the fastest growing sector, and investor interests are protected by a host of policies. While classical producers of minerals and fossil fuels like Australia, Canada, and Saudi Arabia benefited from the 2003-2008 rise in commodity prices (Sturmer, 2010), Tanzania, like other sub-Saharan countries, was burdened by foreign investment regimes that guaranteed that profits largely flowed out of the continent. Despite an overall high economic growth of 7% per annum over the last ten years, Tanzania has failed to translate this economic growth into significant reductions in income poverty or structural industrial development. About one-half of the population continues to live on less than $1.90 a day (The World Bank, 2019). Inequality is fairly high in Tanzania with a Gini coefficient of 0.41, comparable to other African countries such as Senegal (0.403) and Kenya (0.408), though not nearly as high as South Africa (0.63) (The World Bank, n.d.a). While life expectancy gains have been made in the past decade, the average life expectancy is still only 65 years as of 2017. In contrast, billions of dollars in the form of repatriated profits accrue to foreign investors overseas, creating an issue of deep contention and civil unrest as local communities living near mining sites suffer from mining waste environmental degradation. While a modest form of economic nationalism in the mining sector and hints of it in the land sector may be emerging, many of the same features of the neoliberal foreign investment architecture remain.

Tanzania is also one of the top countries globally to have been targeted for foreign investment in large-scale land acquisitions, a dubious position that has sparked civil conflict and accusations of land grabbing and dispossession. In 2007–2008, the spike in agricultural commodity prices catalyzed huge transnational farmland acquisitions that were dubbed by some as a "global land rush." This land rush is driven by deep-seated socio-ecological challenges that are unlikely to abate in the long run. Population growth, growing consumption rates, demand for food, biofuels, and other raw materials have coupled with increasing water scarcity and natural resource constraints as countries globally are seeking to invest in land for food, energy, and environmental security. Increasing demand and limited supplies have also resulted in rising prices, prompting financial speculation and investment for profit purposes. Overall, investor countries have an average GDP per capita four times higher than target countries. In contrast, targeted countries are among the poorest nations in the world and tend to have high incidences of hunger. Investors also tend to seek out countries with weak land institutions that also offer relatively high levels of investor protection. As food and energy security are primary drivers, most investment projects are export oriented and target easily accessible and arable land (Land Matrix, 2018). For Tanzania and Africa at large, this trend has become problematic and has resulted in the acquisition of rural land at a scale unknown since colonial times. Further, African governments appear to be giving fertile land to foreign investors, including governments, at "giveaway prices." In contrast to promises of social and economic development and poverty alleviation, land acquisitions have been associated with lack of democratic oversight and management; loss of livelihoods and access to resources; and conflict between villagers, governments, and investors (Land Matrix, 2018).

Unsurprisingly, Tanzania, like much of Africa in the past several decades, has increasingly witnessed a deepening level of ecologically unequal exchange with the rest of the world while Tanzanian citizens continue to consume relatively little in the way of resources. The following four figures show, as negative values, Raw Material Equivalents of Exports (RME_{ex}) versus Raw Material Equivalents of Imports (RME_{im}), as positive values. RME_{ex} account for the total amount of primary material extraction—both in the domestic economy and in foreign countries—required to produce the exports. RME_{im} account for the total amount of primary material extraction in foreign countries required along the whole supply chain to produce the imports.

As Figures 4.1, 4.3, and 4.4 show, Tanzania is a net exporter in raw material terms in biomass, metals, and non-metallic minerals, which can be interpreted as a form of ecologically unequal exchange for these material categories.[1] (Tanzania, as Figure 4.2 shows, is a net importer of fossil fuels, showing a reliance on external sources for their energy needs.) While Tanzania is overall a net exporter of resources, Tanzanian domestic consumption of materials (DMC)[2] is only approximately 3.4 tonnes per capita in 2015 compared to the world average of about 12 tonnes per capita. As Chapter 2 overviewed, Tanzania, like much of the rest of Africa, finds itself in a typical peripheral position: exporting its resources to the external world while Tanzanian citizens themselves consume relatively little.

Tanzania's Integration into the World-System: Land and Mining in the Colonial Era

The origins of the centralized power of Tanzania's state over national resources began with colonialism. Tanzania's resource-based economy and integration into the world-system began under German subjugation in the 1880s, and the ecological imperialism of today in both the mining and land sectors has its roots in the enduring features established under colonialism. Under German colonial control, Tanzania's economy was organized to export raw materials, mainly agricultural goods. Through violent conquest, forced labor, and laws imposing taxes on the African population, the colonial mode of production was introduced. Roads, bridges, seaports, and railways were built as the infrastructure to extract and transport the surplus from periphery to metropole, and the plantation became a central way of organizing African labor to produce new commodities. By the late 1890s, Africans,

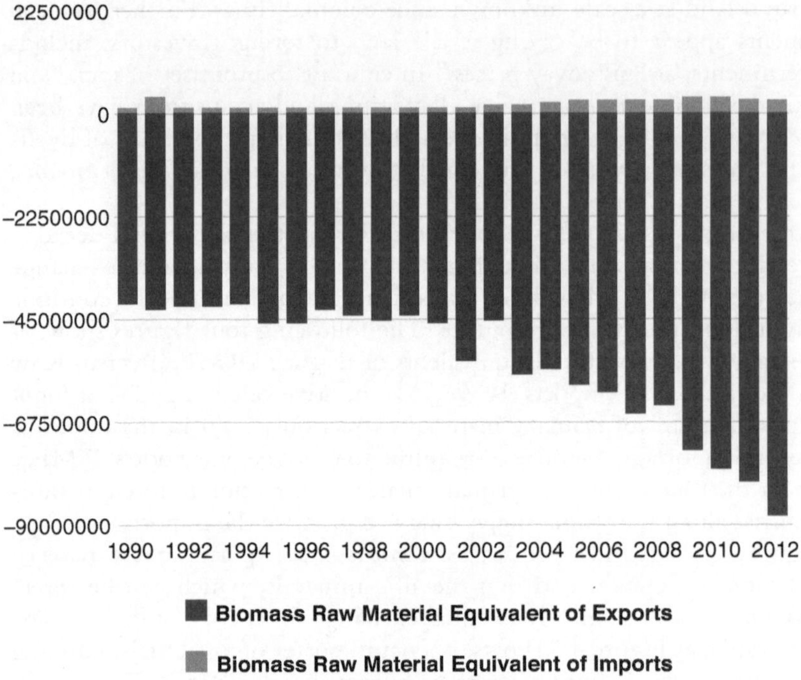

Figuew 4.1

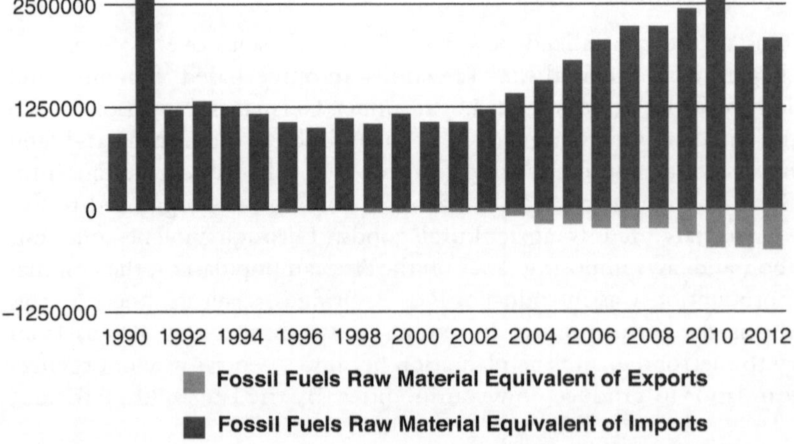

Figuew 4.2

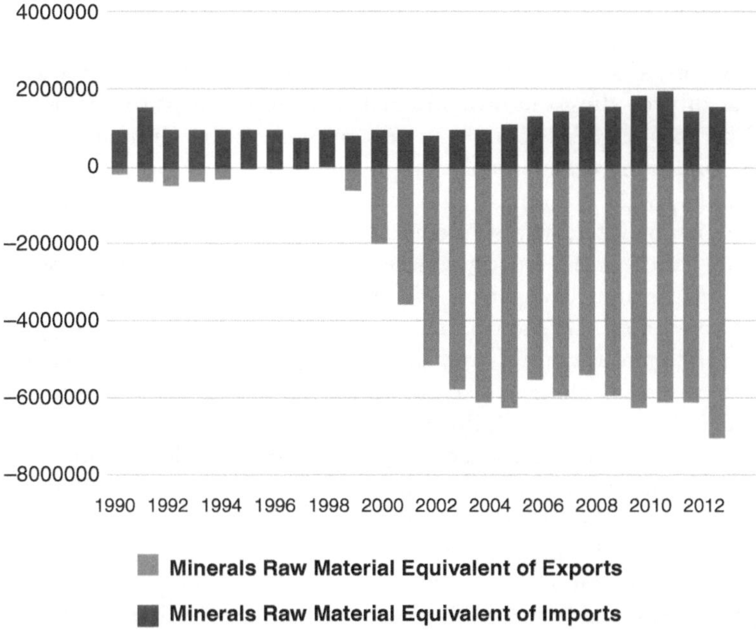

Figuew 4.3

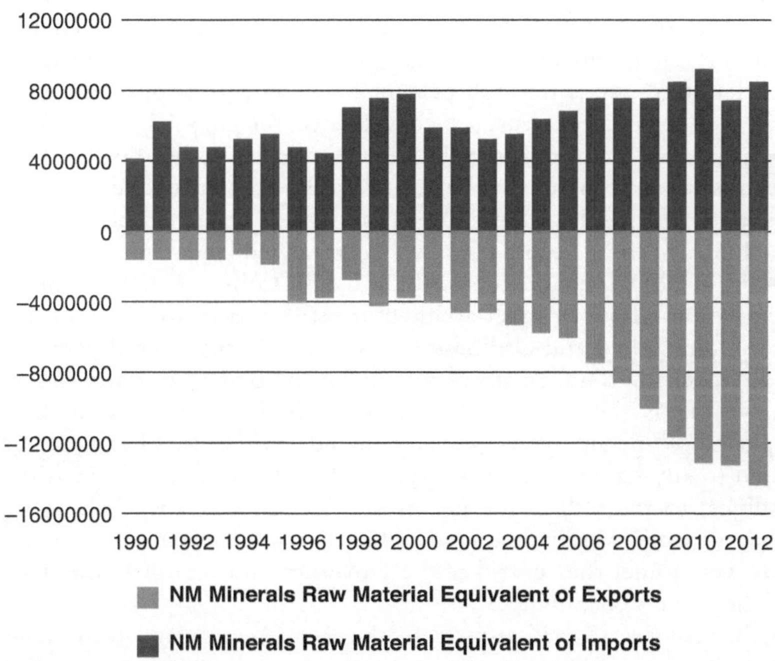

Figuew 4.4

either as peasants or as paid laborers, were forced to cultivate and produce primary commodities, such as sisal, new varieties of cotton, rubber, groundnuts, and coffee (Kaniki, 1980).

Land acquisition was central to the agenda of political control and the economic goal of providing the raw materials for the needs of the colonial metropole. The colonial land regime was established by the Germans from 1885 to 1916. Under the German colonial government, the *Imperial Decree of the 26 of November, 1895* converted all territorial lands into "crown lands." All lands for which private ownership could not be established by documentary ownership were considered ownerless, and while communities could prove ownership through occupation and use, land not continuously used was considered ownerless. Due to this decree, some 1.3 million hectares were alienated from indigenous control, and thereafter German authorities issued freehold grants to settlers along the coast and northern highlands (Land and Natural Resource Tenure in Africa Program, 2010). As a result, conflict over land dispossession underpinned major anti-colonial struggles, beginning with multiple, sporadic resistances in the late 1800s to the Maji Maji War in the early 1900s up until the Meru Land Case and the Kiembe Samaki Uprisings in the mid-1900s (Chachage, 2011).

Today, contentious features of the previously existing land regime remain, particularly the centralized power of the state over land ownership. With the defeat of Germany after WWI, land control and ownership fell under the British, and colonial control over land became even more centralized. The British colonial land regime (1918–1961) essentially assumed indigenous occupants had no ownership rights over land. The property regime established by the British colonial state was intended to facilitate the production of cheap agricultural goods through peasant labor on plantation lands, but Tanganyika[3] was considered a trust territory. Hence, the colonial state had to legitimize its laws and actions in regard to native interests while allowing the British administration to maintain the legal capacity to control and alienate indigenous land. In pursuit of these goals, the British ended up placing all lands in the hands of the state and effectively centralized land administration (Shivji, 2009). In 1923, the British passed the Land Ordinance, the principal piece of legislation whose original architecture still underpins the existing land tenure system. The Land Ordinance installed authority over all land to the colonial Governor. The Governor was given the power to grant "right of occupancy," that is, the right of natives and non-natives to occupy and use land for a period of up to 99 years, and to demand rent for use of any public lands granted to any native or non-native. Further, the ultimate disposal of land was subject to the will of the Governor. Section 2 of the Ordinance declared that all lands were public lands while Section 3 stipulated that all public lands were under the control of the Governor and subject to the disposition of the Governor (Shivji, 2009).

In 1928, in response to criticisms from the Permanent Mandates Commission of the League of Nations, the Ordinance was amended to formally recognize "customary law" (that is, law arising from traditional practices and ownership of land). Nonetheless, customary right was not equated to the same status as "granted right of occupancy" by the state. Hence, despite some recognition of the customary right of occupancy, a dualistic system of land governance evolved whereby rights granted by the state were in practice considered superior to customary rights to land. The rights of customary holders were not entrenched in law, and there were no stipulations as to the rights of customary holders against the rights of the state. Ultimately, land remained public land that was subject to control of the state and disposition of the Governor, and land was not protected by law though natives were legally allowed to occupy land through customary occupancy (Shivji, 2009). Hence, Tanganyika's role as a trust territory was nominally justified through allowing peasant and pastoralist customary landholders to have permissive rights regulated by native law and custom. However, when the colonial political economic interests required alienation, customary occupants could legally be evicted, which resulted in having no land tenure security. With independence, the post-colonial state was to inherit this hierarchically organized, dual land tenure system (Shivji, 2009).

Exploitation of Tanzania's minerals also began under colonial control when the Germans explored for gold around Lake Victoria in the 1890s. While Arab and local traders mined and sold Tanzania's natural resources, such as gold, copper, iron, and salt, German colonialism established the first commercial mines. During the pre-independence era, small- and large-scale mining companies were established and grew in number; they sought to exploit both precious metals and industrial minerals. In the 1920s and 1930s, British and South African mining operations also opened. Mines in Sekenke, Geita, and Mpanda were established for gold, and in Mwadui for diamonds, and mineral production increased consistently in this period throughout the pre-independence period, save for a decline during WWII (Nyankweli, 2012). After the war, mineral exports kept increasing, and by 1959, mineral exports exceeded pre-war production levels. However, just before independence, outputs fell dramatically due the persistently low price of gold as well as investors' fears of economic and political changes (Nyankweli, 2012).

African Socialism: Economic Nationalism and Tanzanian Resources

Like other post-colonial African countries, Tanzania, upon gaining political independence from the British in 1961, was left in a state of economic dependency and neocolonialism. The structure of its trade profile remained essentially the same as established under colonialism—exporting primary commodities (mainly coffee, cotton, diamonds, and sisal) at low prices to capitalist markets and importing finished products and industrial goods at high prices. Trade remained heavily biased toward a few traditional Western partners. Tanzania's means of production remained heavily under the control of Britain, and the West in general. The government continued to depend upon British financial resources, with banking and insurance predominantly British-owned, while in contrast the majority of Tanzanians remained as rural subsistence farmers (Crouch, 1987).

Initially, in the early post-independence years (1960s), the government sought to create an attractive environment for investors. Foreign capital was seen as a necessary component for development, and policies such as the Foreign Investments Protection Act of 1962 and the Preventive Detention Act of 1962 were enacted to attract foreign investors with tax holidays, easy repatriation of profits, and strict labor laws to discipline workers (Shivji, 2009). As a consequence and despite formal political independence, the economy remained under foreign control. However, this situation, coupled with increasing social and economic inequality, led to mounting political tension and dissatisfaction and the desire for economic self-reliance. Nyerere, the first president of the newly independent Tanzania and ideological father of "African socialism," became increasingly convinced of the need for a more equal and self-reliant society. He decided that this necessitated the democratization of institutions at every level, with the state playing the role as representative of the people (Crouch, 1987).

In 1967, Nyerere issued the Arusha Declaration, a series of policy documents expounding new economic and social priorities. The central tenets of the Declaration were socialism, self-reliance, rural development, mass participation, and responsive leadership. The declaration sought to translate socialist theory, in terms of greater social justice and economic independence, into practice. Socialism, according to the Arusha Declaration, was to be built upon the absence of exploitation and the control of the means of production by the peasants and workers. In terms of policy, a more egalitarian society was to be achieved by increased expenditure on social services in rural areas, a more equitable distribution of income, and the facilitation of worker participation in decision-making (Crouch, 1987). Taking cue from other socialist experiments of the era, a command economy was seen as central, especially in achieving greater self-reliance and economic independence. Public ownership was crucial to the socialist project, and all major means of national production were to be owned by peasants and workers through the control of the government. Nationalization began one day after the Arusha Declaration, and foreign commercial banks were the first to be nationalized. In the first week after the Declaration the state took over the six largest foreign-owned import-export houses, all insurance businesses, eight flour milling firms, and the sisal industry. The Tanzanian government also obtained controlling interests in seven MNC subsidiaries[4] (Crouch, 1987). Other measures included government control over investment planning, administrative allocation of foreign exchange and import licensing, price controls administered by the National Price Commission, regulated interest rates and credit rationing, and state control on wholesale trade for some import and domestic commodities (Nyankweli, 2012). Critics on the political right argued that with the Arusha Declaration a number of policies enacted were responsible for directly or indirectly discouraging private (both foreign and domestic) investment. Such policies included nationalization of all means of production, distribution, and exchange; the prohibition of private ownership of small industrial enterprises in villages; and the cracking down on entrepreneurs who had started small-scale enterprises despite these prohibitions (Nyankweli, 2012). Leftist critics, however, argue that while ideologically the Arusha Declaration sought to redistribute wealth and place the means of production within the hands of the producers, in reality economic policies such as the nationalizations expanded the power of the bureaucratic elite.

Typical of the post-independence era of economic nationalism and the New International Economic Order, natural resources were brought under national control as well. The mining sector was brought under state control and nationalized. Private mining, by private persons or companies, was prohibited and only the state mining company STAMICO, a parastatal established in 1972, could conduct exploration and mining for all minerals (Nyankweli, 2012). In terms of land, post-colonial laws largely replicated the essential structure put in place by colonial authorities. In some cases, post-colonial laws even expanded the scope of centralized control over land, paving the way for the alienation and dispossession of land from customary owners in both the eras of economic nationalism and neoliberal reform. For example, the independent government simply modified the 1923 Land Ordinance (that had centralized control under the British) by replacing the word "Governor" with "President." Nyerere then issued a further series of laws that expanded the domain of public land and abolished freehold tenure[5] (Chachage, 2011). The ultimate effect of post-colonial laws regarding land was to further centralize control and place it under the executive power. Under nationalism, the state could dispossess a customary owner because land was considered *mali ya umma* (public property) and all public property fell under the jurisdiction of the president (Shivji, 2009).

From 1967 to 1973, Nyerere's government enacted the controversial Villagization Program (*Ujamaa*) which involved a forced relocation of approximately 80% of the rural population to 5,528 villages (Shivji, 2009). The program aimed to establish large collective farms and modernize agriculture, with large-scale agriculture and pastoralism under parastatals and small-scale agriculture under villagization.[6] Under villagization, the local government was not legally vested with powers to govern land, and villages were often allocated land in public meetings without following any formal procedures. Customary tenure systems were generally ignored, large portions of customary land were alienated, and disputes over existing land rights were largely disregarded (Chachage, 2011). Villagization was acknowledged to have largely failed in its aims, and even worse, in hindsight the process appears to have further eroded land tenure from the domain of customary law and the placement of individual tenure by placing the land under government supervision through detailed regulations, rules, and laws. Parastatals took over nationalized assets including land and held such lands under "rights of occupancy." Such lands had often belonged to customary holders in villages, and villagization destroyed what little was left of the security of "deemed rights." Importantly, the overall direction of the political economy of production of cash crops for export and integration within the world capitalist market was not transformed (Shivji, 2009).

The Era of Structural Adjustments: Neoliberalism and Foreign Investment in Land and Mining

Though nationalism and African socialism defined Tanzania's ideological front in the 1960s and 1970s, in practice the Tanzania's economy moved

> erratically between import substitution and export-oriented industrialization with state capital, a bit of local private capital, and a substantial element of foreign public loans and private management contracts.
> (Shivji, 2009, p. 169)

By the time Nyerere retired from presidency in 1985, the political and economic foundation of nationalist ideology was crumbling. While some mass goods industries like textile, oil, and leather were established with some success, other industries stagnated. Further, like other African countries, Tanzania fell into debt after its period of economic nationalism. Within the government ideological differences had formed; "reformists" wished to open up Tanzania to market forces while "statists" wished to see state dominance continue. In the end, however, Tanzania had to adopt a series of market reforms as the IMF and World Bank imposed preconditions for debt relief. After Nyerere stepped down peacefully from power in 1985, Tanzania underwent a dramatic change in the neoliberal reformist direction, symbolized by the signing of an agreement with the IMF in 1986 for $77.5 million over 18 months to support an economic recovery program (Crouch, 1987).

The overall emphasis of the structural adjustments was to reorient Tanzania's economy toward a market-based, export-led economy (in particular the boosting of agricultural export crop production). Reforms pushed private capital as the main engine of growth, as opposed to import substitution and government intervention in the economy. Major structural adjustment measures included privatization of state-owned enterprises, removal of subsidies, lowering or abolition of tariffs, dismantling of state-marketing boards, liberalization of foreign exchange regimes, reductions in public expenditure, an emphasis on creating a business-friendly environment in terms of FDI, among others (Nyankweli, 2011). With large external debts, Tanzania was highly dependent on multilateral aid and had little bargaining power with regard to debt-relief conditions. With the process of liberalization, marketization, and privation (LIMP), labor, land, and natural resources were liberalized, marketized, and privatized while a number of legal and institutional reforms were introduced (Shivji, 2006).

Tanzania and the Global Rush for Land: An Overview

Neoliberal foreign investment policies and the colonial legacy of centralized control over land have created a precarious and conflict-ridden state of affairs in rural Tanzania. A key argument made by proponents of large-scale land investments is that Africa has the most underutilized fertile land in the world, and Africa would gain in economic growth and development through the influx of foreign capital and technology. This argument has been criticized on a number of grounds. Concerning the alleged bounty of underutilized and available land, critics have argued that in reality systematic empirical data on land availability in Africa remain limited. Further, the meaning of "land availability" is open to interpretation. Although a common argument is that "marginal lands" can be used for large-scale production of agrofuel feedstocks, in reality it is higher value lands, with higher rainfall, access to irrigation, and proximity to markets that investors commonly target. In many cases across Africa, such land is already being used, but as will be discussed, such use often goes unacknowledged as local people on the land often have no formal land rights or access to the relevant law and institutions (Oakland Institute, 2011).

Tanzania is a heavily agriculture-based country with approximately 80% of the population's livelihoods depending on subsistence farming. Food production dominates agriculture with maize, sorghum, millet, rice, wheat, beans, bananas, and potatoes among the major staple crops. The main cash crops include coffee, sisal, cashew, cotton, tobacco, tea, cloves, and oil seeds. Agriculture is dominated by small-scale farmers cultivating farm sizes between 0.9 and 3 hectares. Women make up the majority of the labor force, and farming techniques are characterized by low productivity, leaving Tanzania households vulnerable to climatic and economic shocks. In recent years, such shocks have increased, as Tanzanian harvests have suffered substantially from droughts and floods. The result has been an increase in prices for basic food staples (Oakland Institute, 2011). As of 2020, Tanzania has a population of approximately 56.32 million, and about 94.5 million total hectares of land. Total arable land area is estimated to be only about 15.24% of total land area in 2016 (The World Bank, n.d.).

Land scale acquisitions in Tanzania have resulted in numerous land conflicts in recent years. The Tanzanian government is actively seeking investors in agriculture and other sectors as part of its development and economic strategies. But most of the land sought after and being acquired by foreign investors in Tanzania is already classified as village land. Even if such land is not permanently settled, often it is used for a wide range of rural people's livelihood activities. This includes land used by Tanzania's many pastoralists that is often labeled as barren, idle, degraded, or marginal and therefore potentially available to investors (Oakland Institute, 2011). Moreover, while the Tanzanian government considers available land as meaning that there are no rural communities fully utilizing the land, there are currently no proper guidelines in place for potential future agricultural production and no standard mechanisms for calculating future population growth. As a district officer of agricultural development in the rural town of Lushoto explained, Tanzania has limited land resources already under strain from population growth, and large-scale land investments from foreign investors are further exacerbating this problem. Further, the amount of land actually available is not at all clear according to NGOs nor is it precisely known how much land is acquired by local or foreign investors each year. It is impossible, therefore, to keep investors accountable without publicly accessible information regarding investments, such as readily accessible data that shows how much land is available or has been acquired and granted to local or foreign investors (Oakland Institute, 2011).

While one of the central arguments for land investment in Tanzania (and Africa in general) is the perceived abundance of underutilized land, a growing body of literature has found that large-scale, land-based investments are typically associated with dispossession, loss of resource access rights, and ensuing conflicts. These problems associated with large-scale land investments have prompted critics to dub such transactions as "land grabs." More specifically, the term "land grab" has been defined by the Tirana Declaration[7] as land acquisitions which do one or more of the following:

- Violate human rights, particularly the equal rights of women
- Flout the principles of free, prior, and informed consent of affected land users, particularly indigenous peoples
- Ignore impacts on social, economic, gender relations, and the environment
- Avoid transparent contracts with clear and binding commitments on employment and benefit sharing
- Eschew democratic planning, independent oversight, and meaningful participation

As of 2020, there have been reported cases of 102 land deals in Tanzania that are equal to approximately 1,339,931 ha. Of these deals, 21 are from Asia, 20 are from other African countries, 31 are from Eastern Europe, and 9 are from Northern America. Overall, 32 investors from 17 countries are engaged in large-scale land acquisitions in Tanzania. Investors from the United States of America have the most hectares under contract while investors from the United Kingdom have the highest number of concluded deals. Based on total size under contract, private companies are the major type of investors in Tanzania, followed by state-owned companies. Food crops (40%), agrofuel (16%), forestry (14%), and livestock (11%) constitute the four largest categories of deals, reflecting large-scale land investment trends in other developing countries driven by three main issues: energy security, food security, and environmental security (Land Matrix, 2018).

Concerning energy, land deals, according to a study by the Oakland Institute (2011), are dominated by investments in agrofuels, and both Tanzanian and foreign governments have been promoting this surge in investments. Biofuel investment is typically driven by the growing global demand created by high oil prices, energy security concerns, and global climate change concerns. Now, some of the world's largest oil firms are investing in biofuels in order to profit from this state of affairs. Tanzania's government has promoted biofuel production for its potential to provide a partial energy substitute for costly oil imports and a new source of agricultural income and economic growth in rural areas. Many biofuel investments involve large plantations, though some are carried out by smallholder farmers and locally contracted farmer arrangements (Tanzania Natural Resource Forum, 2009). Investments in Tanzania have also included carbon sequestration initiatives, whereby large tracts of land have been bought in order for foreign countries to secure carbon credits. Foreign investors have also invested in Tanzania to meet the food security concerns of their own domestic countries. Food production investments include investors from the UK, the USA, Singapore, India, the United Arab Emirates, China, Jordan, Saudi Arabia, Turkey, and Bangladesh (Oakland Institute, 2011).

The Neoliberalization of Land: Background and Legalities

In the case of Tanzania, land grabs usually happen through legally sanctioned land acquisition. Within the context of broader neoliberal reforms, a number of legal and institutional reforms paved the way for land privatization and marketization in order to create an atmosphere amenable to foreign investment.[8] The result of such measures was the increase in both foreign and indigenous investment in land. However, the combination of a centralized land administration inherited from colonialism and economic nationalism, legal confusions over land tenure, and increased investment has made land an issue of much conflict between villagers, the government, and investors.

Tanzania's land regime has been problematic for customary holders since colonialism, and continued into the post-independence era. In the neoliberal era, popular discontent over longstanding land issues erupted as early as the beginning of the 1990s. In response to this popular discontent, the government established the Presidential Commission of Enquiry into Land Matters to hear complaints, which led to new land legislation seeking to redress some of the issues. A new Land Legislation was enacted in 2001, specifically the Land Act of 1999 and Village Land Act of 1999. Both acts currently provide the framework for the exercise and administration of land rights. In some areas, there has been substantial reform toward the benefit of customary holders from the prior tenure framework. For example, all Tanzanians above 18 years of age have rights to acquire and own land, and all existing property rights are recognized and protected, including customary titles (Land Rights Research & Resources Institute, 2011).

However, land laws continue to retain problematic features of the old system. Perhaps most significantly, the ultimate ownership of land under the

Land Act remains in the hands of the president as a trustee for all Tanzanians. Ultimately, all aspects of land use and ownership, including rights of occupancy, imposition of development conditions, and land rent, remain under bureaucratic control. Under the Land Act, only the Ministry of Lands, through the Commission of Lands, has the authority to issue grants of occupancy (Land Rights Research & Resources Institute, 2011). Problems arising from centralized executive control over all land in Tanzania are exacerbated by a number of confusions originating from the Village Act and Land Act themselves. Land in Tanzania is divided into three categories: general, reserved, and village land. Reserved land includes all land set aside for special purposes like forest reserves, game parks, and game reserves. This includes about 28% of all land. Under the Village Land Act, which provides the legal framework for the administration of village land, village land is all land within the boundaries of more than 11,000 registered villages.[9] Confusion has arisen from the different definitions of general land and is the source of much conflict regarding the issue of customary tenure arrangements. Under the Village Act, general land is a residual category, that is, any land that is not reserved land or village land. However, under the Land Act, general land includes all public land that is not reserved land or village land, and includes unoccupied or unused village land. The Land Act does not define unoccupied or unused village land but nonetheless places all general land under the authority of the Ministry of Lands as well as Housing and Human Settlements Development thereby leaving a legal loophole that continues to undermine customary tenure of land (Land Rights Research & Resources Institute, 2011). Though the Village Land Act provides that the customary right of occupancy is in every respect equal in status to granted right of occupancy, in practice this is not the case. Government officials do not recognize customary land rights as equal to statutory and do not respect the legal authorities of village government (Land Rights Research & Resources Institute, 2011).

In regard to the issue of land grabbing and foreign investment, the problem lies in the presidential power to transfer "in the public interest" any area of village land to any other category of land (such as general land), whereby public interest also includes investments of national interests. It is the legal process of transferring land from one category to another (*uhawilishaji*) that is at the heart of dispossessing village land into investment land. In essence, the state has the legal right to dispossess village land for foreign investment. Contrary to the argument that neoliberal policies mean removing inefficient state obstacles in order to promote a free market, in reality such policies mean a redefinition of the role of the state, one that guarantees resources are available for the process of capital accumulation.

Although the Village Council and Assembly have the authority regarding the arrangement and allocation of village land, they have no ultimate influence in the president's decision to acquire and transfer any part of their land, especially in the case of large-scale foreign private investment. While affected persons can register their unwillingness to support a transfer, they cannot in actuality refuse the proposal. In the end, the president can resort to lawful expropriation (subject to payment of compensation), even if the result is involuntary settlement. Also while the Village Land Act stipulates that village land may not be transferred until the type, amount, method, and timing of payment of compensation have been agreed upon between the Village Council and the Commissioner, villagers, in reality, often lack the financial and human resources to mount any legal challenge against the government.[10] There are also no clear mechanisms in the Village Act by which communities can appeal or block such reclassifications of their lands. While the law gives village assemblies the power to approve or reject the removal of village land by the state for areas of less than 250 ha, it does not provide for any check on land removal for areas larger than 250 ha (Chachage, 2011). The standard agricultural land lease lasts 99 years at a mere price of 200 shillings ($0.14) per hectare per year, and this price does not vary according to the location of the land or the crops grown. (The price used to be 600 Tanzanian shilling, $0.4 per hectare, but was reduced following investor complaints!) Rent due on land is collected by the Ministry of Lands district staff, and money is incorporated into the government budget. Ten percent of total rent due on the lease every year goes to the Tanzanian Investment Center as a facilitation fee. Leases, however, are supposed to become invalid if investors do not start production within two years and do not ask for extension or give explanation for lack of production (Oakland Institute, 2011).

In sum, criticism of land legislation tends to revolve around two distinct problems. First, the legislation has provided a massive loophole, which has been the source of dispossession and ensuing conflict; the Village Land Act essentially reserves the right of the Present of Tanzania to transfer land from the village sector, transforming it legally into general or reserved land. The second loophole is the inconsistent definition of general land, whereby the Village Land Act defines general land as all public land not reserved or village land while the Land Act defines general land as all public land not reserved land or village land, but includes unoccupied or unused village land. Finally, as an important note, current development policies do not appear to bode well for the issue of land grabbing in Tanzania.

Accumulation by Dispossession: Socio-Ecological Impacts and Conflicts over the Land Issue

Conflict has been endemic to large-scale land acquisition in Tanzania, sparking accusations of land grabbing and anger against the government from NGOs, academics, Tanzanian and international media. Civil society groups have specifically sprung up in order to address the issue of large-scale land acquisition. Among the most pressing issues are accusations of land dispossession by villagers with attendant loss of resource access that have been facilitated by the above discussed problems surrounding customary ownership. Further, according to critics, investment processes lack transparency and accountability, and fair and equal practices. There have even been accusations of corruption within the bureaucratic institutions responsible for land management (REPOA, 2012). The literature also suggests that promised benefits of economic development often fall short of reality.

Studies carried out by international NGOs and Tanzanian civil society groups have found that a number of large-scale land investments have resulted in land dispossession for villagers, with negative consequences for rural livelihoods dependent on land and its resources. The Tanzanian branch of the civil society group, Participatory Ecological Land Use Management (PELUM), issued an extensive report on agribusiness, forestry, and biofuel companies in the Morogoro, Iringa, and Pwani regions. The study found that such ventures posed threats to land access, ownership, and use among villagers and had deleterious effects on villagers' food sovereignty. Once dispossessed of land and made into plantation workers, the report also argued that their labor value was undervalued thereby undermining the commonly made argument that large-scale land investment results in economic opportunities and development. The Oakland Institute Report (2011) found that the controversial Sun Biofuels project in Kisarawe negatively affected over 11,000 people living in 11 villages, in terms of losing land to the investors. Though Sun Biofuels claimed that such land was only bushland and hence unutilized, villagers complain that they were economically dependent on such land for firewood collection. One village lost 40% of its total land area to Sun Biofuels. Overall, the report found that the project had negative impacts on local livelihoods through the loss of land used for collection of natural resources.

The Oakland Institute report also raised the issue of land dispossession for pastoralists, commenting on the historical evidence of land dispossession of the Maasai land in the Arusha area. Pastorals in particular have been affected by land dispossession. Many projects acquire supposedly "idle" or marginal land, assuming it is unoccupied as it is not settled or farmed. For pastoralists such as the Maasai, their claim to land tenure is even more tenuous than settled villagers as land laws leave loopholes for the government to claim ownership of lands neither settled nor farmed. Historically, the Maasai have suffered from land dispossession when in Arusha 40 years ago, they were pushed off fertile grazing land by investors from Holland and South Africa to grow wheat and white beans. As a result, the Maasai are left with only very marginal land. The problem of pastoralists being dispossessed of land remains an ongoing source of conflict. In March 2013, the Tanzanian government, through the Ministry for Natural Resources and Tourism, took 1,500 square kilometers, which are essential dry season grazing land from the Maasai of Loliondo in Ngorongoro District (Just Conservation webpage, 2013). In November 2017 following public outcry and pressure from civil society organizations and international institutions, the government halted the evictions, and the new Minister of Natural Resources and Tourism said that the evictions had been illegally designed without properly following the necessary procedures.

However, according to the International Work Group for Indigenous Affairs (IWGIA), a global human rights group dedicated to the protection of indigenous peoples, the issue of evictions has not been permanently resolved and may escalate quickly again at any point (IWGIA, 2018).

At the heart of the conflict is a false categorization of land as "unused" or "unutilized." In reality, such land often provides important resource services to villagers who use it to collect firewood, charcoal, honey, or fruits or to pastoralists who use such land for seasonal grazing or access to water sources. Finally, like the PELUM report, the Oakland Institute found that plantation labor was underpaid. When BioShape took land from the village of Muvuji, Kilwa, which was fully dependent on maize cultivation, they then employed 70–80% of the villagers to work on its plantation as casual laborers. Workers were paid only two dollars a day, worked six days a week, and were left no time for their own cultivation, but they did not earn enough to sufficiently sustain their families. If people become reliant upon the market in such cases, they become vulnerable to fluctuations in food prices and food security (Oakland Institute, 2011).

According to the literature, the process of large-scale land investments itself is problematic, often violating the principle of free, prior, and informed consent (TNRF, 2019). Aside from the fact that ultimate control resides in the executive power as discussed above, a joint report by the Tanzanian Policy Research for Development (REPOA), the Tanzania Natural Resource Forum (TNRF), and International Institute for Environment and Development (IIED) argued that weak governance in land administration poses a significant threat to land rights. Complex procedures, lack of legal regulations for oversight, transparency, and accountability, corruption at various levels including the local level, general lack of financial and human resources, and the impossibility for the public to access necessary info about investments continuously undermine good quality land administration. The report further argues that even with local participation, local governance bodies tend to mirror social hierarchies in communities and often lack representation from groups that are marginalized (REPOA, 2012).

For example, the Tanzanian Land Rights Research and Resources Institute Haki Ardhi, a civil society group which sprung up to address the land issue in Tanzania, found that villagers in the Kilolo District in Iringa and the Kilwa District in Lindi had faced a series of such issues with the land acquisitions of New Forest Company and BioShape in Tanzania Ltd. The study found that in both cases villagers were inadequately informed as to the amount of village land to be transferred. In the Oakland Institute (2011) study, local people thought they had only "leased" their land, and investors had only sensitized people about potential benefits but not about potential disadvantages. Consultation processes involved no real community participation, and the majority of rural people who had given land away did not fully realize its value at time. Such processes violate the principle of free, prior, and informed consent. Land Rights Research & Resources Institute (2011) has also criticized that land laws contain provisions which allow for corruption and self-enrichment among land administrators that encourage them to acquire profitable or well-resourced village land and pass it on to private companies and rich individuals.

Also of issue is the lack of manifestation of proposed benefits. In a PELUM report that studied the villages in Kilolo District in Iringa and Kilwa District in Lindi, benefits such as new employment opportunities and investments in the communities were limited and short-lived (Chachage, 2011).Though investors have implemented some activities associated with corporate social responsibility, Land Rights Research & Resources Institute (2011) argues that such benefits mask losses villagers would incur in the long run, and strongly suggests that villages could generate more of these benefits by other means. The Oakland Institute likewise found that often promises of employment, social services, and infrastructure between local people and investors are primarily verbal, and therefore it became difficult for anyone to hold the investors accountable (Oakland Institute, 2011).

Associated with loss of resource access and land dispossession is the lack of sufficient compensation, delayed compensation, or unfair compensation for such losses (TNRF, 2019). Before land can be transferred from village to general land so as to be leased to foreign investors, the level of compensation to the affected people is supposed to be decided upon. However, in the Oakland study of Kirasawe, the report found that Sun Biofuels only compensated 152 households for land taken from 11 villages, partially because official compensation doesn't fully cover all land uses and activities. Many market values of land are hidden or difficult to capture in a formal economic valuation sense. Compensation methods being used in Tanzanian do not allow for or take into consideration potential future land use and production activities of local people. Furthermore, following government guidelines, the compensation for land loss is not meant to make a household either better or worse off (Oakland Institute, 2011). Another report, issued by the Tanzanian Forestry Working Group and the Tanzanian Natural Resource Forum (2009), argued that most land obtained or in the process of being obtained by biofuel companies has been village land that was not permanently settled but still used by village members. For example, most of land obtained in areas such as the Kilwa and Kisarawe Districts is miombo woodland with patches of coastal forest and thicket and often used for forest-based economic activities, including commercial charcoal production and the harvesting of forest production for medicines, fuelwood, building materials, and mushrooms. Finally, concerns have been raised about adverse environmental impacts of large-scale biofuel investments on water supplies and forests in coastal areas, which occur when large plantations are established in formerly naturally forested areas. Other indirect impacts have also been noted to occur, such as food prices being adversely affected as land is transferred to biofuel production rather than food production (Tanzania Natural Resource Forum, 2009).

Mining Sector Reforms and the Global Rush for African Minerals

During the years of structural adjustment throughout Africa, mining was identified as a primary sector to galvanize economic growth and was targeted for extensive reforms. It was argued that the mining sector in Africa, suffering from a declining share in the value of world mining output and trade, was underperforming and failing to generate sufficient revenues for development. Poor policies, political interference, lack of investment in geological mapping, poor technical data on mineral endowment, weak infrastructure, and the lack of cheap and reliable energy supplies were seen as hindering the efficient functioning of the mining sector (UNCTAD, 2005). As such, deregulation of Africa's mining sector started in the 1980s in the context of structural adjustment reforms. Broadly, the reforms called for increased liberalization, deregulation, and privatization as means of correcting macroeconomic imbalances, stimulating economic recovery, and establishing a more sustainable growth path. Importantly during this time, the World Bank began to shift from its traditional role of the 1960s as a supporter for exploration and production activities to a supporter of commercialization and privatization of SOEs in the 1980s. In the 1990s, its role evolved to emphasize private sector development and the attraction of FDI. In recent years, the Bank emphasized issues of governance and transparency, pro-poor growth, mitigating environmental and social risks, and protecting rights of people adversely affected by investments in extractive industry.

Overall, reforms have shifted governments' primary objective toward generating tax revenue rather than utilizing the sector to pursue political objectives such as sovereign control of resources as had been the case during the era of state-controlled mining enterprises. Reforms ensured that privatization was considered central to the efficient functioning of mining enterprises. Given the lack of financial and technological resources, as well as the lack of local entrepreneurs, reforms have thus concentrated on attracting capital from foreign mining companies. To this end, African countries were encouraged to create stable legal and fiscal frameworks, including mining codes, contractual stability, guaranteed fiscal regimes, profit repatriation, and access to foreign exchange (UNCTAD, 2005). By end of 1995, under the auspices of the World Bank, 35 countries were reported to have published new mining codes, which reduced tax levels, eased immigration laws for expatriate workers, and granted tax exemptions for imported equipment. Guinea's reforms were introduced in the mid-1990s and were followed later by those of Madagascar, Mali, and Tanzania at the end of 1990s. All phases of reforms followed each other with continuity, and each succeeding phase built upon the set of policies enacted under previous mining regimes (UNCTAD, 2005).

Tanzania's mineral code was introduced in 1998 as a result of a five-year World Bank financed sectoral reform project. It includes the typical elements introduced in reforms, which will be discussed in more detail below. It was argued that Tanzania's mining sector, despite being richly endowed, did not make substantial contributions to the country's economy. This was largely due to its absence of a business-friendly environment and the choice to pursue a state-led socialist economy. According to the World Bank, Tanzania's 1979 Mining Act was problematic—it did not offer private investors a risk-free investment climate. It did not, for example, provide investors adequate security of tenure over mineral rights and supposedly created a climate of uncertainty, arbitrariness, and potential for bureaucratic delays (Nyankweli, 2012). Overall, Tanzania's mining regime was hostile toward private investment, and reforms were intended to create an investor-friendly environment to encourage FDI. As such, reforms have sought to accommodate corporate objectives, such as maximizing profits, minimizing risk, and recovering investments as early as possible. In addition, reforms emphasized policy continuity and predictability, especially toward securing property rights and open markets, and tax regime reformation (UNCTAD, 2005). As a consequence, the 1998 Mining Act allowed 100% foreign ownership, provided guarantees against nationalization and expropriation, and offered unrestricted repatriation of profits and capital. It pegged the royalty rate at a maximum of 3% (the same rate as in Mali and Guinea) and provided waivers in respect of import duties and tax exemptions on imported machinery, equipment, and other inputs. It also waived the requirement (in the 1979 Mining Act) for local procurement of goods and services (UNCTAD, 2005).

As a result of such reforms, Africa has become much more attractive to FDI in its mining sector, especially with high global demand for minerals in the 2000s. Proponents cite the fact that new investment has expanded the capacity of existing producers and new mines have been developed where before the African mining sector stagnated. Places like Mali and Tanzania, which did not have large mining sectors before 1990, now host substantial flows of FDI in large-scale operations. These trends, it is argued, can allow Tanzania's mining sector to become an important engine of development and economic growth, and indeed the mining sector is allocated an especial role in Tanzania's current development policies. Nonetheless, like the issue of land, Tanzania's mining sector has been riddled with conflict. NGOs, civil society groups, and academics have accused Tanzania's mining regime as unjustly giving away Tanzania's precious resources, especially gold, at fire-sale prices to foreign investors with practically no benefit actually "trickling down" to the Tanzanian people. In contrast, Tanzanians, especially those living within the vicinity of mining, bear the burden of environmental degradation and the loss of land access and/or former livelihoods as small artisanal miners. Further, critics argue that on a larger, structural scale the large inflows of FDI and the nature of the current mining regime have fostered a political culture of secrecy, corruption, and undemocratic practices in the governing of Tanzanian resources.

Structural Reforms and the Neoliberalization of Tanzania's Mining Sector: 1990–2017

The years of neoliberalization marked a drastic shift in power from the Tanzanian government to the interests of foreign investors. In 2008, an extensive and comprehensive report was compiled in response to growing public discontent that evaluated and criticized the Tanzanian mining regime. The conclusion of the report was that the Tanzanian government was essentially allowing the foreign plunder of Tanzania resources. The report, *A Golden Opportunity? How Tanzania is Failing to Benefit from Gold Mining*, argued that the mining sector (with focus on the gold sector) was plagued with three main, severe problems: the government is receiving very low tax revenues from gold mining, gold mining is subject to minimal governmental or popular democratic scrutiny and is widely perceived to suffer from associated corruption, and people in gold mining areas fail to benefit significantly and many are actually being made poorer (Curtis & Lissu, 2008).

Government revenues are the primary way in which a country is monetarily compensated from FDI in the extractive sector. As noted, Tanzania's tax regime has its genesis in the neoliberal reforms of the 1980s. The New Mining Act of 1998 was a direct outcome of the five-year World Bank Financed sectoral reform project. As Tanzania had reformed its investment laws to attract FDI, the government had offered a range of incentives to all foreign investors, which critics argue are responsible for the low levels the government actually receives in revenues. The following are some, but not all, of the policies from the 1998 Mining Act criticized by the *Golden Opportunity* report:

- Investors have the ability to repatriate 100% of the profits
- Investors can offset company losses against future tax liability
- Tanzania's mining law stipulates a royalty rate[11] of just 3% on gold, criticized as too low to ensure a fair return to Tanzanians
- Royalty is calculated as a proportion, not of the total production value of minerals but their "net back value" defined as market value of minerals minus cost of transport and cost of smelting or refining in-country
- Mining companies pay 0% duty on imports of mining-related equipment during prospecting up to the end of the first year of production; after this, they pay 5%
- Mining companies enjoy the right to employ an unlimited number of foreign nationals, which compares to a limit of five for non-mining companies. The Immigration Act of 1995 was changed in order to allow this
- The mining laws allow mining companies, unlike other companies in Tanzania, to be exempt from paying capital gains tax
- The cost of all capital equipment incurred in a mining operation can be offset against income from the mine in the year in which it is spent, meaning that mining companies have been able to avoid declaring any taxable income and thus payment of corporation tax

- Foreign mining companies have exclusive ownership of their operations and minerals recovered and the complete power to dispose of them as they wish, including to transfer those rights to other companies without incurring capital gains tax
- Mining companies can operate using foreign bank accounts and are allowed to keep money inside the country that will only be sufficient to keep mining operations going. Thus actual "investment" in a country is limited
- The code allows 100% foreign ownership and provides guarantees against nationalization and expropriation
- Strategic investors"—companies investing more than $20 million, which is typical of mining—can obtain "strategic investor status" and can have individual fiscal agreements with the government, some of which offer special concessions never made public

Unsurprisingly, the above extensive policies have resulted in considerable loss of potential revenue for the Tanzanian government. While an exact figure is near impossible to calculate, the report estimated the amount of revenue loss due to such policies for the gold sector. According to the report, between 1997 and 2005, Tanzania exported gold worth more than $2.54 billion. The government received around $28 million a year in royalties and taxes on these exports, amounting to just 10% over the nine-year period. The authors calculate that Tanzania has lost at least $265.5 million as a result of an excessively low royalty rate, government tax concessions that allow companies to avoid paying corporation tax, and possibly even tax evasion by some companies. The report also claims that this estimate is quite conservative. The report also estimated that the prioritization of large-scale gold mining in the country came at the expense of small-scale artisan miners, around 400,000 of whom lost their jobs (Curtis & Lissu, 2008).

Further, Nyankweli (2012) argues that the government has suffered loss of sovereignty with the 1998 Mining Act. Significantly, in contrast to the 1979 Mining Act, the 1998 Mining Act entitles private license holders to use their mineral rights as collateral and to transfer mineral rights to banks or financial institutions without requiring ministerial approval or consent. This, Nyankweli states, practically enables foreign financial institutions to acquire mineral rights in Tanzania. That is, the Tanzanian government is no longer the sole grantee of mineral rights, and this can be regarded as a significant erosion of Tanzanian sovereignty over its mineral sector. Further, in the 1979 Mining Act, the minister was the only authority in disputes and his decision was final, but in the 1998 Mining Act (Mine Development Agreements Section 10), settlement of any dispute must be done by international arbitration (i.e., the International Convention for the Settlement of Investment Disputes, ICSID).

Also concerning the issue of erosion of sovereignty, the former 1979 Mining Act had provided the Tanzanian government with the right to acquire an interest in any mining venture. In the 1998 Act, this right disappeared. Paradoxically, at the same time as the Tanzanian government suffered the loss of the ability to hold an interest in any mining venture, Nyankweli (2012) states that new provisions in the 1998 Act allow individual Ministry of Mines officials to hold shares in mining companies:

> While the 1979 Mining Act expressly prohibited the Ministry of Mines officials from holding shares in mining companies or mining licenses, this prohibition is dropped from the 1998 Mining Act. This seems to open the door for ministry officials to act with private, rather than state or public interests in mind, and creates additional avenues for private mining companies to try to influence or even directly bribe public officials. (p. 71)

Criticism has also been targeted at the lack of provisions guaranteeing that the mining sector will bring general developmental benefits. In the 1979 Mining Act, general developmental benefits (employment and spill-over effects) were treated as part of the overall package of mining ventures and were included in the approval and licensing process. For example, the 1979 Mining Act required applicants for prospecting and mining licenses to demonstrate their plans for employment and training of Tanzanians. Also, mining license applicants were required to reveal their plans for goods and services to be procured in Tanzania. Such requirements were annulled with the 1998 Mining Act (Nyankweli, 2012).

As a result of the lucrative benefits to foreign investors, Tanzania's mineral sector is the second fastest growing sector after tourism in Tanzania. Mineral deposits in Tanzania include gold, diamonds, tanzanite, ruby, tin, copper, nickel, iron, soda phosphate, gypsum, kaolite, coal, natural gas, and uranium (REPOA, 2012). The growth of gold exports has meant that precious stones and metals now account for about a third of total exports in monetary value, reinforcing Tanzania's position as an extractive, peripheral economy. Since the first large-scale gold mines began production in late 1998, gold mining has been the fastest growing sector of the economy and the largest source of foreign investment (Curtis & Lissu, 2008). Six major gold mines operate in Tanzania, with two foreign mining companies dominating the sector. The Canadian company, Barrick Gold Corporation, operates three mines (Bulyanhulu, North Mara, and Tulawak) and is developing a fourth (at Buzwagi) and the South African-based AngloGold Ashanti (AGA) operates the Geita mine, the country's largest gold deposit. Tanzania has currently proven gold reserves of around 45 million ounces. At current gold prices, the country's potential gold fortune reaches up to $39 billion—over three times the country's annual GDP of $11 billion—without taking into account extraction costs (Curtis & Lissu, 2008).

Even though the Tanzanian mining sector accounts for a large share of total export earnings, the share of mining in GDP is still small. In 2001, the share of mining as a percentage contribution to GDP was only 1.8%, and grew to only 3.3% by 2010 (REPOA, 2012). The small contribution is attributed to the underdevelopment of the sector, which is characterized by low domestic technological capacity, heavy dependency on imported inputs, and weak linkages with other domestic sectors (REPOA, 2012). However, as will be discussed further in depth, critics argue that investment incentives and tax breaks given to investors, compounded by the fact that mining companies retain a large share of their export earnings in offshore accounts, are the major reasons behind the sector's minimal contribution to net national foreign exchange receipts. The sector's contribution to government revenue has been minimal, despite the fact that it has attracted significant FDI stocks. Such low contribution to government revenues is worrisome given that the country's current proven reserves of 45 million ounces are presently being extracted at a rate of over 1.6 million ounces a year for five of the six major mines, and hence reserves may last only another 28 years (Curtis & Lissu, 2008).

Socio-Economic and Socio-Ecological Impacts and Conflicts of the Mining Sector

In addition to loss of government revenue, loss of sovereignty over resources, and the capacity to direct the sale of such resources specifically for development purposes, Tanzania's mining regime has sparked social conflict and discontent among the Tanzanian population. The first major issue is the absence of democratic control over natural resources by the Tanzanian people. Like land, rights to mineral and petroleum resources ultimately belong to the state. Any rights of land occupancy do not extend to mineral and petroleum resources. Instead, such resources are regulated by statutory instruments and their use is administered by the government (REPOA, 2012). Though the Tanzanian state supposedly acts as a trustee for the Tanzanian people, in reality state control over resources has granted elites the privilege of benefitting from resources as opposed to the people. Further, as mining burdens such as environmental degradation and loss of land are primarily shouldered by local communities, violent conflict has arisen between local peoples and the Tanzanian government. For example, in the case of the gold mine at Bulyanhulu mentioned in Chapter 1, conflict between artisanal miners, the gold mining company Barrick, and the government resulted in the deaths of up to 70 people (International Women and Mining Network, 2010).

Public discontent has also festered in regard to the lack of democratic oversight over mining contracts. Mining contracts are shrouded in secrecy with no real democratic scrutiny and lack parliamentary oversight. The Tanzanian parliament has never seen any contracts signed by the government with the mines—except for the Buzwagi contract, which was leaked to the media. As such, elected representatives have no influence over, or even knowledge of, the specific terms given to foreign mining companies to extract the country's resource wealth. Further, according to Curtis and Lissu

(2008), journalists and activists reporting on corruption and mining have been the subject of pressure and even anonymous death threats. Many critics suggest that the favorable treatment given to some mining companies is linked to this corruption.[12] Curtis and Lissu also note that the country's Auditor General estimates that annually over 20% of the government budget is lost due to corruption, theft, and fraud. Curtis and Lissu note that the Tanzania Revenue Authority, which collects taxes, is very prone to corruption and that employees of the Mining Department demand bribes in order to issue mining or prospecting licenses. Further, Tanzania's Economic and Social Research Foundation, in their *State of Corruption* in Tanzania report, acknowledged that the Ministry of Energy and Minerals is prone to corruption, possibly because some officers of the minerals division also own minerals rights (Curtis & Lissu, 2008).

Land dispossession, degradation of land/environment, and loss of access to shared resources such as forests, rivers, and lakes are also associated with gold mining and to some extent tanzanite and diamond mining, creating conflict between communities, mines, and the government. As pointed out by Lugoe (2012) in a report commissioned by the Economic and Social Research Foundation, the Land Act does not define a mineral land among its three categories of general, village, and reserve because mineral land is not known until it is discovered. According to the Land Act Section 22(2), minerals are by definition not a part of land in Tanzania; once resources such as gold are discovered, the land turns into a mineral land and falls under the Minerals Act and policies, which take precedence over land policy and laws that govern rights of occupancy. Upon the discovery of minerals, the land turns into mineral land, overriding all categories of land except conservation areas in the reserved category. This situation is the root cause of many conflicts between mining investors and communities, and it arises from a disharmony between land laws and mineral policies. The discovery of new deposits and issuance of mining licenses almost automatically nullify existing land rights claims, and can result in the relocation of hitherto existing communities against their will.

Further, as the report by the Economic and Social Research Foundation notes, compensation for displacement, environmental degradation, or loss of resource access is often very low, which also sparks dissatisfaction and conflict (Lugoe, 2012). For example, in the North Mara Gold Mine in Tarime District, Barrick Gold Corporation has been accused of forcefully taking villagers' land by dumping millions of tons of waste rock and rubble onto village lands without seeking the community's consent or paying compensation as required by law. This was supposedly done with the active participation of the district administration. As the report notes, Tanzanian communities have lost their lands not only through takeovers but also through degradation as the hazardous land subcategory overrides all three public land categories, and once land is declared hazardous, communities lose all rights (Lugoe, 2011).

The argument for large-scale mining is that it brings economic benefits to local communities—creating employment, importing new technologies, stimulating economic activity by mines that buy local goods and services, and contributing to community development projects. However, while large-scale mines can create jobs, there is extensive evidence that they create only a very small number. This is generally due to few linkages with the broader economy and the fact that transnational corporations also tend to use more capital-intensive technologies and processes than domestic enterprises (UNCTAD, 2005). Further, stipulations such as buying local goods and services have been removed from the mining regime since the neoliberal reforms. The Tanzanian mining law does not require mining companies to buy any percentage of goods and services locally as the 1998 Mining Act had abolished that provision in the 1979 Act as part of the recommendations the World Bank had made to African governments in its *1992 Strategy for African Mining* technical paper (Nyankweli, 2012). Figures suggest that around half of company expenditure goes to local suppliers, which has some positive benefit, but, critics argue, not enough (Curtis & Lissu, 2008).

Tanzania's six major gold mines employ a total of 7,135 people, according to government figures. While Curtis and Lissue (2008) acknowledge that the mining industry, although employing less than 8,000 people, has created 45,000 additional jobs, they also point out that large-scale mining has made many more unemployed. Before the arrival of MNCs, precious metal mining was dominated by small-scale artisan miners who used simple tools and techniques and provided small incomes for a large number of people, generally uneducated and poor. Citing a survey conducted by the World Bank in 1995, which estimated that 550,000 people were directly employed in small-scale mining, Curtis and Lissu point out that large-scale mining may have made around 400,000 people unemployed.

Further, the 1998 Mining Code allows mining companies to employ an unlimited number of foreigners. Government figures show that of the 7,135 people employed in the six major gold mines, 565 or 8% are non-Tanzanians (Curtis & Lissu, 2008). However, expats usually occupy management and supervisory positions and earn very large salaries in comparison with Tanzanian nationals. Further, there have been accusations that mines pay Tanzanians less than foreigners, even when doing the same job. The average pay for mineworkers is between $128 and $240 a month while the pay of the chief executive of Barrick is $9.4 million, when including the basic salary, bonus, and stock options. Further, the organizing of unions is not easy—when unions at Geita mine tried to organize workers in 2002, mine management refused to meet them (Curtis & Lissu, 2008).

Critics also complain that although community development spending is touted as another benefit for large-scale mining, the actual amount spent is small in comparison to local needs or company profits. According to figures provided by Curtis and Lissu (2008), AGA's annual community development spending has averaged around $0.7 million a year while Barrick's appears to be somewhere between $3 and $5 million across all of its mines in Tanzania. Not only are these figures very low compared to the amount of gold exported, they are deductible from taxable income (Curtis & Lissu, 2008). Further, such monetary figures in no way account for the negative socio-ecological externalities associated with the mining sector.

The environmental degradation associated with mining activities and the impact on local communities is a classic example cited by political ecologists and theorists of EUE as the shifting of environmental burdens onto the Global South for the benefit of consumers in the Global North. Typically, extraction activities are associated with very high levels of environmental degradation. Large-scale gold mines in particular generate more waste per ounce than any other mineral. Extracting one ounce of gold requires the removal of more than 250 tons of rock and ore. Piles of infertile soil, effluent from chemical processing plants containing lead and mercury in large quantities, more often remain as waste in the environment. The UN Industrial Development Organization estimated that for every gram of gold recovered, 2–5 grams of mercury is released into the environment (Lugoe, 2011).

Section 10c of the Mining Act 1998 states that development agreements may contain binding provisions related to environmental matters, and the 1998 Mining Act is supposedly an improvement from the 1979 Mining Act in terms of environmental regulations. However, a report by Policy Forum that examined the Tulawaka, Buzwagi, and Geita gold mines' development agreements found that despite environmental legal provisions provided for in the 1998 Mining Act, the government did not actually incorporate any enforceable, environmental terms that adequately address the needs of the local communities. For example, Policy Forum (n.d.) found that there is a distinct absence for mine closure procedures to mitigate negative impacts on local communities.

The laxity of the government in environmental regulation is another root cause of conflict between communities, government, and mines. There are a number of such examples that have garnered high media attention, and for the sake of space, only a few high-profile cases are listed here. For example, between 2005 and 2008 chemical disposals from processing plants at the North Mara mine in Tarime District created environmental and land hazards and adversely affected the surrounding communities. A study conducted by three independent groups found that compared to the standards of the World Health Organization (WHO), USA, and Tanzania, levels of heavy metals were above normal in the area surrounding the mine. Poisonous chemicals, in the form of acid mine drainage, came from the mine's tailing dam and waste rock piles. In addition, the nearby River Thigithe was affected (Lugoe, 2011). The toxic waste from the Mara mining operations is believed to be responsible for killing over 1,350 livestock and negatively affecting the health of over 40 people. Kitula (2006), in a case study of the Geita District, found pressing problems such as pollution of water sources from mercury and cyanide, dust, mine pits, cracking, and the collapse of buildings. Such pollution had caused land degradation, damage to water quality, and harm to livestock and wildlife biodiversity. Kitula also points out that although there is growing awareness of the importance of environmental management among mining stakeholders and government officials, mitigation strategies are offset by conflicts of interest, economic and political, at the central and local levels (Kitula, 2006). At the mining site in Bulyanhulu, where Barrick Gold has been accused for the death of up to 70 people, millions of liters of water are pumped to the mine every hour without consideration for the provision of clean water to the local communities. This mine has been accused of devastating the local ecology with waste rock piles, mine tailings that emit heavy metals into the surroundings, and depleting precious water resources (International Women and Mining Network, 2010). Other studies have likewise found serious issues of land degradation, water degradation, and air degradation due to mining. Such environmental degradation causes major adverse effects on the whole population's health, not to mention associated effects such as the spreading of malaria through creation of stagnant water and the spread of HIV and STDs through migrant workers (Nyankweli, 2012).

Twenty-First Century-Anti-Imperialist Resistance in Tanzania? Government, NGOs, and Grassroots Movements

In all extractive economies, the government is the crucial extra-economic actor that either resists or colludes with imperialist pressures; the government can itself be the face of a broader anti-imperialist movement, the grudging partner pushed into submission by debt and dependency, or the enthusiastic partner where government elites and foreign investors collude. What characterizes the neoliberal state in extractive economies is the reconfiguration of the state's top-down, centralized governmental control over resources to support the interests of foreign investors; the state is the crucial intermediate actor in ecological imperialism. In the neoliberal years, control over Tanzania's resources has centralized not so much in the government at large but in certain relevant ministries whose actions were not subject to democratic oversight by the Tanzanian people nor elected officials in parliament. The Mining Act of 1998, importantly, gave the Minister of Energy and Minerals, in particular, the discretionary powers to award and revoke mining licenses, enter into Mining Development Agreements, and defer royalties. Further, it is illegal to disclose any information obtained from reports between mining companies and the Minister or any other authority. The secretive nature of land and mining deals, and the public discontent and conflict surrounding them are simply the visible manifestations of the non-democratic control of resources. This does not mean that the Tanzanian government has always been univocal in regard to the issue of foreign investment—some members of the Tanzanian government have in fact been vocal dissenters against what they considered a neocolonial situation. Some members of parliament have actively protested against various aspects of how foreign investment in the extractive sector is governed. But again, in a demonstration of unequal balance of power, outspoken critics on the mining issue have been penalized. For example, in 2002 the Tanzanian government charged two environmental activists and an opposition political leader with sedition for speaking out about allegations of widespread human rights abuses at the Bulyanhulu Gold Mine.[13] For the Tanzanian people, this issue of lack of democratic control is closely tied with another problem, the lack of practical legal channels for addressing the grievances of citizens and communities. To the extent that such legal channels exist, they are too difficult for ordinary citizens to access.

One of the fundamental contentions of neoliberals is that the state is prone to corruption; hence, it is better to leave most societal and economic functionings to the market and private individuals. The obsession of the World Bank and Western donors centers on the ideals of good governance and accountability. *Yet neoliberal policies appear to have fostered the very class structure classically criticized by dependency theorists—the growth of a sort of comprador class whose interests overlap with the interests of foreign investors.* As the Marxist theorist Baran had argued, in underdeveloped countries there is a powerful bloc of mercantile interests attached to foreign capital particularly in the export and import sectors. As the above case studies on land and mining demonstrate, in the neoliberal era the interests of foreign capital and the interests of the comprador bourgeoisie continue to overlap (Brewer, 1990). Certainly, the lack of democratic control over resources and the secretive nature of land and mining contracts seem to foster corruption among the government elites. However, what seems to elude the mainstream critique of corruption is the relationship between corruption and neoliberal foreign investment policies. As noted, it was not until the reforms and the 1998 Mining Act that ministers were allowed to hold shares in mining companies. Neoliberal policies have made investments in lucrative sectors like gold a veritable windfall for extractive transnationals and have created an environment that incentivizes government elites to award investment deals for substantial kickbacks. Yet perhaps an even more important point is that even if corruption could be eliminated, policies that benefit foreign capital over the Tanzanian people would still be perfectly legal. The issue is not one solely of corruption, but it is also the lack of effective democratic control and a broader politico-economic structure that ensures the flow of both profits and resources from periphery to core.

However, in response to years of public discontent, conflict, and pressure from civil society groups, Tanzania has slowly moved toward more restrictive demands on foreign investors in order to retain higher levels of profits in the mining sector beginning with the 2010 Mining Act. There are hints that once again a "Polanyian counter-movement" at the national level, reminiscent of the era of economic nationalism, may be emerging. After years of discontent and public outcry, the drafting of the 2010 Mining Act included weeks of consultation with civil society organizations, members of Parliament, companies, and other stakeholders (Olan'g, n.d.). The 2010 Mining Act included such policies as raising royalty rates on gold from 3% to 4% and allowing the government the right to take a stake in any strategic mining operation, which would be determined by type of minerals and level of investment. All companies were forced to list on the local stock exchange and to set aside a certain percentage of their production for processing, smelting, or refining within the country. No foreign firms were to be granted licenses for gemstone mining without entering a 50–50 partnership with a Tanzanian company, and mining contracts, while granted for the life of the mine, are to be subject to performance review every five years (Ng'wanakilala, 2010). The act also made it mandatory for the government to set aside specific areas for small-scale miners, in the effort to avert conflicts between artisanal miners and big mining companies.

In 2017 under the rhetoric of African nationalism and vows to defeat imperialism, Tanzania's President Magufuli and the Tanzanian government enacted further changes to the 2010 Mining Act. On July 1, 2017, Tanzania enacted the Finance Act, which imposes a 1% clearing fee on all minerals exported from Tanzania. President Magufuli has suspended the issuance of new mining licenses pending implementation of the laws and stated the government would review all existing mining licenses granted to foreign investors (Jones Day, 2017). The government now has the power to renegotiate terms in mining contracts that it considers "unconscionable," including those relating to international dispute resolution mechanisms. It immediately banned the exportation of unprocessed minerals. It gave the state 16% of the equity (non-dilutable free-carried interest shares) of all existing and future mining projects and suggested this could rise to 50% in the future. Tanzania also hiked royalties on gold, copper, silver, and platinum exports from 4% to 6%. It increased the royalty on uranium exports from 5% to 6%. The new regulations allow the government to reject a company's own valuations if it believes the prices are too low. It also said it planned to impose a 1% clearing fee on the value of exported minerals. The corporate income tax rate is now set at 30%. Furthermore in January 2018, the government issued regulations that an "indigenous Tanzanian company" must have 5% ownership of any project before a new mining license is granted. Also, foreign miners must only conduct their business through Tanzanian banks (Mitchell, 2019).

Conclusion

This chapter focused on the neoliberalization of land and the mining sector in Tanzania and the central role of the state as an intermediate actor in ecological imperialism. While state power was centralized during colonialism and reinforced during economic nationalism, the state under neoliberalism has been reconfigured to meet the needs of foreign investors and provide the legal structures for laissez-faire capitalism. As one of the primary sectors targeted in Africa, land is especially vital to the topic of ecological imperialism. In the current ecological crisis, land represents the outcome of global food insecurities, energy crises, and climate change. This has incentivized large-scale land investment on the one hand and the marginalization and dispossession of land and livelihoods of indigenous peoples and small farmers on the other hand. Mining is another crucial area of focus in the study of ecological imperialism in the periphery. It is one of the most lucrative forms of economic activities in the periphery. Aside from agricultural activities, it is the central sector through which resources and windfall profits are extracted from the periphery. Mining in Tanzania, and throughout the periphery, has long been associated with uneven development, enclave economies, and the creation of a comprador elite whose interests align more closely with foreign investors.

Neoliberal policies, beginning with the structural adjustments from the World Bank and IMF, combined with a long legacy of colonialism and neocolonialism have created the perfect storm in peripheral economies such as Tanzania during an era of global ecological crises. The common win-win rhetoric promoted unfortunately ignores on-the-ground realities and long-standing historical power dynamics. In the land sector, it ignores the fact that investors target the best-quality arable land, and behind almost every land grab there is a water grab. In reality, this land is often already occupied, and the selling of such lands leads to accumulation by dispossession. In the mining sector, the win-win rhetoric ignores the realities of billions of dollars of lost profit, the loss of the capacity of the Tanzanian state to regulate the mining sector for development purposes, and the environmental degradation from primary extractive activities. While hints of economic nationalism are now emerging in Tanzania, it is too early to tell the outcome of this incipient economic nationalism, and how gains, if any, will go to the Tanzanian people without direct redistributive mechanisms from the mining sector to the people.

References

Chachage, C. (2011, May). *Land acquisition and accumulation in Tanzania*. International Land Coalition: Commercial Pressures on Land. https://landmatrix.org/media/uploads/commercialpressuresonlandorgresearch-papersland-acquisition-and-accumulation-tanzania.pdf

Crouch, S.C. (1987). *Western responses to Tanzanian socialism, 1967-83*. Farnham: Gower Publishing Co.

Curtis, M., & Lissu, T. (2008). *A golden opportunity? How Tanzania is failing to benefit from gold mining*. Dodoma: Christian Council of Tanzania (CCT).

International Women and Mining Network/ Red Internacional Mujeres y Mineria (RIMM). (2010). *Women from affected mining communities speak out: Defending land, life, & dignity*. International Women and Mining Network. https://landportal.org/node/13967

IWGIA. (2018, May 22). Half a million of indigenous peoples' livelihoods threatened in Tanzania. https://www.iwgia.org/en/news/3252-indigenous-peoples-livelihood-threatened-tanzania

Jones Day. (2017, August). *Tanzania overhauls mining law, fines investor US $190 billion: Is your investment protected?* JonesDay.com. https://www.jonesday.com/en/

insights/2017/08/tanzania-overhauls-mining-laws-fines-investor-us190-billion-is-your-investment-protected

Just Conservation. (2013, March 24). *The Tanzanian government insists on grabbing Maasai land in Loliondo.* https://justconservation.org/the-tanzanian-government-insists-on-grabbing-maasai-land-in-loliondo

Kaniki, M.H.Y. (1980). *Tanzania under colonial rule.* London: Addison-Wesley Longman Ltd.

Kitula, A.G.N. (2006). The environmental and socio-economic impacts of mining on local livelihoods in Tanzania: A case study of Geita District. *Journal of Cleaner Production, 14*(3–4), 405–414. https://doi.org/10.1016/j.jclepro.2004.01.012

Land Matrix. (2018). Tanzania country profile. https://landmatrix.org/resources/tanzania-country-profile/

Land and Natural Resource Tenure in Africa Program, & Resources Institute. (2011). Focus on land in Africa: Tanzania lesson brief, gender and land rights. Land Portal Foundation. https://landportal.org/resource/africa/focus-land-africa-tanzania-lesson-brief-gender-and-land-rights

Land Rights Research & Resources Institute. (2010). *Accumulation by land dispossession and labor devaluation in Tanzania: The case of biofuel and forestry investments in Kilwa and Kilolo.* https://landportal.org/node/43970

Lugoe, F. (2011). *The land factor in Mining Gold Reserves in Tanzania.* Africa Portal. https://www.africaportal.org/publications/the-land-factor-in-mining-gold-reserves-in-tanzania/

Lugoe, F. (2012). *Governance in mining areas in Tanzania with special reference to land issues.* Economic and Social Research Foundation. esrf.or.tz/docs/GOVERNANCEINMININGAREASINTANZANIA.pdf

Makwarimba, M., & Ngowi, P. (2012). *Making land investment work for Tanzania: Scoping assessment for multi-stakeholder dialogue.* REPOA, TNRF, & iied. https://www.tnrf.org/LBI-report.pdf

Mitchell, J. (2019, December 12). Mining overhaul fails to dent Tanzania's investment appeal. fDiIntelligence. https://www.fdiintelligence.com/article/74361

Nyankweli, E. (2012). Leiden University Repository. Foreign direct investment and poverty alleviation in Tanzania. https://openaccess.leidenuniv.nl/handle/1887/20160

Ng'wanakilala, F. (2010). Tanzania faces industry opposition to its new mining law. Mines and Communities: Home. http://www.minesandcommunities.org/article.php?a=10087

Oakland Institute. (2011). *Understanding land investment deals in Africa: Country Report Tanzania.* https://www.oaklandinstitute.org/sites/oaklandinstitute.org/files/OI_country_report_tanzania.pdf

Olan'g, S. (n.d.). *New mining law in Tanzania: Legislative and CSOs' capacity play critical role.* Natural Resource Governance Institute. https://resourcegovernance.org/sites/default/files/RWI_Case_Study_Tanzania_Mining_Bill.pdf

Policy Forum. (2011). *Parliamentary advocacy in the extractive industries: An illustrative guide for civil society.* Agora: Portal for Parliamentary Development. https://www.agora-parl.org/resources/library/parliamentary-advocacy-extractive-industries-illustrative-guide-civil-society

Policy Forum Tanzania. (n.d.). The demystification of mining contracts in Tanzania. *Policy Forum.* Retrieved March 1, 2013, from www.sdsg.org/wpcontent/uploads/2010/02/Article-re-Mining-Contracts-in-Tanzania.pdf

Policy Forum Tanzania. (2012). *Revenue losses owing to tax incentives in the mining sector: Policy recommendations*. Actionaid and Tax Justice Network-Africa. http://hdl.handle.net/20.500.12018/226

REPOA. (2012). *Poverty and human development report, 2011*. Dar es Salaam, Tanzania. https://media.africaportal.org/documents/PHDR_2009_text.pdf

Shivji, I. (1975). Peasants And class alliances. *Review of African Political Economy, 2*(3), 10–18. https://doi.org/10.1080/03056247508703253

Shivji, I.G. (2006). *Let the people speak: Tanzania down the road to neo-liberalism*. Dakar: Codesria.

Shivji, I.G. (2009). *Where is Uhuru? Reflections on the struggle for democracy in Africa*. Cape Town: Pampazuka Press.

Stürmer, M. (2010). *Let the good times roll? Raising tax revenues from the extractive sector in Sub-Saharan Africa during the commodity price boom*. German Development Institute/Deutsches Institut für Entwicklungspolitik (DIE). https://www.die-gdi.de/en/discussion-paper/article/let-the-good-times-roll-raising-tax-revenues-from-the-extractive-sector-in-sub-saharan-africa-during-the-commodity-price-boom/

Tanzania Investment Center. (n.d.). Tanzania Investment Center. www.tic.co.tz

TanzaniaInvest. (2012, December 2). New Tanzania Mining Law Benefits Citizens. TanzaniaInvest.com. https://www.tanzaniainvest.com/mining/new-tanzania-mining-laws-benefit-citizens

Tanzaniainvest.com. (2010). *New Tanzania Mining Law Passed*. Tanzaniainvest.com. https://www.tanzaniainvest.com/mining/new-tanzania-mining-law-passed

Tanzania Natural Resource Forum. (2009). *Developing commercial biofuels through securing local livelihoods and land rights*. https://www.tnrf.org/en/node/9587

Tanzania Natural Resource Forum. (2012). *Land rights and the rush for land: Findings of the global commercial pressures on land research project*. iied, cirad, International Land Coalition. http://www.tnrf.org/node/22623

The World Bank. (2019, December 11). Tanzania's path to poverty reduction and pro-poor growth. https://www.worldbank.org/en/country/tanzania/publication/tanzanias-path-to-poverty-reduction-and-pro-poor-growth

The World Bank. (n.d.a). *Gini Index (World Bank Estimate)*. The World Bank Data. https://data.worldbank.org/indicator/SI.POV.GINI?locations=ZG&most_recent_value_desc=false

The World Bank. (n.d.b). *Arable land (% of land area)- Tanzania*. https://data.worldbank.org/indicator/AG.LND.ARBL.ZS?locations=TZ

United Nations Conference on Trade and Development. (2005). *Economic development in Africa: Rethinking the role of foreign direct investment*. New York: United Nations.

Notes

1 In a previous article (Frame 2016), I calculated Tanzania's physical trade balance. The PTB measures the physical trade surplus or physical trade deficit of a country. It is calculated as imports minus exports based upon the physical weight of imports and exports as they cross a nation's borders. For the years covered, Tanzania had a PTB surplus. At the time of the chapter I had surmised that, surprisingly, Tanzania was *not* experiencing ecologically unequal exchange. However at the time, the necessary calculations for calculating a Raw Material Equivalents Trade Balance (RTB) were not available. The Raw Material Trade Balance measures the physical trade surplus or physical trade deficit of a country, including domestic and foreign extraction of materials needed along all supply

chains to produce the imports and exports. RTB equals imports in Raw Material Equivalents (RME_{im}) minus exports in Raw Material Equivalents (RME_{ex}). Hence, the RTB is arguably a more comprehensive measure of ecologically unequal exchange. When the RTBs for Tanzania's various resources were calculated, Tanzania was a net supplier of resources to the rest of the world.

2 Domestic material consumption measures the total quantity of materials directly used within an economic system. DMC equals the sum of domestic extraction and imports minus exports.

3 From 1962 to 1964, Tanzania was known as the Republic of Tanganyika. In 1964, Tanganyika joined the islands of Zanzibar to form the United Republic of Tanganyika and Zanzibar, changing its name to Tanzania.

4 However, for practical reasons Nyerere still sought to reassure potential investors that private investment would be welcome in any new or existing industry not listed as reserved for public ownership and that minority private participation might be permitted in several of the listed industries. Consequently, some sectors of the economy were 100% government owned, in other sectors private and government partnership existed, while in other sectors some enterprises were privately owned (Crouch, 1987).

5 For example, the Freehold Titles (Conversion) and Government Leases Act of 1963 converted freehold titles (<1% of land) to 99-year leaseholds with development conditions. The Rights of Occupancy Development Conditions Act of 1963 obligated lessees to pay rent. The Rural Farmland (Acquisition and Regrant) Act of 1965 empowered the government to acquire undeveloped private land and transfer it to people who would occupy and develop it (in practice, land transferred to state corporations, parastatals, and cooperatives) (Chachage, 2011).

6 The post-independence village settlements actually had their genesis in modernization theory and development plans from the World Bank and USAID. As Shivji notes, the first five-year plan adopted immediately after independence was based on the World Bank report *The economic development of Tanganyika.* Modernizing traditional peasants or pastoralists meant removing them from traditional surroundings so as to integrate them in the world capitalist market through production of cash crops for export. The transformation approach recommended by the World Bank involved settling selected farmers in villages supervised by the government agency the Rural Settlement Commission. A similar philosophy informed the *Fallon Report* published by USAID, which was the basis of the Range Development Act in 1964 (Shivji, 2009).

7 In November 1995, over 1,000 representatives of civil society, governments, and multilateral institutions came together in Brussels, Belgium for a conference on hunger and poverty. In 2003, this coalition was renamed the International Land Coalition and created the Tirana Declaration.

8 One major reform was the Tanzania Investment Act no. 26 of 1997 that established the Tanzania Investment Center (TIC), the institution currently responsible for granting derivative rights to land to foreign investors.

9 Village land constitutes nearly 70% of all lands in Tanzania and provides customary rights of occupancy automatically to village lands in perpetuity. By the Village Act, village land is under the managerial authority of the Village Council elected by the Village Assembly, which includes all residents aged 18 years and above. As Tanzania is still largely rural, most Tanzanians own land through customary law (Chachage, 2011).

10 Land acquisition is legally restricted to Tanzanian citizens unless investment is involved. Under the Tanzania Investment Act, 1997, which replaced the 1990 National Investment Act, the Tanzania Investment Centre (TIC) is mandated with identifying and providing land to investors. Land is vested with the TIC

and transferred to investors on the basis of a derivative title, and at the end of the investment project, it is supposed to revert back to TIC.

11 Royalties are the most common instrument for taxing the extractive sector. Royalties tax the fiscal dues on the basis of either the volume (unit royalty) or the value (ad valorem royalty) of production or exports. For governments, royalties ensure a relatively stable stream of revenue, but for producers, royalties constitute additional costs that have to be paid irrespective of profit levels. Very high royalties are thus a major deterrent to investment (Sturmer, 2010).

12 In the website Tanzanian Corruption Tracker, a Tanzanian NGO has written a number of articles on corruption and the Tanzanian mining sector.

13 Rugemeleza Nshala and Tundu Lissu of the Lawyers' Environmental Action Team (LEAT) and Augustine Mrema, Chairman of the Tanzanian Labor Party, raised concerns over allegations of killings, illegal evictions, and destruction of livelihoods at the Bulyanhulu Gold Mine in August 1996. Tundu Lissu has since become a vocal member of parliament (MP). Another example includes Mr. Zitto Kabwe, the MP for Kigoma, who in 2006 was suspended for disclosing the details of a mining contract.

5 Emerging Economies in the Global Ecology

Semi-Peripheral and Regional Sub-Imperialism

In the past several decades, the capitalist global economy has witnessed a world-systemic shift as global capital and productive activities have relocated from core economies to formerly peripheral economies through the activities of transnational corporations shifting their manufacturing processes overseas in search of cheaper sources of labor. The industrialization of semi-peripheral "emerging economies" constitutes a central feature of neoliberal globalization and current-day imperialism with profound planetary ecological consequences. Despite this world-systemic change, the industrializing semi-periphery remains undertheorized in terms of both imperialism (Bond, 2018) and ecologically unequal exchange (Frame, 2018). By overviewing recent world-systems literature on the growth of the industrializing semi-periphery, extant empirical literature from the sustainability sciences, and a short case study of China's growing influence in Southeast Asia, this chapter seeks to lay preliminary theoretical foundations for semi-peripheral ecological imperialism and ecologically unequal exchange.

In the US media, the growing presence of emerging economies such as China in overseas investments is an increasing competitive concern, and the spate of anti-Chinese media articles whips up one-dimensional portraits of Chinese imperialism overseas. However, the reality of the situation is more complex. Ecological sub-imperialism emanating from emerging economies is qualitatively different from core imperialism. For one, emerging economies are competing in a capitalist world-system still dominated by core economies. They also serve as manufacturing platforms to transnational corporations largely headquartered in the Global North. While semi-peripheral states may be industrializing, major profit-oriented activities still congregate in core economies. Empirical studies have shown that while such countries have emerged as economic powers, they have not gained core status in terms of wealth. Importantly, from the perspective of ecological imperialism, the industrialization of the semi-periphery has resulted in some of the most egregious forms of environmental destruction as TNCs from the developed countries have outsourced materially and energy-intensive production processes through global production chains. In the industrializing semi-periphery, the exploitation of cheap labor and the degradation of Nature are intimately interlinked

DOI: 10.4324/9780429261305-5

in one process—the production of global consumer goods, many of which are exported to the Global North. This dual exploitation of labor and Nature in the semi-periphery has bolstered the unsustainable consumption patterns of consumers in the developed countries and the profits of Northern TNCs and is a defining feature of contemporary ecological imperialism.

Yet while the overall structure of the capitalist world-system remains core dominated, the industrialization of semi-peripheral countries has introduced new dynamics in how ecological imperialism operates in the 21st century. With the establishment of capitalist relations of production in emerging economies, these countries have transformed into their own centers of accumulation, seeking to attain core status through establishing spheres of geopolitical influence and economic integration both regionally and into more peripheral areas globally. This system has generated a form of ecological sub-imperialism and semi-peripheral ecologically unequal exchange. At a regional level, semi-peripheral industrializing countries can wield as much power and influence, or more, than core countries over their peripheral neighbors. Despite anti-imperialist rhetoric, semi-peripheral ecological imperialism challenges neither the essential dynamics of capitalist expansion driven by global labor arbitrage nor the historical patterns of ecological imperialism.

As will be discussed in regard to China's expansion in Southeast Asia, the ecological sub-imperialism of the semi-periphery strongly mimics the historical trajectory of imperialism from capitalist core economies. All semi-peripheral powers, not only China, have entered into a global context whereby, as discussed in previous chapters, peripheral Natures have already been cracked open through hundreds of years of colonialism and the neocolonialism of structural adjustments. The structures created from this—land dispossession, the collusion between foreign investors and authoritarian regimes in the interest of resource exploitation, and the systemic degradation of Nature under the aegis of economic development—remain fundamentally in place. While new forms of economic integration and cooperation outside the influence of the traditional Western powers have been created, ultimately, these new forms of economic integration strongly mimic the neoliberal agenda of free trade and strong protection for investors. Capitalist expansionary dynamics underpin both core ecological imperialism and semi-peripheral ecological imperialism.

First, all emerging economies must obtain the resources to support their industrialization as well as the growing consumption of their own populations. They must also build markets overseas to absorb their manufactured goods. The result is patterns of ecologically unequal exchange between the imperial power and the region of its influence. Second, also mimicking a pattern from colonial history, is the release of built-up capital surpluses in the form of large-scale infrastructure projects, many of which support the extraction of resources in the periphery. This is a hazardous trend for the environment in the periphery. Third, there is a nascent movement toward the shifting of low-technology production overseas that are environmentally polluting. As emerging economies have destroyed and continue to destroy their environments for the unsustainable consumption of core consumers and the profits of TNCs headquartered in the Global North, they are simultaneously replicating ecological sub-imperialism overseas. The industrializing semi-periphery now straddles an ambiguous category of both exploiter and exploited.

Defining the Semi-Periphery: Orthodox Interpretations and New Complexities

A holistic theory of ecological imperialism must recognize the significance of the semi-periphery in the global accumulation of capital and the global ecology by linking ecological imperialism to major structural changes taking place in the semi-periphery for the past several decades. In orthodox world-systems theory, the capitalist world economy is structured into three interrelated tiers, each with specific characteristics and functions. Core countries are characterized by highly developed forces of production, including high-paid labor, capital-intensive production, and technological advancement. Accordingly, they appropriate a disproportionate share of the benefits of the international division of labor. In contrast, peripheral countries are characterized by the export of raw materials, and low-level forces of production, including low-paid labor and labor-intensive production. Semi-peripheral countries tend to contain a mixture of both core and peripheral economic activities, and while able to appropriate a relatively greater share of the global surplus than the periphery, semi-peripheral countries nonetheless appropriate less surplus than core countries. Semi-peripheral countries, in world-systems theory, occupy an ambiguous role of being both exploited and exploiter and are important in stabilizing and legitimizing the capitalist world-system (Wallerstein, 1974). Chase-Dunn and Hall (1997, p. 78) define the semi-periphery as:

1. Regions that mix both core and peripheral forms of organization
2. Regions spatially located between core and peripheral regions
3. Regions spatially located between two or more competing core regions
4. Regions in which mediating activities linking core and peripheral areas take place
5. Regions in which institutional features are intermediate in form between those forms found in adjacent core and peripheral areas

Other theorists such as Arrighi et al. (2003) have emphasized that it is not so much the particular mix of economic activities in defining what is core, semi-peripheral, or peripheral but the capability of a state to appropriate the benefits of the world division of labor. This is determined, they argue, primarily by a state's position in the global hierarchy of wealth. The further up in the hierarchy of wealth a state is, the better positioned its rulers and subjects are in the struggle for benefits. *While semi-peripheral states may be industrializing, major profit-oriented innovations, and the profits associated with them, tend to cluster in "zones of prosperity" within core countries*. By the time new products and techniques are adopted by the poorer countries they tend to be subject to intense competition and no longer bring the high returns they did in wealthier countries. Arrighi (1990) found for the 1938–1983 period that there was a stable hierarchy of wealth in the global economy. He identified, based on world distribution of GNP per capita, three distinct clusters of countries (high, middle, and low) and found that long-term upward/downward mobility of countries from one cluster to another was exceedingly rare. In other words, despite changes in levels of industrialization throughout the semi-periphery and periphery, the capacity of non-core states to capture the global surplus did not change significantly.

However, more recent empirical studies find that in the last several decades of the 21st century a more complex configuration of the world-system has emerged. Karataşlı (2017), for example, finds that the 21st-century capitalist world-system more accurately reflects a "quadri modal" distribution. While during the period of US hegemony (1930s–1990s), the three-tiered structure of the world-system remained relatively stable, a new four-tiered (i.e., quadrimodal) structure starting at the turn of the 21st century has emerged. The transformation dynamics are occurring primarily because of the upward mobility of a major section of the periphery (particularly China) to a semi-peripheral position. Previously, excess global capital had moved from core countries to other core countries, or to rising semi-peripheral countries. The current capitalist world-system, however, is characterized by the relocation of global capital and productive activities from North America and Western Europe (and even semi-peripheral countries) to the peripheral regions of Asia. Other peripheral countries, such as India, now constitute an "upper peripheral zone." In contrast, a "lower peripheral zone," which consists of countries such as Afghanistan, Bangladesh, and many countries in sub-Saharan Africa, is actually falling further behind.

The Industrializing Semi-Periphery in the 21st-Century Global Accumulation of Capital and the Global Ecology

The relocation of global capital and productive activities from core economies to formerly peripheral economies, and the industrialization and graduation of such economies to the category of the semi-peripheral or emerging, constitute central features of neoliberal globalization and imperialism with profound planetary ecological consequences. In the late 1960s and 1970s, U.S. capital faced a profit squeeze arising from multiple threats, including wage increases, increasing governmental regulation, competition from Western Europe and Japan as rising industrial powers, and, as discussed in the previous chapter, Third World economic nationalism that threatened U.S. access to cheap raw materials and energy. In response, most large U.S. companies decided to establish production sites in low-income countries, seeking out low-wage workers and weakening the bargaining power of U.S. workers at home (Reuss, 2013). By the late 1960s and 1970s, global outsourcing of manufacturing, including the production of intermediate goods as well as the export of finished goods to firms and consumers in imperialist countries, marked the beginning of neoliberal globalization (Smith, 2016).

Transnational corporations are responsible for the bulk of international trade and investment flows and are the chief economic actors in the era of neoliberal globalization. Significantly, most are headquartered in the Global North. From a world-systems perspective, one major difference between the historical rise of core countries and the rise of semi-peripheral or emerging economies is the fact that emerging economies are jockeying for position in a hierarchical global economy already dominated by the transnational corporations of the Global North. The management of TNCs and the higher value-added activities of product development, scientific research, corporate research and development, financial services, and so on concentrate in certain countries and regions within those countries. Since these activities generate the greatest incomes and profits, wealth concentrates in certain countries and regions of the world (Van Den Berg, 2017). As Smith (2016) documents extensively in his work on imperialism from a labor perspective, Northern capital, through transnational corporations, is highly dependent on exploiting Southern low-wage labor for the production of global consumer goods.[1] Such nations have reoriented their economies to the export of manufactures and also play host to Special Export Processing Zones. According to Smith, the structure of the global economy is increasingly marked by three crucial trends: the concentration of imperialist banks and finance capital; a process of concentration among Northern industrial and commercial capitals, many of them lead firms in value chains in which the actual production is performed by workers for distant Southern suppliers; and a process of disintegration of production processes and their dispersal to Southern nations in the quest for super-exploitable labor.

From a world-systems perspective, the value chains set up by TNCs are exploitative structural relationships in which a vast array of unequal exchanges occurs among nodes of the chain and across zones of the world economy. The capitalist world economy is connected through millions of chains of production and exchange, from extraction through final consumption. Within each node of each commodity chain, a certain amount of surplus is generated (Ciccantell & Smith, 2009).

However, the surplus generated is unevenly distributed among the states in the world system so that even developing countries with large economies such as China are not able to secure as large a surplus as the developed countries, reflecting their semi-peripheral, or even peripheral, status (Li, 2003). Analyzing multiple network analysis of various types of international commodity trade between 1965 and 2000, Smith and Mahutga (2009) find that while it is true that some newly industrializing countries have successfully engaged in industrial upgrading in which there is a shift from commodities such as textiles, apparel, and footwear to higher value-added items many peripheral countries remain primarily export platforms for low-technology, labor-intensive goods made by low-wage, unskilled workers. Through these value chains, the structure of the world economy—the overall core-semi-periphery-periphery layering—is replicated.

While a considerable amount of literature on imperialism has been written about core dominance and the super-exploitation of the cheap labor of the industrializing semi-periphery, core dominance over semi-peripheral Nature has been equally important. The economies of the semi-periphery are a mixture of both industrial and traditionally peripheral activities centered on the extraction and export of natural resources. In contrast to many of the countries of the lower periphery where ecological imperialism often manifests as direct control of resources through foreign direct investment, such as found in sub-Saharan Africa, direct control of semi-peripheral resources through outward FDI from core economies may or may not occur. For example, Petronas, the corporation vested with the entire oil and gas resources in Malaysia, is wholly owned by the Government of Malaysia and serves as an important source of revenue for the state. As will be discussed, many semi-peripheral countries exploit their own resources through domestic companies while actively expanding their control over the resources of more peripheral countries through South-South FDI.

Nonetheless, tremendous environmental degradation has accompanied the industrialization necessary for emerging economies to become the recipients of the outsourcing of transnational corporations headquartered in the Global North. *Inextricably linked to this industrialization is the exploitation of semi-peripheral Nature as TNCs from the developed countries have outsourced materially and energy-intensive production processes through global production chains.* In the industrializing semi-periphery, the exploitation of cheap labor and the degradation of Nature are intimately interlinked in one process—the production of global consumer goods, which largely serve to bolster the unsustainable consumption patterns of consumers in the developed countries. The outsourcing of the materially and energy-intensive processes of global supply chains has resulted in the shifting of a variety of environmental burdens to the industrializing semi-periphery.

One of the more studied forms of environmental pollution shifting from core to industrializing semi-peripheral countries is CO_2 emissions. A 2003 study by Grimes and Kentor (2003) examined the impact of foreign investment dependence on carbon dioxide emissions between 1980 and 1996. In a cross-national panel regression analysis of 66 less developed countries, the authors found that foreign capital penetration in 1980 had a significant positive effect on the growth of CO_2 emissions. They postulated that, in general, foreign investment is more concentrated in those industries that require more energy. In addition, transnational corporations may relocate highly polluting industries to countries with fewer environmental controls and poorer infrastructure.

A later study of 113 countries and 57 industries by Davis and Caldiera (2010) finds that in 2004 23% of global CO_2 emissions, or 6.2 gigatonnes

CO_2, were traded internationally, primarily as exports from China and other emerging markets to consumers in developed countries. In some wealthy countries, including Switzerland, Sweden, Austria, the United Kingdom, and France, greater than 30% of consumption-based emissions were imported, with net imports to many Europeans of greater than 4 tons CO_2 per person in 2004. (The net import of emissions to the United States in the same year was somewhat less, accounting for 10.8% of total consumption-based emissions and 2.4 tons CO_2 per person.) In contrast, 22.5% of the emissions produced in China in 2004 were exported, on net, to consumers elsewhere. The authors state that the net effect of international trade is the export of emissions from China and other emerging markets to consumers in the United States, Japan, and Western Europe. Davis and Caldeira (2010) argue,

> Thus, despite apparent decarbonization of the energy supply in some countries, consumption of internationally traded goods tends to equalize the carbon intensity of energy consumed worldwide. Finally, we note that consumption-based accounting of emissions acts to further decouple population and emissions by shifting substantial emissions from emerging markets such as China and India to much less populous developed countries. In terms of global equity, the prosperity of developed countries was not only founded on two centuries of fossil fuel emissions, but also in some cases is now being maintained by emissions produced in developing countries.
>
> (p. 5691)

A study by Wiebe et al. (2012) examined both CO_2 emissions and materials (resources) in terms of their embodiment in trade. Specifically, it focused on six major emerging economies—Brazil, Russia, India, China, South Africa, and Argentina (BRICSA)—and the influence of consumption in OECD countries on the development of CO_2 production and material extraction in these countries. What they found was quite revealing. On the one hand, OECD countries were almost able to stabilize their domestic emissions production and materials extraction between 1995 and 2005 while also increasing their GDP. That is, the OECD countries realized a decoupling of monetary drivers and physical production; however, these trends did not hold true from a *consumption* standpoint. Rather, *the outsourcing of environmentally intensive stages of production was one of the main causes of decoupling in the OECD countries.* The study also found that increasing demand in the OECD countries is one important driver for growing CO_2 emissions and resource use in the emerging countries of BRICSA. The authors argue that their study confirms the increasingly important role of international trade for the environmental performance of countries, illustrating that the OECD countries have improved their performance partly due to shifts of environmental pressures into BRICSA. This increase is more pronounced for emissions, metals, and minerals but is also visible for fossil fuels and biomass. China plays by far the most important role in this process, followed by Russia.

To my knowledge, there has been no wide-scale study attempting to calculate a monetary figure for the environmental "externalities"[2] that were shifted onto the industrializing semi-periphery through global production chains. However, a short study by Clelland (2014) notes that given the extensive environmental resources and degradation used in the production of Apple iPad the savings to Apple of not paying for some ecological externalities is $190 per iPad, nearly double Apple's operating profit margin. As Clleland notes, the unaccounted-for environmental externalities and labor exploitation embodied in global commodities that are consumed by core consumers have created a kind of core consumer aristocracy. Finally, it should be noted that this capacity of TNCs from the Global North to shift environmental burdens onto semi-peripheral industrializing countries was no accident. As a study by Frey (2003) points out, the establishment of export processing zones, which have few regulatory restrictions on production practices and offer many other concessions to TNCs, resulted in the transfer of some of the core's most hazardous products, production processes, and wastes.

In sum, the multinationalization of production from transnational corporations of the Global North, and the exports sent to the Global North have driven the engine of demand in emerging economies for several decades. As we saw in the above discussion, the overall environmental consequence was the shifting of pollution-based industries overseas and the draining of semi-peripheral resources, enabling both the (relative) conservation of Northern environments and unsustainable consumption of global resources. While this system may be reaching a crisis as demand for exports from the U.S., in particular, has been slowing down in recent years (Ghosh, 2016), some of the most salient forms of environmental degradation in the first two decades of the 21st century semi-periphery nevertheless stem from this shift in the capitalist world-system.

Semi-Peripheral Ecological Sub-Imperialism: Case Study of China in Southeast Asia (ASEAN)

While the overall structure of the capitalist world-system remains core dominated, the industrialization of semi-peripheral countries has introduced new dynamics in how ecological imperialism operates in the 21st century beyond the historical binary core/periphery relation created during colonialism. With the firm establishment of capitalist relations of production globally, these countries are becoming their own centers of accumulation as such countries seek to attain core status, establish spheres of geopolitical influence, and economically integrate with the rest of the world on terms favorable to their continued accumulation of capital, leading to a rise in South-South foreign investment and trade. As Gray and Gills (2016) have noted, the rise of South-South cooperation has engendered divisive interpretations, with some who lauding the potential of Southern economic development and liberation from Northern domination. Others, however, criticize the success of the South as ultimately subsumed within the existing global capitalist development paradigm (see for example the work of Nilsen and Holdt (2019), that critiques the political, economic, and social in the rise of the BRICS countries). This system has generated a form of semi-peripheral ecological imperialism and semi-peripheral ecologically unequal exchange, a trend I first began to suspect in a short, earlier study on land grabbing in Cambodia (Frame, 2018). To an increasing extent, ecological imperialism and the resultant global ecological crises in general are being driven by a kind of sub-imperialism emanating from semi-peripheral emerging economies.

As will be discussed in regard to China and Southeast Asia, several important dynamics underpin the ecological imperialism of the semi-periphery that strongly mimics the historical trajectory of imperialism from capitalist core economies to the periphery. First, semi-peripheral emerging economies are constructing new forms of economic integration on terms favorable to obtaining the resources necessary to support their industrialization and growing consumption of their own populations, and also to absorb their manufactured goods, resulting in patterns of ecologically unequal exchange. Second, such economic integration acts to release built-up surpluses of capital in the form of large-scale infrastructure projects in the periphery, with dubious environmental consequences; third, there is evidence of an incipient movement toward shifting low-technology production overseas that are environmentally polluting.

Ultimately, despite anti-colonialism rhetoric, semi-peripheral imperialism challenges neither the essential dynamics of capitalist expansion driven by global labor arbitrage, nor the historical exploitation of the Nature of peripheral countries by core economies. As Bond (2018) noted in his writings on sub-imperialism, BRICS firms have become some of the most super-exploitative corporations engaged in accumulation not only on their home turf but also in Africa. Bond also aptly comments,

> The BRICS bloc—given the nature of its ruling classes (and particularly with the right now in ascendency in Brazil and in India)—has no ideological alternative to imperialism. The domestic policies adopted by the BRICS states can be described as *neoliberal with southern characteristics*—with a focus on sales of commodities, low wages to workers along with the recycled surplus turned over as credit to the North, even as the livelihood of their own citizens is jeopardised, and even as they have developed new markets in other, often more vulnerable, countries which were once part of the Third World bloc....

This section examines the case study of China's growing influence in the ten-member Association of Southeast Asian Nations (ASEAN) region. While much literature has examined China's growing presence in Africa and the rush for resources, relatively less attention has been paid to Southeast Asia. Within the capitalist world-system, China has emerged as one of the main global production and manufacturing hubs for OECD countries. As the 2012 study discussed above, China, among the BRICS economies studied, has played the most important role as a recipient country for the environmental shifting of pressures from OECD countries (Wiebe et al., 2012). It is also the largest carbon producer and consumer. According to a World Wildlife Fund and International Institute for Sustainable Development (IISD) report (Rutherford, Lazarus & Kelly, 2008), China's economic rise has transformed it into one of the world's greatest consumers of natural resources, leading to the rapid increase in Chinese overseas FDI (OFDI) flows that stretches all the way to Africa and Latin America. China's demand for goods and services is increasingly met by global supply chains involving countries situated in far geographical distances where processes at each stage in the production chain create environmental impacts.

China: A Biophysical Overview

China's own domestic environment has been sacrificed in the pursuit of its rapid economic growth and industrialization. As Figure 5.1 shows, China's domestic extraction (DE), which comprises all biotic and abiotic raw materials extracted from the domestic environment and further used in production processes, has increased sharply from 1970 to 2017.[3] In the period of 1970–2017, domestic extraction increased by a staggering 1,460.4%, from approximately 2 billion tonnes in 1970 to approximately 33 billion tonnes in 2017. World extraction in 2017 was a little over 90 billion tonnes, meaning China's domestic extraction accounted for about a third of the world's extraction of resources (WU Vienna, 2020)! Non-metallic minerals had the largest share in overall material extraction in 2017 (68.5%), followed by biomass (12.1%), fossil fuels (12.1%), and metal ores (7.3%). Again, however, it is important to note that according to a report by Wiedmann et al. (2013) a substantial part of the country's infrastructure (more than one-third of the domestic extraction related to construction materials) is related to consumption in other countries.

It is useful here to compare China's immense increases in domestic extraction with Europe (Figure 5.2) and North America's (Figure 5.3) relatively modest increase, showing a relative stabilization in domestic extraction of resources. Japan (Figure 5.4) even shows an overall decrease in domestic extraction.

Behind these numbers is a development model of rapid industrialization and economic growth ultimately based on environmental destruction, social decay, and primitive accumulation (Muldavin, 2012). China's heavy demand for resources and energy to fuel its rapid industrialization has spurred its own domestic land grabs through land and resource acquisitions by state and non-state actors. Such domestic land grabbing has led to wide-spread landlessness and loss of livelihoods, with an estimated 75 million landless peasants and 200 million migrants and widespread social unrest. In response to fears of declining legitimacy, Muldavin (2012) maintains, the leadership has attempted to

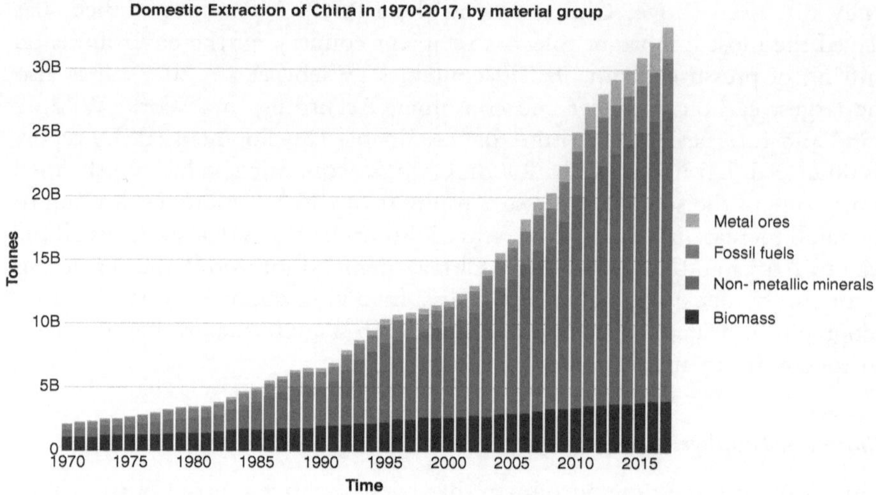

Figure 5.1 Domestic Extraction of China in 1970–2017, by Material Group

Source: WU Vienna (2020): Material flows by material group, 1970–2017. Visualization based upon the UN IRP Global Material Flows Database. Vienna University of Economics and Business. Online available at materialflows.net/visualisation-centre

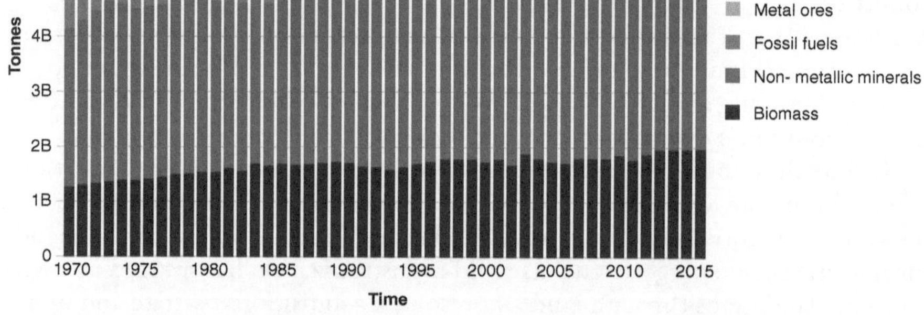

Figure 5.2 Domestic Extraction of Europe in 1970–2017, by Material Group

Source: WU Vienna (2020): Material flows by material group, 1970–2017. Visualization based upon the UN IRP Global Material Flows Database. Vienna University of Economics and Business. Online available at materialflows.net/visualisation-centre

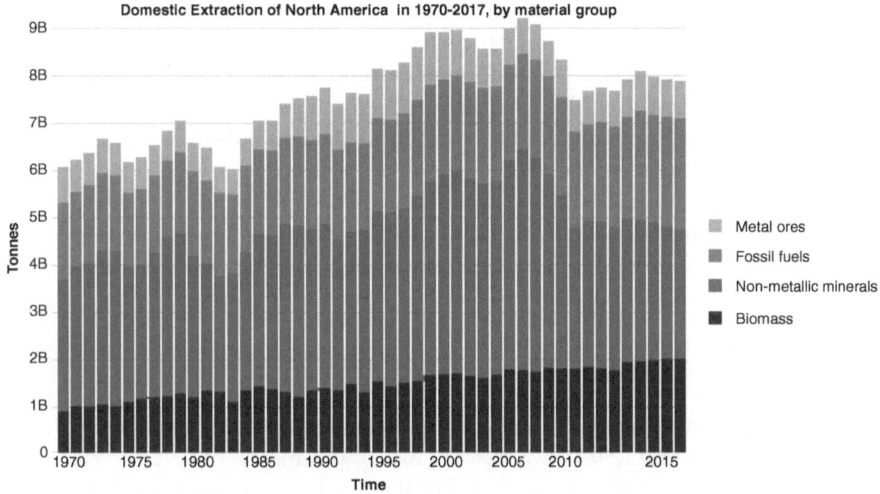

Figure 5.3 Domestic Extraction of North America in 1970–2017, by Material Group
Source: WU Vienna (2020): Material flows by material group, 1970–2017. Visualization based upon the UN IRP Global Material Flows Database. Vienna University of Economics and Business. Online available at materialflows.net/visualisation-centre

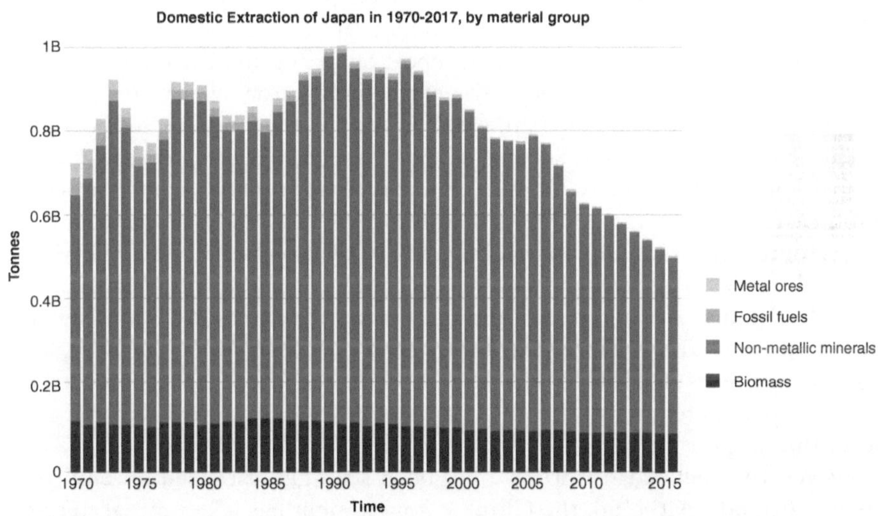

Figure 5.4 Domestic Extraction of Japan in 1970–2017, by Material Group
Source: WU Vienna (2020): Material flows by material group, 1970–2017. Visualization based upon the UN IRP Global Material Flows Database. Vienna University of Economics and Business. Online available at materialflows.net/visualisation-centre

intensify the development model of continuous high growth, bringing about further environmental and social degradation. In response to this contradiction, China is engaging in international land grabs as a "geographic fix"—that is, a fix to internal crises and contradictions through expansion overseas. By externalizing resource demand through global sourcing and production, China is attempting to decrease domestic environmental destruction and land losses while maintaining rapid capital accumulation and continued industrialization (Muldavin, 2012). In doing so, however, Muldavin argues that China is replicating its own domestic problems through investments around the world, challenging China's international legitimacy with environmental degradation, social destruction, and unrest resulting from land and resource grabs overseas.

By 2010, China's annual OFDI flows were more than 70 times greater than its flows in 2000. In both 2009 and 2010, the Export-Import Bank of China and the China Development Bank together lent more than the World Bank did to developing countries (Dyer et al., 2011). China's Tenth Five-Year Plan (a plan that outlines the country's economic and social planning initiatives and goals) that covered 2001–2005 encouraged the country to "go global" and promoted investment abroad to increase international competitiveness (Government of China, 2001). The "go global" strategy is one of the main drivers of China's dramatic increase in investment over the past decade as the country seeks to access natural resources, stimulate exports, and build markets abroad. Latin America, Africa, and Asia all received significant or growing amounts of China's OFDI between 2005 and 2011.

Like many other countries' overseas investments, a significant portion of China's investments go to the energy and natural resources sectors. According to a World Resources Institute (WRI) report by Leung and Zhao (2013), 8.3% of China's OFDI in 2010 went to the extractives sector, which commanded the third highest amount of Chinese OFDI after the business services and financial sectors. A substantial part of China's OFDI is directed toward the Global South, where many Chinese companies have found opportunities in resource-rich developing countries. China's overseas interests range from natural resources like minerals and oil in Africa to hydropower in Southeast Asia.

Notably, in 2013, China launched its ambitious Best and Road Initiative (BRI) aimed at strengthening trade links with at least 64 countries. Its terrestrial route aims to integrate Central Asia, Russia, India, Pakistan, and Europe, while its maritime route runs along the coast of Asia, East Africa, and Europe. Increasingly, the BRI reaches beyond Asia and Europe; it is becoming a global strategy for China (World Wildlife Foundation, 2017). However, the Belt Road Initiative has been strongly criticized on environmental grounds. Although the Chinese government has taken initial steps to incorporate environmentally sustainable, or green, strategies and objectives into BRI, they largely remain in very high level and conceptual terms (Zhou et al., 2018). The report argues that Chinese energy and transportation investments in the BRI countries from 2014 to 2017 fail to align with the green priorities communicated in BRI countries' Nationally Determined Contributions (NDCs).[4] Rather, most Chinese deals in energy and transportation over the period reviewed were tied to carbon-intensive sectors and did not show a strong alignment with the low-carbon priorities included in the BRI countries' nationally determined contribution (Zhou et al., 2018). Further, according to a World Wildlife Fund report (2017a), the BRI area includes many different environmentally important areas such as protected spaces, key landscapes, Global 200 Ecoregions, and biodiversity hotspots that cover the distribution range of flagship species, as well as areas that are important for delivering ecosystem services that provide social and economic benefits to people. The report states that there is "significant potential overlap" between the terrestrial BRI corridors and areas that are important for biodiversity conservation and for the provision of social and economic benefits to people, which poses risk for potentially negative impacts of infrastructure development.

Expansion as release value for overaccumulated surplus capital is a fundamental dynamic of imperialism, discussed in greater length in Chapter 6. In the case of China, a major driving force behind outgoing FDI has been its massive foreign reserves accumulated since the early 2000s. Invested mostly in US government debt, China's reserves were generating low returns. In response, a consensus emerged that China would be better off investing in other types of assets overseas and the amount of outgoing FDI and aid rose dramatically. The "go global" strategy is one of the main drivers of China's dramatic increase in investment over the past decade as the country seeks to access natural resources, stimulate exports, and build markets abroad (Wang, 2016).

Finally, another dynamic of Chinese investment overseas includes the relocation of low-technology industries abroad, mimicking the pattern of Western countries in the second half of the 20th century. Following general global patterns to shift low technology abroad, iron, steel, and cement industries are being moved to provinces in the west of China and to the BRI-participating economies, allowing China to reduce air pollution in Beijing to some extent. China's new environmental "polluter pays" regulations have reduced profits in cement industries within China, giving them a market incentive to move out along the Silk Road. The policy to shift operations of old iron and steel, for example, to BRI countries is associated with China's metals industry moving into cleaner, higher-tech, steel products and metal trading (OECD, 2018).

Figure 5.5 shows China's RME_{im} from 1990 to 2013. RME_{im} account for the total amount of primary material extraction in foreign countries required along the whole supply chain to produce the imports. As the graph demonstrates, China's reliance on imported materials has, in tandem with its economic growth and growth in domestic extraction, grown dramatically.

Figure 5.6 displays China's RME_{ex}. RME_{ex} account for the total amount of primary material extraction—both in the domestic economy

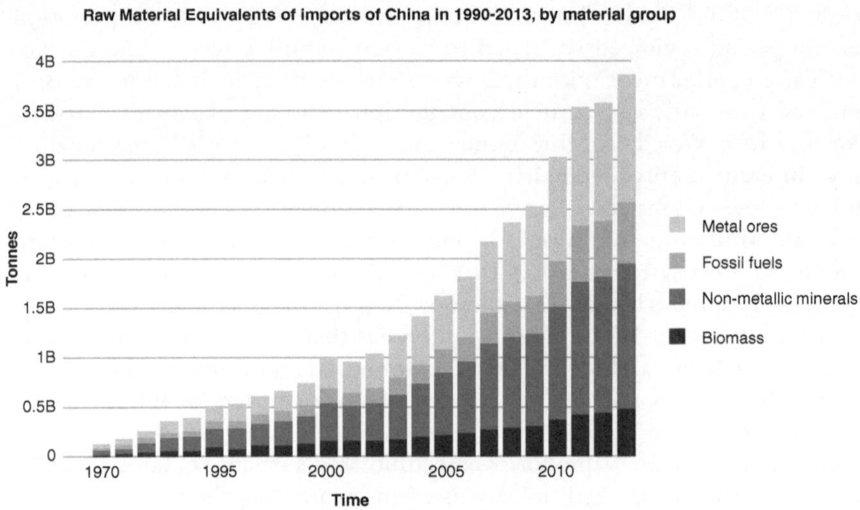

Figure 5.5 China's Raw Material Equivalents of Imports 1990–2013, by Material Group

Source: WU Vienna (2020): Material flows by material group, 1970–2017. Visualization based upon the UN IRP Global Material Flows Database. Vienna University of Economics and Business. Online available at materialflows.net/visualisation-centre

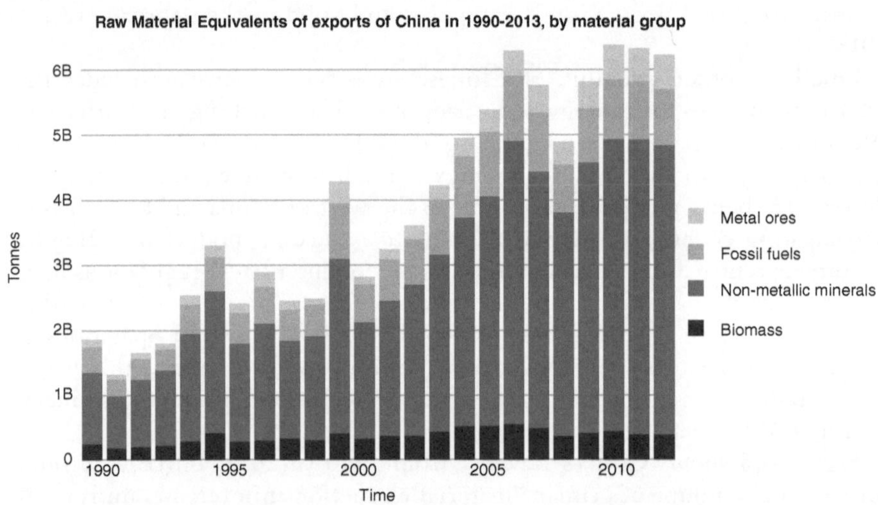

Figure 5.6 Raw Material Equivalents of Exports of China from 1990 to 2013, by Material Group

Source: WU Vienna (2020): Material flows by material group, 1970–2017. Visualization based upon the UN IRP Global Material Flows Database. Vienna University of Economics and Business. Online available at materialflows.net/visualisation-centre

and in foreign countries—required to produce the exports. China's RME_{ex} have, in general, also increased since 1990 and in aggregate are greater than China's RME_{im}, primarily due to China's high export of non-metallic minerals.

However, even as many criticize China's expansion overseas through initiatives such as the BRI and the relocation of environmentally polluting industries, it is impossible to disentangle the role of Northern multinationals and IFIs in this process. China is a major industrial platform for many global corporations subcontracting overseas. As Muldavin (2012) argues, China plays an important role for such corporations by opening up new areas for resource flows, keeping global prices down for some commodities, and facilitating super profits for such global corporations. *Transnational corporations, Muldavin insists, have in essence subcontracted China to extract resources from Africa, Asia, and Latin America, which further obscures the linkages between the social and ecological costs of extraction, production, and consumption.* For example, China's enormous need for timber resources has led to decimation of its own forests, both as a consequence of increasing domestic demand and internal consumption but also for the global subcontracting factories on its industrial platform supplying IKEA, Walmart, and others. In response, China has shifted timber sourcing to Siberia, Southeast Asia, Central Africa, and Latin America, once again displacing some of the impacts through a geographic fix. Similar comparable trends could be found in the cases of mineral extraction and processing, lands for agribusiness, large-scale infrastructure projects, and so on. As Muldavin (2012) further points out, it was the very policies of such institutions as the World Bank that set the stage for China's domestic primitive accumulation and subsequent going-out investments. The International Finance Corporation (IFC) and the Export-Import Banks (ExIm) encouraged FDI in China and pushed the idea of China as a global subcontracting platform. From 1981 onward, the World Bank has pushed privatization and market-oriented policies in all sectors of China's economy. It has also provided support for infrastructure development, an important factor behind displacement, land loss, and dispossession within China.

Nonetheless, though Northern corporations may be implicated in China's overseas expansionary dynamics, increasing levels of domestic consumption also play a role. Figure 5.7 shows China's Raw Material Consumption per capita from 1990 to 2013. RMC captures the amount of domestic and foreign extraction of materials needed along all supply chains to produce the final products consumed *within* a country. RMC equals the sum of Domestic Extraction plus imports in Raw Material Equivalents (RME_{im}) minus exports in Raw Material Equivalents (RME_{ex}). China's increase in RMC per capita illustrates the growing environmental pressures China's domestic consumption places domestically and abroad.

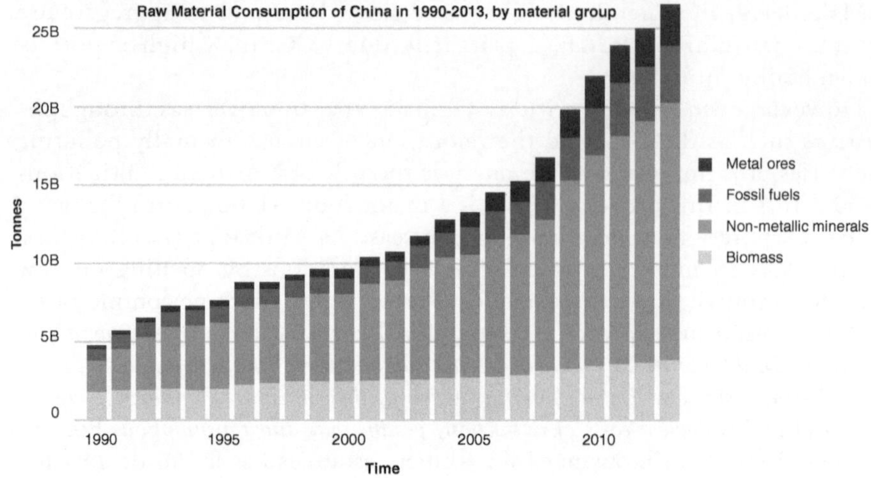

Figure 5.7 China's Raw Material Consumption 1990–2013, by Material Group
Source: WU Vienna (2020): Material flows by material group, 1970–2017. Visualization based upon the UN IRP Global Material Flows Database. Vienna University of Economics and Business. Online available at materialflows.net/visualisation-centre

China-ASEAN Case: The Political Economy of Regional Ecological Sub-Imperialism

One major way in which the capitalist world-system has changed with the growth of semi-peripheral emerging economies is the extent to which such economies can be dominant powers at a regional level, even more so than core economies, exerting a type of *regional* sub-imperialism. China's rising economic power in particular has implications for the study of the semi-periphery and ecological imperialism. Similar to Minqi Li's argument on China's semi-peripheral position and imperialism (see, for example, Li 2021), I suggest China is best classified as a semi-peripheral country in the capitalist world-system with complex implications for the subject of ecological imperialism. As Li states:

> The currently available evidence does not support the argument that China has become an imperialist country in the sense that China belongs to the privileged small minority that exploits the great majority of the world population. On the whole, China continues to have an exploited position in the global capitalist division of labor and transfers more surplus value to the core (historical imperialist countries) than it receives from the periphery. However, China's per capita GDP has risen to levels substantially above the peripheral income levels and, in terms of international labor transfer flows, China has established exploitative relations

> with nearly half of the world population (including Africa, South Asia, and parts of East Asia).
>
> (Li, 2021, n.p.)

The regional sub-imperialism between China and the ten-member Association of Southeast Asian Nations is being consolidated by initiatives outside the scope of core influence, such as the China-ASEAN Free Trade Agreement (CAFTA) and China's Belt Road Initiative. However, again it is impossible to disentangle the role of Northern institutions in creating the foundational neoliberal political context necessary for ecological imperialism to operate. Institutions such as the World Bank and IMF have pushed export-led development centered on natural resource extraction in Southeast Asia for decades, cracking open the resources for both Northern and sub-imperial TNCs.

China and ASEAN have increasingly deepened their regional cooperation and economic integration in the past two decades with promises of economic development and protection from Western dominance and dependency. In 2020, China emerged as ASEAN's largest trading partner, with total imports and exports equal to $516,879,313,584 (ASEANStatsDataPortal, n.d.). China is also increasing its role as a donor country to Southeast Asia in the form of government-sponsored investment, concessional loans, grants, and debt cancellation. China-ASEAN trade patterns are complex and do not mimic a simple neocolonial division of labor, as might be the case with China and Africa; ASEAN is a diverse set of Southeast Asian nations all at varying degrees of economic development, economic power, and industrialization. Rather, China's trade pattern with ASEAN is characterized by a production fragmentation partnership with components passing from economy to economy before being manufactured, normally in China, into a final tradable product (Xianbai, 2020). Nonetheless, while not mimicking a simple neocolonial division of labor, access to ASEAN resources is a vital aspect of China's expansion into Southeast Asia.

As for any semi-peripheral power, China's actions in Southeast Asia take place in a political economic context that was initially constructed by the neoliberal economics policies of core economies and their core-dominated international institutions. Like Latin America and Africa, Southeast Asian nations underwent significant structural adjustments dictated by the IMF, World Bank, and WTO, which created economies primed for export-led development with an emphasis on attracting foreign investment, particularly in natural resource sectors. As elsewhere, the results for the poorer, more peripheral countries of Southeast Asia, such as Cambodia,[5] have been the heavy exploitation of resources by foreign investors and elites, conflict-ridden land grabs, and rapid degradation of the environment. Like Latin America and Africa, such exploitation of resources occurs in a nexus between often corrupt, authoritarian regimes, and investment deals that lack democratic oversight or are done in complete secrecy. Further, not just Chinese investors but also intra-ASEAN investors from higher income economies such as Malaysia,

Thailand, and Vietnam are prominent investors, alongside the traditional colonial powers from the developed world. In Frame (2018), an article on land grabbing in Cambodia, I had written that large-scale land in Southeast resembled a totem pole, with the higher income countries grabbing up land in the lower income countries. For decades the World Bank pushed for deregulation and market liberalization in Cambodia, with the International Finance Corporation providing the financial and technical support. In 2003, the Cambodian government amended its 1994 Investment Law ensuring a wave of deregulation meant to encourage FDI inflows. These reforms included cuts on certain import duties, renewable land leases of up to 99 years, and no price controls on goods or services produced by investors. Unsurprisingly, the reforms triggered sharp increases in FDI, including in agriculture and natural resource extraction. Relatedly, land conflicts between 2000 and 2014 impacted over 500,000 Cambodians (Frame, 2018).

In Indonesia, the World Bank, through various forms of assistance and funding, has fostered sweeping liberalization policies in foreign direct investment and a development agenda heavily focused on natural resource extraction for over five decades. In Indonesia, too, this has had devastating effects on forests and the lives of over 40 million indigenous people living on forested lands under customary tenure, with millions of hectares of customarily managed forests handed over to foreign private firms. Lax regulations for companies to develop large expanses of land have fueled social conflicts over natural resources and widespread deforestation with the expansion of the oil palm, mining, and logging industries (Oakland Institute, 2018). Another example concerns Laos and Cambodia, where Deutsche Bank and the World Bank's International Finance Corporation are implicated in land grabbing through the backing of two giant Vietnamese rubber companies, Hoang Anh Gia Lai (HAGL) and the Vietnam Rubber Group (VRG). Both companies, according to a Global Witness report, operate through a web of subsidiaries which help hide the identity of their true owners (Global Witness, 2013). The World Bank funding has also pushed for market liberalization in Cambodia, triggering an increase in FDI that has been associated with egregious forms of land grabbing (Oakland Institute, 2013). Such examples are far from exhaustive, but they do serve to underscore the foundational role of Northern Institutions in neoliberalizing Southeast Asian Natures.

Whatever the role of Northern international financial institutions, it seems unlikely that China is departing from these fundamental dynamics in its engagement with its regional neighbors. Instead, as Patrick Bond (2018) notes, the BRICS emerging economies have no ideological alternative to neoliberalism, that is, no real ideological alternative to capital accumulation built upon ultra-low wages and ecological devastation. This does not mean emerging economies have embraced wholly free market economic policies domestically in terms of the removal of the role of the state in the economy. In China the state continues to play a central role in the economy as the respective states did for other Asian countries such as Japan and South Korea in their economic development. Further, as will be discussed, state-owned banks such as the Export-Import Bank of China and state-funded insurance companies such as Sinosure are key players in China's expansionary Belt and Road Initiative. However, one could argue that China's regional integration policies are ultimately neoliberal in nature, that is, promoting trade liberalization and emphasizing the rights and protection of foreign investors while taking advantage of the neoliberalization of Southeast Asian Nature that occurred under Northern institutions. As such, China's expansionism is a distinct blend of state-driven policy with neoliberal characteristics. The ASEAN-China Free Trade Area (ACFTA) was signed into agreement in 2010 and has included a number of upgrades since then. Overall, the goals of ACFTA are to progressively liberalize and promote trade in goods and services as well as create a transparent, liberal, and facilitative investment regime (ASEAN.org, n.d.). ACFTA coincided with China's "Going Out" Strategy (2004) and the Tenth Five-Year Plan for National Economic and Social Development (2001–2005), both of which were specifically intended to meet its growing demand for natural resources by spurring outward investment through subsidizing investment by Chinese companies in overseas natural resources acquisition. In addition to ACFTA, ASEAN, being one of China's largest trading partners with vast natural resources and geographical proximity to China, is a key priority for China's Belt Road Initiative. More than 60% of Chinese overseas direct investment to BRI countries from 2013 to 2015 went to ASEAN member states (Gokken, 2018).

While clothed in the language of economic development, these trends, critics argue, have worsened the resource exploitation and environmental degradation. In Cambodia, Laos, and Vietnam there has been the partial withdrawal of International Financial Institutions such as the World Bank and the Asian Development Bank (ADB). These IFIs have developed international standards and best practices for investment in projects with potentially large social and environmental impacts, such as hydropower, mining, and industrial agriculture. This has left an investment vacuum that has been gradually filled by largely Asian financiers, particularly Chinese companies, that are not bound to similar standards in their overseas activities (Rutherford et al., 2008).

Chinese state-owned enterprises are becoming major investors in Cambodia, Laos, and Vietnam and are fueling natural resource extraction. Most of the Chinese projects are designed and implemented by Chinese companies and backed by the China Exim Bank[6] and Sinosure,[7] which are involved in the majority of China's overseas investments. While not an exhaustive overview, the following are significant examples of this trend. In terms of extractive activities, China is expected to remain a large market for minerals and a key investor in the region. In Laos along the Bolaven Plateau and in the Central Highlands of Vietnam, China is starting to invest in large tracts of land for bauxite mining in order to export aluminum for its growing construction, transportation, and packaging industries. The China

Nonferrous Metals International Mining Co. Ltd. (CNMIC) is active in copper mining in Vietnam and bauxite mining in Laos. Chalco (Aluminium Corporation of China), partnering with Thai and Laotian companies, has begun an environmental impact assessment for bauxite mining in the same area as CNMIC in Laos and is also engaged in Vietnam. Other mining investments and/or exports in the three countries include gold, copper, iron, zinc, and coal (Rutherford et al., 2008).

Aside from extractive activities in metals and minerals, China is also invested in hydropower projects in Southeast Asia. In Laos and Cambodia, China is involved in roughly 21 hydropower projects either as an investor or as a developer. The Sinohydro Corporation, the largest hydropower dam building company in China, is developing numerous hydropower projects in both Laos and Cambodia. And the China Southern Power Grid Company Limited is either active or exploring opportunities in all three countries. Until recently, agricultural production in Cambodia and Laos was largely for local consumption and lacked intensive inputs and practices. Now, however, China is providing a major source of investment capital for agricultural inputs in the two countries and is a principal market for goods in all three. Commodities such as cassava, sugarcane, corn, palm oil, cashews, and eucalyptus, among others, are major sources of investment by China. China's rising demand for natural rubber, for example, has already led its southern neighbors to convert large areas of land to rubber production. China is a major investor in rubber production in Laos, although less so in Cambodia. And while China's investment in Vietnam's rubber sector is presently negligible, China is already the principal market for its rubber exports (Rutherford et al., 2008).

Environmentalists and other civil society groups are raising concerns over a number of such Chinese investments in Southeast Asia. Concerns include specifics such as environmental impacts of Chinese-backed hydropower projects along the Mekong River and deforestation and biodiversity in areas such as the Pan Borneo Highway (The ASEAN Post Team, 2019). More broadly, the World Wildlife Fund (2017b) finds over 1,700 critical biodiversity spots and 265 threatened species will be adversely affected by the BRI. A study published in the *Current Biology* journal quantifies invasion risks of 816 alien terrestrial vertebrates along 121 China's Belt and Road Initiative countries and 14 invasion hotspots facing a high invasion risks with both high introduction risk and habitat suitability overlap, a majority of which falls along the 6 proposed BRI Economic Corridors (Liu et al., 2019).

China, ASEAN, and Ecologically Unequal Exchange

As discussed in previous sections, China's growth has been built on steeply increasing levels of domestic resource extraction and increasing levels of imported resources, even as it continues to export high amounts of resources. While much more research needs to be conducted on ecologically unequal exchange between semi-peripheral and peripheral countries, there are a few studies that provide provisional empirical evidence. Yu et al. (2014) examine the hypothesis of ecologically unequal exchange for the case of China, revealing the complex "*middling*" position of such emerging semi-peripheral countries. On the one hand, the authors find that China is the world's largest exporter in terms of producing goods for consumption in developed countries. The authors examine value-added and four environmental indicators [sulfur dioxide (SO_2) emissions, greenhouse gas (GHG) emissions, water, and land] by using a global multi-region input-output model. Overall, they find that *developed regions, such as North America, the EU, and East Asia (including Japan and South Korea), externalize environmental impacts through importing goods produced in China*. On the other hand, they find that *less developed regions, such as Southeast Asia, South Asia, and Africa, export large quantities of goods and associated SO_2 and CO_2 emissions, land and water to China*. Further, these regions only gain relatively small shares of economic value in exchange. Overall, the authors emphasize that China's economic growth, having resulted in environmental degradation domestically, is now externalizing these environmental pressures in other developing countries. Another study on ecologically unequal exchange by Shandra et al. (2019) looks specifically at the effects of China on other low- and middle-income nations in terms of forest loss. They find that forestry exports sent from low- and middle-income nations to China are related to increased forest loss in those exporting nations. Overall, they argue that China, a middle-income nation, is exploiting forests of other low- and middle- income nations in a manner similar to high-income nations as it tries to protect its own forests while meeting its needs for wood, fuel, paper, and pulp from abroad to stimulate its economic growth and satisfy its changing consumption patterns.

The following preliminary findings are suggestive of a developing pattern of ecologically unequal exchange developing between China and ASEAN, though more in-depth studies involving assessment along entire value chains would need to be conducted to answer definitively. According to the United Nations International Trade Statistics Database (UNCOMTRADE) data, ASEAN exports substantially more natural resources to China than China exports to ASEAN. In 2019, ASEAN, with a population of approximately 661.5 million people, exported to China 377 million tonnes of resources, 203 million tonnes of fossil fuels, 125 million tons of metals and minerals, 31.3 million tonnes of agricultural products, 16.7 million tonnes of forestry products, and 371,000 tonnes of fertilizers. From 2014 to 2019, the export of metals and minerals grew by 10%, fossil fuels by 7.3%, and forestry products by 2%. During this time period, there were no categories of resources whose exports were declining from ASEAN to China. In 2019 the top exporters, in descending order, were Indonesia, Philippines, Malaysia, Myanmar, and Vietnam. ASEAN's total export to China has grown substantially; in 2000, ASEAN exported 25 million tonnes of natural resources to China, and by 2019, it reached 377 tonnes (Chatham House, n.d.).

In contrast, in 2019 China, with a population of approximately 1.398 billion people, exported only 77.2 million tonnes of resources to ASEAN: 26.8 million tonnes of metals and minerals, 33.6 million tonnes of fossil fuels, 8 million tonnes of agricultural products, 7.2 million tonnes of fertilizers, and 1.4 million tonnes of forestry products. Top importers included, in descending order, Singapore, Vietnam, the Philippines, Malaysia, and Indonesia.

In sum, the above statistics are indicative of ecologically unequal exchange occurring between China and ASEAN. However, it should be kept in mind that these statistics only cover the import and export of natural resources. Comprehensive analysis of ecologically unequal exchange requires assessment along the entire value chains that make up all exports and imports. So, for example, while ASEAN is exporting more natural resources to China than vice versa, the statistics quoted here do not account for Chinese domestic resources that may be embodied in the manufacturing goods being exported from China to ASEAN.

Another angle to assess ecologically unequal exchange is large-scale land investments. Land grabbing has become a serious social and environmental issue in Southeast Asia. The neoliberalization of land laws has favored the interests of investors, and the guarantee of investor protection by national governments has accelerated land grabbing and all the associated socio-ecological costs. For China-ASEAN, land grabbing occurs primarily in one direction, from China to Southeast Asia, and not vice versa. According to the data provided by the Land Matrix in 2020, China invested in 12,929,041 hectares in ASEAN, while ASEAN nations as a whole have only invested in 158,014 hectares in China. Table 5.1 shows China's land investment in ASEAN nations by country and sector in 2020 as well as total ASEAN hectares invested in China in the last column.

Table 5.1 Chinese Large-Scale Land Investments in ASEAN Nations 2020

	Total Hectares Invested in Each Country	*Agriculture Deals*	*Industry Deals*	*Timber Deals*	*Tourism Deals*	*Renewable Energy Deals*	*Mining Deals*	*Total ASEAN Hectares Invested in China*
Brunei	0	0	0	0	0	0	0	0
Myanmar	655,046	21	2	0	0	2	2	0
Cambodia	138,700	23	3	9	2	1		0
Timor-Leste	0	0	0	0	0	0	0	0
Indonesia	95,231	5	0	0	0	0	0	13,000
Laos	10,720,769	42	7	5	1	0	3	0
Malaysia	600	3	0	0	0	0	0	0
Philippines	1,250,385	8	0	0	0	1	0	0
Singapore	0	0	0	0	0	0	0	145,000
Thailand	0	0	0	0	0	0	0	0
Vietnam	68,310	3	6	0	0	0	1	0
Total	12,929,041	105	18	14	3	4	6	158,014

Source: Compiled from the Land Matrix open access database in 2020

As the table shows, China has been a heavy investor in mainland Southeast Asia by investing largely in large-scale land deals related to agricultural sectors but also in deals related to industry, timber, mining, renewable energy, and tourism. Activist groups have criticized Chinese large-scale land investment as making corruption worse, debilitating governance, violating human rights, and damaging the environment in Southeast Asia. As discussed above, domestic environmental issues coupled with increasing domestic demand are pushing China's large-scale land investments elsewhere. For example, according to one report, as Chinese farmland increasingly diminishes, Chinese agricultural firms are looking to produce elsewhere, such as Laos. And, as Chinese demand for cars grows, the country is expected to consume 30% of the world's rubber by 2020. To meet its needs, Chinese companies have recently looked to produce rubber on Laotian land (Local Act Thailand, n.d.).

Conclusion

By the 21st century, capitalism's expansionary tendencies have resulted in a world-systemic shift with the industrialization of the formerly peripheral economies and their shift into a semi-peripheral status as emerging economies. A major feature of neoliberal globalization, this shift, as well as the resource competition with the Global North, has had profound planetary ecological consequences. Yet in the current capitalist world-system, the position of semi-peripheral emerging economies is anything but clear; semi-peripheral emerging economies occupy an ambiguous position as both imperialized *and* holding imperial power. While core economies underwent industrialization and the original stages of capital accumulation abetted by slavery, colonialism, and neocolonialism, emerging economies are competing in a capitalist world-system still dominated by core economies. Importantly, emerging economies also serve as manufacturing platforms to transnational corporations largely headquartered in the Global North, a consequence that has led to the vast degradation of their own Nature.

Nonetheless while the overall structure of the capitalist world-system remains core dominated, the industrialization of semi-peripheral countries has produced major changes in how ecological imperialism operates in the 21st century. Semi-peripheral emerging economies have transformed into their own loci of accumulation, seeking to attain core status through establishing spheres of geopolitical influence and economic integration both regionally and more broadly into peripheral areas globally. This system has arguably generated a form of ecological sub-imperialism and semi-peripheral ecologically unequal exchange. As the case study of China-ASEAN discusses, semi-peripheral industrializing countries can wield as much power and influence, or more, than core countries over their peripheral neighbors. Despite anti-imperialist rhetoric, semi-peripheral ecological imperialism challenges neither the essential dynamics of capitalist expansion driven by global labor arbitrage nor the historical exploitation of the Nature of peripheral countries. All economies competing under capitalist relations of production seem to repeat similar expansionary patterns: resource acquisition overseas to obtain the resources to support their industrialization as well as the growing consumption of their own populations, the building of overseas markets to absorb their manufactured goods, and the release built-up surpluses of capital in the form of large-scale infrastructure projects—many of which support the extraction of resources in the periphery. As emerging economies have destroyed and continue to destroy their environments for the unsustainable consumption of core consumers and the profits of TNCs headquartered in the Global North, while also engaging in their own form of ecological sub-imperialism overseas, the industrializing semi-periphery now straddles an ambiguous category of both exploiter and exploited.

References

Arrighi, G. (1990). The developmentalist illusion: A reconceptualization of the semi-periphery. In W.G. Martin (Ed.), *Semiperipheral states in the world-economy* (pp. 11–42). Westport, CT: Greenwood Press.

Arrighi, G., Silver, B., & Brewer, B. (2003). Industrial convergence, globalization and the persistence of the North-South divide. *Studies in Comparative International Development*, *38*(1), 3–31.

ASEAN.org. (n.d.). *Framework agreement on comprehensive economic co-operation between the association of South East Asian nations and the people's.* ASEAN. Retrieved December 13, 2021, from https://asean.org/wp-content/uploads/2021/08/Framework-Agreement-on-Comprehensive-Economic-Co-Operation_ASEAN-Rep-of-China.pdf

ASEANStatsDataPortal. (n.d.). https://data.aseanstats.org/trade-annually

Bond, P. (2018). *Towards a broader theory of imperialism.* Review of African Political Economy. http://roape.net/2018/04/18/towards-a-broader-theory-of-imperialism/

Chase-Dunn, C., & Hall, T. (1997). *Rise and demise: Comparing world-systems.* Boulder, CO: Westview Press.

Chatham House. (n.d.). *Resourcetrade.earth.* Data | resourcetrade.earth | Chatham House. Retrieved December 13, 2021, from https://resourcetrade.earth/

Ciccantell., P., & Smith, D. (2009). Rethinking global commodity chains: Integrating extraction, transport, and manufacturing. *International Journal of Comparative Sociology*, *50*(3–4), 361–384.

Clelland, D.A. (2014). The core of the apple: degrees of monopoly and dark value in global commodity chains. *Journal of World-Systems Research*, *20*(1), 82–111. https://doi.org/10.5195/jwsr.2014.564

Davis, S.J., & Caldeira, K. (2010) Consumption-based accounting of CO_2 emissions. *PNAS*, *107*(12) 5687–5692. https://doi.org/10.1073/pnas.0906974107

Dyer, G., Anderlini, J., & Sender, H. (2011, January 17). China's lending hits new heights. *Financial Times.* Retrieved July 2019, from http://www.ft.com/intl/cms/s/0/488c60f4-2281-11e0-b6a2-00144feab49a.html#axzz2PFJ8gwuU

Frame, M. (2018). The role of the Semi-Periphery in ecologically unequal exchange: A case study of land investments in Cambodia. In R.S. Frey, P.K. Gellert, & H.F. Dahms (Eds.), *Ecologically unequal exchange: Environmental injustice in comparative and historical perspective* (pp. 75–106). Cham: Palgrave Macmillan.

Frey, R.S. (2003). The transfer of core-based hazardous production processes to the export processing zones of the periphery: The maquiladora centers of Northern Mexico. *Journal of World-Systems Research*, *9*(2), 317–354. https://doi.org/10.5195/jwsr.2003.236

Ghosh, J. (2016). *The "emerging economies" today*. Triple crisis: Global perspective on finance, development, and environment. http://triplecrisis.com/the-emerging-economies-today/

Global Witness. (2013, May 13). *Rubber barons*. https://www.globalwitness.org/en/campaigns/land-deals/rubberbarons/

Gokkon, B. (2018, July 18). Environmentalists are raising concerns over China's belt and road initiative. *Pacific Standard*. https://psmag.com/environment/environmental-concerns-over-chinese-infrastructure-projects

Government of China. (2001). *10th five-year plan for national economic and social development (2001–2005)*. Retrieved July 2018, from http://www.people.com.cn/GB/shizheng/16/20010318/419582.html

Grey, K., & Gills, B.K. (2016). South-south cooperation and the rise of the global south. *Third World Quarterly*, *37* (4), 557–574.

http://dx.doi.org/10.1080/01436597.2015.1128817

Grimes, P., & Kentor, J. (2003). Exporting the greenhouse: Foreign capital penetration and CO? Emissions 1980–1996. *Journal of World-Systems Research*, *9*(2), 261–275. https://doi.org/10.5195/jwsr.2003.244

Hielscher, L. (2019). *Sinosure - Belt and Road Initiative*. Belt and Road Initiative. Retrieved January 10, 2022, from https://www.beltroad-initiative.com/sinosure/

Karataşlı, Ş.S. (2017). *Sociology of Development*, *3*(2), 163–196. https://doi.org/10.1525/sod.2017.3.2.163

Land Matrix. (n.d.). Land Matrix. Retrieved July 13, 2020, from https://landmatrix.org/

Leung, D., & Zhao, Y. in collaboration with Hu, T., & Ballesteros, A. (2013). *Environmental and social policies in over seas investments: Progress and challenges for China*. World Resources Institute. http://pdf.wri.org/environmental_and_social_policies_in_overseas_investments_china.pdf

Li, M. (2003). The rise of China and the demise of the capitalist-world economy: Exploring historical possibilities in the 21st century.

Li, M. (2021). China: Imperialism or semi-periphery? *Monthly Review*. https://monthlyreview.org/2021/07/01/china-imperialism-or-semi-periphery/https://guilfordjournals.com/doi/10.1521/siso.69.3.420.66524

Liu, X., Blackburn, T.M, Song, T., Li, X., Huang, C., & Li, Y. (2019). Risks of biological invasion on the belt and road. *Current Biology*, *29*(3), 499–505. https://doi.org/10.1016/j.cub.2018.12.036

Local Act Thailand. (n.d.). *Land grabbing and impacts to small scale farmers in Southeast Asia Sub-Region*. International Institute of Social Studies. Retrieved December 13, 2021, from https://www.iss.nl/sites/corporate/files/CMCP_60-Samranjit.pdf

Moore, J.W. (2015). *Capitalism in the web of life: Ecology and the accumulation of capital*. London: Verso.

Muldavin, J. (2021). *Land from the tiller: China's role in global processes of land dispossession*. Conference paper. Land Deal Politics Initiative, Institute of Social Science, Cornell University, Ithaca, NY.

Nilsen, A.G., & Holdt, K.V. (2021). *Rising powers, people rising neoliberalization and its discontents in the Brics countries*. New York: Routledge.

Oakland Institute. (2013). *World Banks bad business in Cambodia.* https://www.oaklandinstitute.org/world-banks-bad-business-cambodia

Oakland Institute. (2018). *Indonesia: The World Bank's failed Asian miracle.* https://www.oaklandinstitute.org/indonesia-world-bank-failed-east-asian-miracle

OECD. (2018). *China's belt and road initiative in the global trade, investment and finance landscape.* OECD Business and Finance Outlook. https://www.oecd.org/finance/Chinas-Belt-and-Road-Initiative-in-the-global-trade-investment-and-finance-landscape.pdf

Reuss, A. (2013). Labor and the global economy. *Dollars and Sense.*

Rutherford, J., Lazarus, K., & Kelley, S. (2008) *Rethinking investments in natural resources: China's emerging role in the Mekong region.* Heinrich Boll Stiftung Cambodia, World Wildlife Fund, iisd, International Institute for Sustainable Development, Institut international du développement durable. http://d2ouvy59p0dg6k.cloudfront.net/downloads/china_study_executive_summary.pdf

Shandra, J.M., Restivo, M., & Sommer, J.M. (2019). Appetite for destruction? China, ecologically unequal exchange, and forest loss. *Rural Sociology, 85*(2), 346–375. https://doi.org/10.1111/ruso.12292

Smith, D.A., & Mahutga, M.C. (2009). Trading up the commodity Chain? The impact of extractive and labor-intensive manufacturing trade on world-systems inequalities. In J. Bair (Ed.), *Frontiers of commodity chain research* (pp. 63–82). Palo Alto, CA: Stanford University Press.

Smith, J. (2016). *Imperialism in the 21st century: Globalization, super-exploitation, and capitalism's final crisis.* New York: Monthly Review Press.

The ASEAN Post Team. (2019, December 24). China's BRI negatively impacting the environment. *The ASEAN Post.* https://theaseanpost.com/article/chinas-bri-negatively-impacting-environment

The Export-Import Bank of China. (n.d.). *The introduction.* The Export-Import Bank of China. Retrieved January 10, 2022, from http://english.eximbank.gov.cn/Profile/AboutTB/Introduction/

Van Den Berg, Hendrik. (2017). *International economics: A heterodox approach* (3rd edition). New York: Routledge. https://wwf.panda.org/wwf_news/?161282/Rethinking-Investments-in-natural-resources-Chinas-emerging-role-in-the-Mekong-region

Wallerstein, I. (1974). *The modern world system I: Capitalist agriculture and the origins of the European world-economy in the sixteenth century.* New York: Academic Press.

Wang, H. (2016). *A deeper look at China's "Going Out" policy.* Center for International Governance Innovation. https://www.cigionline.org/publications/deeper-look-chinas-going-out-policy/

Wiebe, K.S, Bruckner, M., Giljum, S., Lutz, C., & Polzin, C. (2012). Carbon and materials embodied in the international trade of emerging economies: A multiregional input-output assessment of trends between 1995 and 2005. *Journal of Industrial Ecology, 16*(4). https://doi.org/10.1111/j.1530-9290.2012.00504.x

World Wildlife Foundation. (2017a). *The belt and road initiative WWF: Recommendations and spatial analysis.* http://awsassets.panda.org/downloads/the_belt_and_road_initiative___wwf_recommendations_and_spatial_analysis___may_2017.pdf

World Wildlife Foundation. (2017b, November 2). *WWF and greening the belt and road initiative.* https://www.wwf.org.hk/en/?19680/Feature-Story-WWF-and-Greening-the-Belt-and-Road-Initiative

WU Vienna. (2020). *Visualisation centre*. Materialflows.net. materialflows.net/visualisation-centre

Xianbai, J. (2020). *The rise of China-ASEAN trade amid trans-Pacific decoupling*. CGTN. https://news.cgtn.com/news/2020-03-19/The-rise-of-China-ASEAN-trade-amid-trans-Pacific-decoupling-OXZHjem1c4/index.html

Yu, Y., Feng, K., & Hubacek, K. (2014). China's unequal ecological exchange. *Ecological Indicators*, 47, 156–163.

Zhou, L., Gilbert, S., Wang, Y., Muñoz Cabré, M., & Gallagher, K.P. (2018). *Moving the green belt and road initiative: From words to actions*. World Resources Institute (WRI) & BU Global Development Policy Center. https://files.wri.org/s3fs-public/moving-green-belt-and-road-initiative-from-words-to-actions.pdf

Notes

1 However, this pattern of North-South trade occurs primarily between industrialized countries and a group of 24 developing countries. Africa and the Middle have not, overall, made this transition to export-oriented industrialization and remain reliant on the export of primary commodities.

2 It would be an interesting exercise to try to calculate such externalities, but Moore's (2015) critiques of the use of the term "externalities" in economics in general are on the mark. Capitalism does not just create negative side effects that can somehow be eliminated through better policy; rather, capitalism systematically exploits the free gifts of Nature to survive. This exploitation is inherent to how it operates, and enables the expansionary tendencies of capitalism.

3 2017 being the latest available data.

4 The Paris Climate Agreement requires all participating governments to agree to "nationally determined contributions" that specify the extent to which each country will reduce their carbon emissions.

5 See, for example, the wealth of information on land grabbing, dispossession, socio-political conflict, deforestation on Cambodia's main human rights organization's website, LICADHO https://www.licadho-cambodia.org/topic/land

6 The Export-Import Bank of China is a state-funded and state-owned bank dedicated to supporting China's foreign trade, foreign investment, and international economic cooperation (The Export-Import Bank of China, n.d.).

7 The China Export Credit & Insurance Corporation (Sinosure) is a state-funded insurance company established in 2001. It is a significant player in the making of projects along the BRI since it provides a safety net critical to Chinese investors (Hielscher, 2019).

6 International Finance in the Global Ecology

One of the most paradoxical features of the 21st-century capitalist world-system is the rapid escalation of global ecological crises coupled with a tremendous accumulation of capital in the financial sector. The wealth of Nature and the stability of important Earth systems, has deteriorated sharply while the profits of the financial sector and what Marx termed "interest-bearing capital" have swelled. Previous chapters have focused on how neoliberal development policies created the political economic foundations of ecological imperialism through trade and investment policies that favor the interests of TNCs, while reinforcing an international division of labor characterized by ecologically unequal exchange. This chapter addresses the third component of neoliberal globalization, the liberalization of the financial sector together with the financialization of the economy that is marked by the rise of a hegemonic financial class. This chapter theorizes several key ways that financial capital exacerbates the global socio-ecological crises in the contemporary era of financialization. It begins with several of Marx's insights into the nature of "interest-bearing capital"—that is, interest-bearing capital as originating from previously exploited surplus value—and critiques the movement to "green finance."

In the capitalist mode of production, the fundamental relationship between ecological imperialism and interest-bearing capital is its role in enabling the expansion of capitalist activities. As Marx in *Capital Volume III* (1999) had noted, the financial system acts as a mechanism of concentration of multiple streams of revenues from non-reinvested industrial profits to the savings of workers. Through the financial system, these multiple scattered, small funds, unable to act on their own accord, become a concentrated "money power" at the disposal of the financial class. Today the vast hoards of money capital circling the global for rates of highest return exacerbate the fundamental contradiction of an Earth system characterized by diminishing capacity and the endless quest for economic growth. In the hierarchical international division of labor of the world-capitalist system, this concentrated and internationalized money power, the locus of which is in the developed countries and emerging economies, enables the processes of enclosure and accumulation by dispossession through the disciplining mechanism of debt as well as the

DOI: 10.4324/9780429261305-6

funding of neoliberal development policies. With financial liberalization and the entanglement of a wide variety of financial actors globally with corporations operating in the natural resource sectors of the Global South, the Natures of the Global South have become a site for the accumulation of global capital. The Natures of the Global South are thoroughly integrated into the circuits of the global financial sector. Behind virtually every environmentally damaging extractive industry—whether the industry is domestically based or a TNC—stands a diverse array of international financial actors. As long as extractive, environmentally damaging industries remain profitable, the financial sector follows.

Neoliberalism and Financialization

The neoliberal era is characterized by the remarkable growth and political economic power of the financial sector, along with the emergence of a super-wealthy financial class and a surge of accumulation as financial capital. In the literature, this trend is often referred to as "financialization," a multifaceted term with a number of meanings. At times, financialization is used to describe the growth of the private financial industry's share of national income, while simultaneously its contribution to the real economy has diminished (Van Den Berg, 2017). According to one study, the financial services sector in 1950 was 2.8% of GDP and later in 2014 it grew to 7.3%. Further, the sector has become more concentrated: the top five banks in 1970 held 17% of aggregate bank assets, but by 2010, they held 52% (Konczal & Abernathy, 2015). At other times, financialization refers to how finance has become more important in the non-financial business sector. For example, the work of Lapavitsas and Mendieta-Munoz (2016) calculates the steady increase of financial profits as a percentage of corporate profits of U.S. domestic industries since 1955. Financialization is also used to describe the broader implications for society, such as the influence of finance on the real economy and the growing influence of finance in shaping business behavior. Households, for example, have become financialized as financial transactions have penetrated into the realm of household revenue for both borrowing and saving. This trend has become a significant source of profit for banks. Others have used the term "financialization" to discuss the rise of a rentier class whose economic and political power derives from the ownership of capital (Palley, 2007).

The essential issue at hand is the shift in the nature of contemporary capitalism to favor the interests of the financial class, which has been enabled by a host of economic, institutional, legal, policy and ideological changes. This shift, according to a number of scholars (Foster & Holleman, 2010), Sweezy (1994), has led to a growing proportion of the capitalist class that now derives its wealth from finance as opposed to production. Peet locates the origins of this shift in the neoliberal policy regime that arose in response to the Keynesian democracy crises and the stagflation of the early 1970s.

By interpreting the cause of the crises as a problem of state intervention in the economy, Peet (2011) argues that neoliberalism represents the interests of a certain fraction of capital, one that favors the withdrawal of the nation-state from macroeconomic management in interest of the working class to re-intensified state intervention on the side of finance capital. According to Peet, in contrast to the post-WWII Keynesian era of strong unions and increasing wages of the working class, the working class in the neoliberal era has witnessed stagnating wages in the face of de-unionization, declining government spending on social services, the downward pressure of globalization on wages, advances in technology that make lower-skilled labor redundant, and tax reforms benefiting the wealthy. In the era of neoliberal financialization, wealth accumulation is primarily being captured by super-wealthy families, CEOs, upper managers, and entrepreneurs. Post-Keynesian research on financialization has also directly linked stagnating wages of US workers to the increased funneling of corporate profits to shareholders (Konczal & Abernathy, 2015).

Wealth inequality has increased dramatically in the past 35 years. Overall, the share of wages as total income has shrunk relative to capital income. Since 1970, the share of total income from wages in the U.S. has fallen from about 72% to less than 64%. This drop is one of the factors in rising inequality in the U.S. (Goodwin et al., 2013). In the US, the top 1% of the population own more than half of all stocks and mutual funds, and the top 10% own more than 90% of all stock and mutual funds. Further, the top 10% also hold more than 60% in pension accounts. Over the past three decades, America's most affluent families have added to their net worth while those at the bottom have dipped into "negative wealth," meaning the value of their debts exceeds the value of their assets (Inequality.org, n.d.).

The neoliberal policies that have fostered this shift in hegemonic power to the financial class and the turn toward the financialization of the economy and society are numerous. Post-Keynesian research emphasizing the "shareholder revolution" of the 1980s has argued that CEOs prioritize the transfer of cash to shareholders over the regular, important investment in productive expansion and wages. According to one study, corporations at the height of the 2007 bubble paid out 9% of GDP in stock buybacks and dividends to shareholders. This was the highest rate in the last 70 years and is more than 1.7 times the corporate earnings of that year (Konczal & Abernathy, 2015). Importantly, policies of financial liberalization have removed barriers to capital accumulation at a global level. Financial capital has been freed from its national restrictions whether as international investment (the acquisition of real assets located in one country by citizens, firms, or governments of another country) or as international finance (international borrowing or lending). Beginning in the early 1970s, market economies around the world began removing government oversight of their financial sectors. The process accelerated in the 1980s, and most market economies had largely deregulated their financial sectors by the mid-1990s. The liberalization of the financial sector included the liberalization of capital accounts, which allowed banks and corporations to freely borrow money abroad, and the removal of restrictions on capital outflows and repatriation of profits. Financial liberalization also included the liberalization of domestic financial sectors, and liberalization of markets in stocks and other securities that allowed foreigners to freely invest and repatriate profits. Further, it has created few restrictions on the types of financial instruments that can be bought and sold, and minimal controls on leverage (Daly & Farley, 2011). Other significant policies include the creation of a whole host of new financial instruments, massive consumer credit to fuel consumption, and the role of the stock market in driving growth. Advances in information technology have also abetted in the emergence of a truly unified global capital market (Bello, 2006).

In sum, financialization is marked by rising inequality and the hegemonic rise of a super-wealthy financial class. Relatedly, it has also resulted in the overaccumulation of capital channeling into the financial sector. As Peet (2011) points out, huge surpluses are accruing in the hands of relatively few people who cannot possibly consume such surpluses, and therefore they must save and invest. Some Marxist scholars link financialization and neoliberalism as a whole to a chronic, underlying structural crisis of capitalism, that of overaccumulation and overproduction.[1] Chesnais (2017), for example, argues that the contemporary era of capitalism is characterized by large amounts of capital looking for profitable investment in a setting of underlying overproduction and low profits. At a global level, Chesnais traces sources of overaccumulation to processes that date back to the 1960s and 1970s and continue until today. He cites factors such as the servicing of government debt in numerous countries, the play in Keynesian terms of the declining marginal propensity to consume of high-income brackets, the accumulation of rent and surplus value in Middle East and Asian Sovereign Funds, and, as accumulation falters, the overaccumulation of non-reinvested corporate profits. Baran and Sweezy (1966) link the overaccumulated capital with the structure of the contemporary capitalist economy, which they term "monopoly capitalism," that is, capitalism dominated by monopolists and oligopolists rather than competitive capitalism. The huge surpluses generated in monopoly capitalism are captured by monopolists/oligopolists. Today, this overaccumulated capital, failing to find profitable outlets in the real economy, is not being reinvested in production but is instead being hoarded and fueling financial accumulation (Foster, 2007; Chesnais, 2017).

A thorough investigation of the nuances of such arguments on overaccumulation of capital and the financial sector is beyond the space of this book; however, what is significant is that the rise in the hegemony of the financial sector has produced one of the most paradoxical and deleterious features of the current capitalist world-system. On the one hand, the escalation of a global socio-ecological crisis is marked by the rapid destruction and depletion of extra-human Nature, and, on the other hand, a tremendous accumulation of capital in the financial sector is incessantly circling the globe in search of the highest yields. In the face of this crisis/paradox, the questions that remain are: in what ways does this pose a serious problem for global socio-ecological sustainability? How does the workings of the financial system exacerbate the ecological contradictions of capitalism? What role does financial capital play in ecological imperialism?

Some financialization literature focuses on the restructuring of entire categories of social life that have been securitized and turned into a kind of capital. Correspondingly from the environmental side, a number of scholars have noted the ways in which new areas of the environment are increasingly "financialized." They term this the "financialization of Nature." The financialization of Nature involves a process whereby Nature is broken down into its constitutive elements, monetized, and traded, transformed into yet another form of investment for speculative capital. For example, land, water, and even specific ecosystem services such as carbon sinks are monetized and traded (Lohman, n.d.; World Rainforest Movement, 2012; Friends of the Earth, 2015). Such "financialization of Nature" appears to also be happening under the guises of environmental conservation through a reconceptualization of conserved Nature in monetary and tradable terms (Sullivan, 2013). The problem with such financialization, according to the critics, is that it rationalizes human and non-human Nature to conform to an economic system that privileges price over other values, profit-oriented market exchanges over the distributive and sustainable logics of other economic systems (Sullivan, 2013), and subjugates all socio-ecological processes to the short-term logic of financial profit.

Other authors have looked at the dynamics of specific financial institutions and the environment, such as private equity funds that are particularly aggressive in their global infrastructure operations and push for ultra-high rates of return despite social and environmental costs (Bracking, 2012; Hildyard, 2012). Still others have noted how environmental and financial crises combine to create perverse dynamics of resource grabbing. For example, particularly for the case of land and water, climate change and land degradation have resulted in food price spikes. With the search for safe investments following the 2007–2008 financial crisis, investors have targeted large-scale land investments overseas as lucrative and safe investments. This dynamic has, in turn, resulted in land grabbing, dispossession, and all the other negative issues discussed throughout this book (Klare, 2012; Sassens, Davis et al., 2015).

What the following sections seek is to deepen and expand the current literature by drawing attention first to the fundamental characteristics that are unique to financial capital as "money-as-commodity" and how these characteristics inherently conflict with the global ecology, and second to how financial capital operates in the capitalist world-system as a mechanism of ecological imperialism. To do so necessitates returning to some fundamental propositions by Marx in his observations of interest-bearing capital and addressing some relevant insights from ecological economics.

Financial Capital and Ecological Imperialism

The Expansionary Role of Interest-Bearing Capital and a Critique of "Green" Finance

In the most basic sense, financial capital is implicated in every environmental crisis because it is precisely what enables and drives the expansion of capitalism, both domestically in its country of origin and globally in the case of imperialism. Interest is the root of profit in the financial sector, and Marx's observations of the role that interest-bearing capital plays in the accumulation process in capitalism remain highly relevant for understanding the dynamics of global socio-ecological crises today. As Marx (1999) wrote on interest-bearing capital in *Capital Volume III*, money itself under capitalist relations of production can be transformed into capital; money can become a potential means to the production of profit. In other words, money becomes a commodity whose price is interest, which yields a profit within a specific period of time. Marx points out that *what is new in capitalism is that a large number of loans serve the enrichment of the debtors: they borrow money to use it as capital.* This form of credit, which only existed as an exception in pre-bourgeois societies, is the typical form of credit for capitalist enterprises. The special form of circulation of modern interest-bearing capital is M-M-C-M'-M" in which the first M represents the advance of money from the lender to the industrialist, the second M represents the use of this money to finance a profit-yielding production process, and M' and M" represent a double return that first goes to the industrial capitalist and then goes from the industrial capitalist to the lender. The return to the industrial capitalist contains a profit (in the case of successful valorization), and the return to the lender contains interest, which is paid from this profit (Heinrich, 2004).

Quite simply, finance of some sort is implicated in nearly every economic activity because finance is the source of funding, and nearly every economic activity under capitalism (from extraction to production to distribution to consumption) has troubling implications for the environment. As Marx points out (Vasudevan, 2017), with credit the expansion of individual capitalist enterprises need not be limited to the reinvestment of their retained earnings. Thus, the system of credit accelerates the expansion of the scale of production, development of technology, and creation of the world market. Further, large financial actors in contemporary capitalism have been shown to hold significant corporate control globally (Vitali et al., 2011; Fichtner et al., 2017). If the machinations of the global capitalist economy are destroying the planet, then interest-bearing capital as credit and the central source of funding are the lifeblood that enables the economy and expands it. Financial capital intensifies the global ecological crises—a system built on debt and the repayment of that debt with interest that is locked into endless growth. This is why, as following sections will explain, international negotiations on climate change (the Paris Climate Agreement) and biodiversity loss (Aichi

Biodiversity targets) that seek to rein in the activities of financial capital fall drastically short in doing so.

Marx's second relevant insight to the topic at hand is that the capitalist financial system functions as a massive engine of centralization and concentration. Marx had argued that the essential nature of financial profits is an appropriation of unpaid labor time, which when non-reinvested back into the process of production coalesces into what he termed "hoard form" or "latent money capital." This coalescence of non-reinvested money then becomes available as loanable money. In other words, profits that are not reinvested in the sphere in which they were realized are now available for investment in other branches. Similarly, all revenue streams that are not immediately spent, including ground rent and savings from workers, also assume the form of deposits and can be loaned out by the banking system. With the growth of the banking system, the volume of financial assets and securities will also expand. This results in the proliferation of what Marx calls "fictitious capital." Fictitious capital refers to tradable titles that constitute claims on future flows of income and surplus. In contemporary capitalism, many forms of revenue coalesce (aside from the hoarding of industrial profit), such as workers' savings, land rent, and the servicing of Third World debt, and are centralized not only through banks, but through a wide variety of financial institutions (Chesnais, 2017).

The significance, in a *political* economic sense, is, as Marx stated, that small amounts of revenue, which by themselves are incapable acting as money capital, merge together into larger masses and form a money power—a money power that flows back into financial institutions and enriches the capitalists who can lend and profit from it in terms of both money and power (Chesnais, 2017). In other words, interest-bearing capital, which has its basis in the exploitation of labor-power as well as the exploitation of Nature, concentrates and centralizes as a money power under the service of a specific faction of capital—the financial class. Under the control of the financial class, this money power provides the continuous funding, the dynamism and the push, for the endless expansion of capitalism.

Ecological economics also offers the relevant criticism that financial assets, as mere mathematical abstractions, have no real relation to biophysical reality. Like IOUs, financial assets can be exchanged for real wealth; they entitle their owners to a share of the real wealth that society produces, current and in the future. But also like IOUs, financial assets are simply a measure of debt. This is problematic because as abstractions financial assets can seemingly increase without limit in the short run. Unlike the production of real wealth, which necessitates the resources, the land and water for production, the fuel for transportation, and the sink capacities to absorb wastes, financial assets are not constrained by biophysical realities. The short-time growth in financial assets can sustain the illusion that the economy continues to grow even as the resources essential to economic production become more scarce. Ultimately, however, financial assets for society as a whole are debts to be paid back out of future real growth. In the short term, economic production can deplete natural capital to keep pace with financial sector growth, but only at the cost of far more catastrophic crises in the future. When the value of present real wealth plus biophysically constrained production capacity is no longer sufficient to serve as liens to guarantee the exploding debt, the debt must implode. Financial crises, ecological economics criticizes, are bound to emerge when biophysical limits become binding. In the end, it is the rest of society which pays the cost both socially and ecologically (Daly & Farley, 2011).

The massive amount of capital in the financial sector and the conflict between the imperatives of financial capital and the needs of sustainability have not escaped policy makers. In more recent years, there have been a number of key policy attempts to rein in and "green" finance. Proponents of "green finance" argue that financial capital should be aligned with sustainability objectives in terms of not undermining environmental objectives as well as funding a global transition toward sustainability (Fleming, 2020). For many reasons, green finance would obviously be a good idea. However, the extent to which this is possible on a global, systemic scale is questionable. Ultimately such stored-up funds in the financial sector are *capital*, and, in the Marxian sense, capital as commodity whose primary objective is to yield M′. While there are growing amounts of finance dedicated to sustainability objectives, numerous studies document how the financial sector as a whole does not operate according to sustainability objectives but continuously undermines it. For example, two of the major planetary boundaries most at risk are biodiversity loss and climate change, and the movement to green finance has done little to alter how the financial sector, as a whole, continues to fund activities pushing these boundaries to crises.

The planet is in the midst of a Sixth Great Extinction in which as many as 30–50% of all species are possibly heading toward extinction by mid-century. However, according to an Organisation for Economic Co-operation and Development (OECD) report (2019) on finance and biodiversity loss, the awareness, commitment, and action for protecting biodiversity by the business sector are very limited. The report states that progress in integrating biodiversity in business and investment decisions remains limited across most corporations, investors, and insurers. Forty-six percent of Financial Times Stock Exchange (FTSE) companies that have a medium to high impact on biodiversity have no policies in place to manage exposure to biodiversity loss. And even though green bonds are rapidly scaling up, they focus primarily on climate change and seldom include biodiversity-relevant finance. Overall, the report estimates that the global finance needed to meet the 20 Aichi Biodiversity Targets[2] by 2020 was estimated at about $150–440 billion per year. In contrast, the global financial flows allotted to protect biodiversity were estimated at about only $52 billion in 2010. Furthermore, based on conservative estimates, financial flows that are harmful to biodiversity (for example, fossil-fuel subsidies and government support to environmentally harmful agriculture) outweigh financial flows for the conservation, sustainable use, and restoration of biodiversity by a factor of ten. In all, the report states that biodiversity and natural-capital assessments often remain an academic exercise, with limited business applications beyond a few industry leaders (OECD, 2019). Only very recently, in 2021, has a more global initiative launched, aimed toward biodiversity protection. The international Taskforce on Nature-related Financial Disclosures (TNFD) is a new global initiative which aims to give financial institutions and companies a complete picture of their Nature-related risks. Its stated task is to develop a framework for corporations and financial institutions to report on Nature-related physical and transition risks that include immediate, material financial risks, Nature dependencies, and impacts and related organization and societal risks (Summerhayes, 2021).

There appear to be several currents in the efforts to green finance. On the one hand, grassroots or bottom-up efforts by NGOs and other civil society groups supply some of the most valuable research linking the financial sector to on-the-ground processes of environmental destruction, dispossession, and the effects on indigenous populations and others in the Global South. These grassroots efforts seek to hold the financial sector accountable and make visible what would largely remain hidden without their investigative work.[3] On the other hand, there is the top-down, pro-market response by the financial sector itself (in part as a response to the criticism from the bottom-up movement). While it is absolutely necessary for the financial sector to be regulated, it is hard not to be a bit cynical about the pro-market-based efforts of the financial sector to become "green" despite the rapidly proliferating rhetoric. While the TNFD website (TNFD, n.d.a), for example, states that its framework will support a shift in global financial flows away from "Nature-negative outcomes" and toward "Nature-positive outcomes," the language on the website is revealing. Much of the language on the website revolves around the high dependency of the global economy on Nature and the fears that Nature loss *represents significant risk to corporate and financial stability*. In fact, much of the green finance movement by the financial sector is couched in terms of "risk to corporate and financial stability." Though the TNFD website states that the Taskforce is informed by stakeholders such as NGOs and research organizations, the Taskforce itself consists of approximately 30 members from industry. One has to wonder about conflict of interests in such cases. For example, the TNDF forum includes BNP Paribas (TNFD, n.d.b), a top investor and creditor in deforestation-risk sectors globally like soy, beef, palm oil, timber rubber, and paper.[4] Further, in the face of the new enthusiasm for green finance, we must recognize that the financial sector has for decades funneled trillions of dollars and received trillions of dollars in profit from activities that are highly environmentally destructive. Only now, after much damage has already been done and the Earth is on the brink of imminent ecological crises, is the financial sector beginning to grapple with the effects of finance on the environment, and it is largely doing so out of concern for how "Nature-based risks" affect the finance sector. Finally, while it is too early to assess the ultimate outcome of initiatives like the TNDG, it, like the Paris Climate Agreement, is a voluntary initiative. Its primary purpose is to give companies a "complete picture of their environmental risks"—not to enforce an international regulation of financial capital that would lawfully prevent investment in environmentally destructive activities.

The situation for climate change is, when examining the financial sector as a whole, also severely lacking. According to the current scientific consensus, limiting warming to the desired 1.5°C threshold will require deep and rapid transitions in the energy, land, urban, industrial, and infrastructure systems. Global emissions must peak between 2020 and 2030, reach net zero around 2050, and then continue to decline through 2100. Scenarios based on 2°C allow for another 10–20 years before emissions must reach net zero (Larsen et al., n.d.). Parties to the United Nations Framework Convention on Climate Change (UNFCCC) agreed, with the 2015 Paris Agreement, to the aims of "holding the increase in global average temperature to well below 2°C above pre-industrial levels" (Article 2.1a) and to "increasing the ability to adapt to the adverse impacts of climate change and foster climate resilience" (Article 2.1b). Article 2.1c of the Paris Agreement calls for "making finance flows consistent with a pathway toward low greenhouse gas emissions and climate-resilient development" (UNFCCC, 2015).

The recent UNFCCC 2018 Biennial Assessment and Overview of Climate Finance Flows (UNFCCC, 2018) did find that there has been a scaling up of climate finance flows, i.e., financial resources dedicated to adapting to and mitigating climate change. It estimates an 18% increase in new investments in the 2015–2016 period compared to 2014, or approximately $680 billion annually. However, aside from the problematic fact that the Paris Agreement is an entirely voluntary international agreement and that nations are not even currently meeting their carbon reduction emissions, while climate finance flows may be increasing, but they remain relatively small when compared to broader finance flows. Further, another report on tracking finance flows by the OECD (2019) critiques the UNFCCC. While the UNFCCC monitors public- and private-led initiatives for mobilizing finance toward activities that *contribute* to climate objectives, they fail to monitor finance that *undermines* climate policy objectives (Jachnik et al., 2019).

What kinds of financial flows continue to undermine the objectives of the Paris Agreement? Private banks, for one, have been identified as major actors in the report compiled by a consortium of NGOs, *Banking on Climate Change: Fossil Fuel Finance Report Card 2019* (Rainforest Action Network et al., 2019), which adds up the lending and underwriting from 33 global banks to the fossil fuel industry as a whole. The report finds these private banks, primarily Canadian, Chinese, European, Japanese, and from the US, have financed fossil fuels with $1.9 trillion since the Paris Agreement was adopted (2016–2018). The report also finds that overall these banks gave $600 billion to these companies that are *expanding* fossil fuel production at a time when, according to the Paris Agreement, humanity must undertake a major shift and begin the phase out of fossil fuel usage. The report also graded banks' overall future-facing policies regarding fossil fuels, assessing them on restrictions on financing for fossil fuel expansion and commitments to phase out fossil fuel financing on a 1.5°C-aligned trajectory. It found that while some banks have taken important steps, overall major global banks have "simply failed to set trajectories adequate for dealing with the climate crisis" (Rainforest Action Network et al., 2019).

Overall, one-third of equity and fixed income assets issued in global financial markets can be classified as belonging to the natural resource and extraction sectors as well as carbon-intensive power utilities, chemicals, construction, and industrial goods firms (Tooze, 2019). As Tooze (2019) states, if we are to stabilize temperatures below catastrophic levels, the vast majority of the world's known fossil fuel reserves will have to stay in the ground. Leaving that energy untapped will mean as much as $28 trillion in lost revenue for oil, gas, and coal companies over the next 20 years. Decarbonization would essentially strand those assets, resulting in losses in asset values for the energy sector of $1 trillion to $4 trillion. In the broader industrial sector, the stranded asset risks could rise to $20 million (Tooze, 2019). BlackRock, holding $6.5 trillion in assets, in particular has come under fire from activist groups, as the world's largest investor in new coal plants. The financial giant's reserves in the fossil fuel industry contributed to 30% of all energy-related carbon emissions from 2017 (SumofUs, 2019). It is no surprise then that the top-down, pro-market rhetoric of greening finance centers so heavily on "reducing Nature-based risk."

Further, according to another study on the role of finance and climate (Galaz et al., 2015), avoiding dangerous climate change requires taking account of the non-linear, threshold dynamics, i.e., tipping points. To avoid such tipping points, reducing greenhouse gas emissions is insufficient; the resilience of specific biomes, particularly the Amazon tropical forest in Brazil and boreal forests in Canada and Russia, must be maintained. However, most current green financial initiatives focus primarily on various ways to reduce emissions through divestment, renewable energy, energy efficiency, and low-carbon transport. Galaz et al. (2015) find that international banks and institutional investors such as insurance companies, asset managers, and pension funds hold significant stocks in key companies responsible for deforestation in these biomes associated with a potential tipping element. The authors also point out how, by their very size, these financial actors have potential to influence companies. However, analysis of the voting behavior of the Big Three (BlackRock, Vanguard, and State Street) shows that these global investors tend to vote against proposals related to Environmental, Social, and Governance (ESG) issues proposed by activist shareholders.

Finally, it must be pointed out that the sheer complexity and opaqueness of global supply chains, operating in many countries with major differences in environmental rules and regulations, stymie the genuine greening of finance. For finance to be truly sustainable, all the economic projects that finance is supporting must, logically, be sustainable. This means that if a financial institution is funding a particular corporation, the entire supply chain of that particular corporation must be proven to be sustainable. And for the entire supply chain to be sustainable, every activity of the supply chain—from extraction to production to distribution—must be sustainable across all measurements of sustainability (not just a reduction of carbon emissions but also in terms of biodiversity loss, deforestation, the disposal of pollution and waste, etc.). However, how many economic activities under global capitalism genuinely meet these sustainable criteria?

Money Fetishism and Ecological Crises

In an era of ecological crises one of the most perplexing and pernicious characteristics of interest-bearing capital is that it bears no mark of its origin, neither the social relations of production from which it originated nor its biophysical roots. Marx had applied this insight to commodities in general, but considered the fetishism of interest-bearing capital as the most extreme. The concept of fetishism in regard to interest-bearing capital may seem merely philosophical or psychological, but there are concrete legal and economic structures that maintain it. As Chesnais (2017) remarks,

> Yet with the fabulous expansion of fictitious capital and transactions on financial markets, money fetishism pervades contemporary capitalism … The banker's and investor's aspiration to autonomy pervades twenty-first century capitalism. But the autonomy of interest-bearing capital and the fictitious forms of capital it takes is necessarily but partial and temporary. The autonomy can never free itself from an ultimate dependency on the effective production and realization of surplus value. The dependency is sheltered by the social and political power of financial capital and the protection it has received from governments.
>
> (pp. 86, 88)

In Ch. XXIV of *Capital Volume III*, Marx wrote of the peculiar and mystifying quality of interest-bearing capital as interest appears to be merely the fruit of the ownership of capital. In contrast to the profit of enterprise, which is more obviously the result of capital functioning in the production process, interest-bearing capital is seemingly removed from the production process. Thus, interest and the profit of enterprise appear to be qualitatively different amounts, originating from different sources. This illusion is strengthened, according to Marx, by the fact that the rate of interest develops on the market as a uniform quantity not dependent upon the individual capitalist (Heinrich, 2004). This results in a highly inverted perception of reality. As Marx (1999) remarked,

> The relations of capital assume their most externalized and most fetish-like form in interest-bearing capital. We have here M-M′, money creating

> more money, self-expanding value, without the process that effectuates these two extremes ... Capital appears as a mysterious and self-creating source of interest- the source of its own increase ... The result of the entire process of reproduction appears as a property inherent in the thing itself. In interest-bearing capital, therefore, this automatic fetish, self-expanding value, money generating money, are brought out in their pure state and in this form it no longer bears the birthmarks of its origin.
>
> (p. 520)

Nonetheless, interest-bearing capital for Marx is ultimately nothing but a portion of the surplus value which the capitalist extorts from the laborer and must pay to the owner and lender of the capital he has borrowed (and the capitalization of the free gifts of Nature, as this chapter will discuss). Marx criticized his contemporary political economists as mistakenly regarding interest-bearing capital as a "self-regulating automaton," a "mere number that increases itself" in which the source of profit is no longer discernible (Marx, 1999). In reality the seemingly inherent capacity of interest-bearing capital to automatically accumulate in geometrical progression rested on the continued domination of capital (itself a product of past labor) over living surplus-labor, a domination dependent on the particular social relations of the capitalist mode of production. Chesnais (2017) extends this argument on finance capital to contemporary capitalism by pointing out how all manner of financial instruments, from bonds and shares to non-interest banking profits as well as various commissions and fees paid to banks by corporations and high-income bracket households, are essentially drawing rights on previously produced surplus value.[5]

This concept of money fetishism must be extended to recognize not only the source of interest as surplus value but also the underlying exploitation of Nature embedded in the capitalist production process. *The "extreme fetishism" of financial capital obscures surplus value as the source of interest, but it also hides the processes of enclosure and accumulation of dispossession that is discussed throughout this book.* While the environmentally degrading activities of extractive transnationals are relatively visible, the interest accruing to the 401(k)s of middle-class American workers appears to have no relation to the environment whatsoever.

Psychologically, the repercussions of this money fetishism separate and alienate the holder of interest-bearing capital from the source of the interest. This psychological disconnect is bound to have repercussions in how seriously society undertakes movements toward sustainability.[6] But aside from an inverted perception of reality, the distance that separates the holder of interest-bearing capital from its socio-ecological roots is reinforced by political and social institutions that favor financial capital over societal and environmental interests. Financial flows are on the whole either not regulated or poorly regulated in regard to social and environmental concerns and lack transparency. While neoliberal financial liberalization has granted financial capital the power to scour the Earth in search of the highest yields, there is currently no overarching international regulation on international financial flows in regard to environmental and social sustainability. Further, there is substantial variation across financial institutions on basic definitions of "sustainability" and "green."

Chapter 7 delves more deeply into these issues for the case of palm oil and deforestation, but the following are some additional examples. A World Resources Institute report (Larsen et al., n.d.) analyzed the role of Multilateral Development Banks (MDBs) in supporting the Paris Agreement. MDBs have a critical role to play in helping countries meet the temperature goal laid out in the Paris Agreement. MDBs are major finance providers to developing countries. They also directly or indirectly mobilize additional finance by acting as lead investors and attracting others to invest alongside them. MDBs set standards that are often followed by other financial institutions, companies, and governments through the projects they invest in and the policies they apply. The MDBs have, on paper, committed to supporting the implementation of the Paris Agreement. At the One Planet Summit in December 2017, MDBs and the bilateral and national development banks that are members of the International Development Finance Club (IDFC) reaffirmed "their joint commitment to align their financial flows with the Paris Agreement" (Larsen et al., n.d.).

The biggest issue, according to the report, is that while MDBs are scaling up their climate-focused finance, they have not aligned their overall portfolios with the Paris Agreement's goals. That is, they are not ceasing to invest in high-emissions activities that drive the climate crisis and do not take climate-resilience considerations into account. While the MDBs in the report all identified certain categories of projects and technologies they would not finance, all banks still had allowed some form of activity that was directly misaligned with the Paris Agreement temperature goal. For example, the African Development Bank, Asian Development Bank, Asian Infrastructure Investment Bank, European Investment Bank, and Inter-American Development Bank had no specific exclusions on activities involving coal. The Inter-American Development Bank and Asian Infrastructure Investment Bank had no specific exclusion on activities involving oil, and the World Bank had no specific exclusion on activities involving logging. Further, the report noted that in cases where MDB finance is intermediated through other institutions, such as commercial banks, public development banks, micro-finance institutions, and insurance companies, MDBs lack control over the final use of funding, making it difficult to assess their impact on climate change mitigation. MDBs provide a significant share of their funding through financial intermediaries (around 20–50% depending on the MDB).

The degree to which private banks have adopted sustainability policies also varies widely across individual institutions. In November 2018, the United Nations Environment Program Finance Initiative and a coalition of 28 banks from around the world launched the Principles for Responsible Banking (PRBs) for global public consultation. The new principles seek to align the banking sector with the Paris Climate Agreement and the UN Sustainable Development Goals (SDGs), setting out a new framework that will hold the banks accountable for their environmental, social, and economic impacts. Endorsing banks will need to consistently meet transparency requirements, set adequate targets, and demonstrate progress or risk being removed from the list of signatories. To date, almost 250 banks have joined the movement, representing about a third of the global banking industry (United Nations Environment Programme, n.d.). However, as the massive databank of the NGO BankTrack demonstrates, hundreds of banks continue to be involved in projects that undermine sustainability objectives globally.[7]

Finally, academic work has criticized the methods that financiers use in evaluating the environmental impact of their investments. Bracking (2012) argues that private equity firms, which are dominant investors in the resource-based economies of Africa, and their partners in development finance institutions, employ largely "performative technology" in the environment and development assessment and have only marginal relation to the material world they seek to measure and protect. She argues that the calculative technologies used are dissociated, incomplete, partial, and largely seek to legitimize private equity funds.

At a global level, both the psychological and institutional opacity of money fetishism simply serves to extend the distance between those who benefit from economic activities that destroy the environment and those who shoulder the burdens. It is one more layer added to an unequal dynamic that already includes the distance between, for example, wealthy consumers in the Global North and the marginalized in the Global South who bear the burden of this consumption. It is, in other words, one more channel for the usurpation of global Natures and the funneling of profits to a specific class. One may argue that because of money fetishism and the general complexity of the global economy what may be the most crucial dynamics of contemporary capitalism are hidden. The connections between the exploitation of the working class and the growth of financial profits, the staggering inequality of global wealth, the contradictions of faltering real investment, the overaccumulation of capital in the financial sector, and the role of financial capital in perpetuating the processes of enclosure and accumulation by dispossession overseas are completely obscured to most analyses.

Finance and Ecological Imperialism: Seminal Developments in the Neoliberal Era

In the neoliberal era of financialization, where a ridiculously small minority of the world's population hold the vast majority of wealth—and specifically in the financial form—surpluses from exploited labor and exploited Nature are somehow being funneled upward to a hegemonic financial class. Relations of dependency, the hierarchy of the international division of labor, the concentrated monopoly power of footloose and powerful TNCs, etc. (in other words, the workings of imperialism in a capitalist world-system as described in this book) ensure this to be the case. Historically in the capitalist world-system, the financial sector played two major roles when it comes to imperialism—first, as recipient of the surpluses derived from the workings of imperialism, and, second, as enabler and driver of imperialism. This section overviews some of the most seminal developments in the neoliberal era where financial capital has played a critical role in enabling contemporary ecological imperialism, and also where rules and regulations have been rewritten to extend the reach of financial capital for appropriating Global South Natures.

Role of Multilateral Development Banks and Other International Financial Institutions

Since colonialism, finance as loans and debt has functioned as a key source of power of the industrialized North over the peripheral South. Finance has been a crucial component enabling the continuation of capital accumulation by Northern-based multinationals and instrumental in influencing the economic and political policies of the periphery. For example, in the 19th century, with the growth of modern industry and global financial markets, abundant credit was extended to the colonial regions of Africa and Asia and neocolonial regions of Latin America to finance the imports of large US, German, British, and French manufacturers. Later during the Second Industrial Revolution, loans were extended to finance the massive investments undertaken to build the railways, ports, roads, and other infrastructures needed to obtain tropical products and raw materials that were demanded by the colonial powers. Governments from colonial and neocolonial regions borrowed to build needed infrastructure that was often built by foreign companies. Such loans typically had strings attached, with credit extended on condition that bulk of loan be used to purchase equipment from the lending nation as well as to import the necessary labor. Whatever benefits may have ensued from the increased future production of raw materials dissipated in the face of future interest payments and special loan fees (Cypher, 2017).

Luxemburg (Chesnais, 2017) pointed out the connection between such loans, imperialism, and the restoration of the conditions for accumulation for capitalism in the imperial countries. According to Luxemburg, loans allowed realized surplus value, which could not be capitalized in the colonial powers, to be invested in productive capital overseas, such as in railway construction and waterworks. In these productive overseas activities, industrial materials were supplied by the country where the capital originated. Luxemburg saw international loans and debt as a key means of political domination between imperialist and semi-colonial countries. Loans and debt also served as a release of overaccumulated capital and ensured the continuation of capital accumulation through external means. International loans converted the money of non-capitalist groups into capital, transformed money capital into productive capital, and transferred accumulated capital from old capitalist countries to young ones. Ultimately, however, the interest on such loans had to be paid by the citizens of the colonized countries.[8]

These issues remain relevant today. As discussed repeatedly throughout this book, following the developing world debt crises of the 1980s, IFIs such as the World Bank and other international financial institutions such as the IMF have been central in precipitating the transformation of Global South Natures along laissez-faire pro-market lines and thereby creating the foundation of ecological imperialism. To repeat briefly here, it was ultimately through the structural adjustment policies of the IFIs that the incipient economic nationalism of the Third World and their push for resource sovereignty were defeated. The IFIs structural adjustment policies reemphasized the ideology of static comparative advantage, economic growth through intensive exports, and the downsizing of the state particularly in regard to social safety nets and environmental regulation. As part of loan conditions, the World Bank has often required nations to increase agricultural and natural resource exports, liberalize trade in extractive industries, and cut government spending for conservation to receive a structural adjustment loan. The World Bank has also provided investment loans for projects in agriculture, forestry, mining, and infrastructure. All of these trends are well known, and larger-scale empirical studies have studied the link between IFIs loans and environmental problems. For example, Shandra et al. (2008) found that higher levels of IMF structural adjustment are associated with more deforestation. Shandra, Shircliff, and London (2011) found that low- and middle-income nations that receive a World Bank International Finance Corporation loan tend to have higher rates of deforestation than low- and middle-income nations that do not receive such a loan.

Further, it is impossible to separate the actions of these institutions from the wider global financial community; multilateral development banks such as the World Bank are centralizing agents for other financial actors, directly or indirectly mobilizing additional finance by acting as lead investors and attracting others to invest alongside them. MDBs set standards that are often followed by other financial institutions, companies, and governments through the projects they invest in and the policies they apply. Many private banks look to the IFC for leadership in their lending procedures and use the IFC Performance Standards to guide them.

Liberalization of International Finance and International Investment

While the actions of IFIs such as the World Bank and the IMF were instrumental in creating the political economic context for ecological imperialism through liberalizing trade and foreign investment laws, financial liberalization is the third critical pillar of neoliberal globalization. The usual criticisms of financial liberalization have focused on such issues as increasing financial instability and currency speculation. However, from an ecological perspective, the Nature of the Global South under neoliberal globalization has become a site of accumulation for global financial capital through the entanglement of a wide variety of financial actors with corporations in the natural resource sectors. In many cases the corporations are multinational but many are also domestically based and receive funding from a wide variety of global financial institutions.

Alongside liberalization of trade and foreign investment, the previous decades have also seen the deregulation of capital controls globally, the expansive development of the international capital market,[9] and the exponential increase of international financial flows enabled by these factors. Prior to the neoliberal era of financial deregulation, capital controls, which limit the amount of money that can be brought into or out of a country, were enforced strictly. Capital controls limited the extent to which a country's firms and residents could invest overseas, put funds in a bank abroad, or finance the setting up of factories overseas. In contrast to the post-WWII era of strict controls, there are relatively few capital controls left in the world. By the 1970s and 1980s, the ideological stance against capital controls dominated as economists shifted in favor of free trade and fewer government restrictions. Starting with the industrialized First World, countries progressively dismantled barriers to private capital flows across their borders and the IMF was instrumental in getting developing countries to lift their capital controls. The growth of new technology also made capital controls harder to enforce (Krugman & Obstfeld, 2006).

As a result, the scale of transactions in the international capital market has grown more quickly than world GDP since the early 1970s. In the early 1960s, most banking business was purely domestic, involving the currency and customers of the bank's home country. Two decades later many banks were deriving a large share of their profits from international activities. Other financial actors, such as commercial banks, corporations, and non-bank financial institutions (insurance companies, pension funds, mutual funds), have become important players in the international capital market as they have moved into foreign assets to diversify their portfolios. International trade in assets—bonds and deposits, shares of stocks, currency options, or the purchase of foreign real estate and direct acquisition of a factory in another country—is utilized as a way of reducing risk through portfolio diversification abroad. For developing countries, the orthodox justification for capital control liberalization is that it allows countries scarce in capital to utilize the savings from other countries in order to fund large development projects. Overall, this allows businesses and governments to have more places where they can get funding and investors more choices of where to best put their money (Krugman et al., 2018).

The problems of ecological imperialism associated with globalized financial capital are, of course, wholly outside the box of orthodox considerations. The standard textbooks on international economics make no mention of these issues (Krugman et al., 2018). For example, the capacity for companies operating in natural resource sectors to obtain funding globally creates a situation in which, as long as such companies are profitable, they can obtain funding no matter their environmental or social record. As Chapter 7 discusses, in the case of palm oil, some European banks, wary over the environmental and social repercussions of palm oil production, have started withdrawing their financing; however, investors from Southeast Asia are filling the void. As Chapter 7 argues, financial liberalization and the tremendous growth of global capital markets have opened a Pandora's box. In this context the Earth's manifold resources are enclosed, privatized, and marketized by the architecture and rules of international trade and foreign investment, and absorbed into the territory of international financial capital through global capital markets.

Overaccumulated Capital in the Financial Sector and Ecological Imperialism

The link between the export of excess capital and imperialism has been a central theme of classical theories of imperialism. Since the early neocolonialism of places like Latin America in the 19th century, the internationalization of finance has acted as a pressure release valve for the overaccumulated capital that has flowed into the financial sector. It has acted as an external fix that allows realized surplus value, which cannot be capitalized in the country of origin, to be invested in productive capital overseas. This dynamic is no less important today, but there have been some significant changes in the past several decades, most notably the deepening of capitalist relations of production globally and consequently, emerging economies becoming important loci of accumulation.

For emerging economies, at least a portion of the overaccumulated capital in their financial sector flows into Global South projects that directly fund extraction, build the infrastructure necessary for it, or is directly involved in speculation and enclosure of ecological commons, such as land. Consider, for example, the case of China's "going out policy," whose ecological incentives and repercussions were discussed in Chapter 5. One driving force of China's outgoing FDI has been its massive foreign reserves accumulated since the early 2000s. Invested mostly in US government debt, China's reserves were generating low returns. In response, a consensus emerged that China would be better off investing in other types of assets overseas and the amount of outgoing FDI and aid rose dramatically. The "go global" strategy is one of the main drivers of China's dramatic increase in investment over the past decade as the country seeks to access natural resources, stimulate exports, and build markets abroad (Wang, 2016).

Finance in the Hierarchy of the Capitalist World-System

Unsurprisingly, capital in the financial sector mirrors the hierarchy of the world-system, meaning it is primarily concentrated in core Northern countries. In 2017 the combined assets of the 500 biggest asset managers reached \$93.8 trillion, but the top 20 firms in 2018 controlled a record 43% of assets. Managers in North America represented 58.1% of assets while European managers controlled 31.8% of assets, and Japanese managers controlled 4.8%. The rest of the world controlled a mere 5.2% of assets (Segal, 2018). European, US, Japanese, and Chinese banks constitute the world's top 50 largest banks (Sanders, 2018). In contrast, funding sources in regions like sub-Saharan Africa, where resource industries are dominated by foreign multinational corporations, are also dominated by foreign wealthier countries. BankTrack, for example, has tracked the financing of nine major extractive projects in sub-Saharan Africa that are riddled with social and environmental problems, from land grabbing to issues of political corruption and environmental degradation. The vast majority of funding comes from European, US, and Asian financiers.

With the growth of capitalist relations of production globally, it must be emphasized how emerging economies are growing as important loci of accumulation and how their financial reserves are being funneled into natural resource sectors throughout the Global South. While Chapter 7 goes into more detail with the case of Asian investors in the palm oil sector, Table 6.1 shows the top ten financiers behind deforestation-risk companies in West and Central Africa, Latin America, and Southeast Asia for beef, soy, palm oil, pulp and paper, and timber. In Table 6.1 we can see that while investors from traditional core economies such as Japan, the EU, the UK, and the US are still significant players, investors from emerging economies such as Brazil and Malaysia are now prominent.

Table 6.1 Top Ten Creditors and Investors 2013–2021 in Deforestation-Risk Companies

Creditors	*Credit (USD Millions)*	*Headquarters*	*Investors*	*Investment (USD Millions)*	*Headquarters*
Banco de Brazil	47,436	Brazil	Permodalan Nasional Berhad	5,710	Malaysia
Bradesco	13,037	Brazil	Employees Provident Fund	4,162	Malaysia
Rabobank	8,671	Netherlands	BNDES	2,934	Brazil
Mizuho Financial	8,109	Japan	BlackRock	2,066	United States
Itau Unibanco	7,770	Brazil	Vanguard	1,894	United States
JPMorgan Chase	7,584	United States	KWAP Retirement Fund	1,274	Malaysia
Malayan Banking	7,504	Malaysia	Lembaga Kemajuan Tanah Persekutuan (FELDA)	1,110	Malaysia
HSBC	6,795	United Kingdom	Fidelity Investments	1,079	United States
Santander	6,685	Spain	Government Pension Investment Fund (GPIF)	862	Japan
BNP Paribus	6,089	France	Government Pension Fund Global	582	Norway

Source: Data compiled from the Forests & Finance website https://forestsandfinance.org/

Conclusion

Neoliberalism, enabled by a host of economic, institutional, legal, policy, and ideological changes, has resulted in a shift in contemporary capitalism to favor the interests of the financial class. Financialization has led to proliferating inequality, particularly of wealth, and the rise of a hegemonic financial class that holds much of its wealth as financial assets rather than productive activities. This shift has led to a number of important consequences for Nature and ecological imperialism. As tremendous surpluses are accruing in the hands of relatively few people who cannot possibly consume them and must also save and invest, contemporary capitalism is characterized by a build-up of capital accumulated within the financial sector. With financial liberalization and the growth of global capital markets, the previously exploited surplus value of ordinary workers in the Global North and the Global South, and the surpluses of exploited Nature, are concentrated and turned into a form of money power at the hands of a hegemonic global financial class. Circling the globe in trillions of dollars, this money capital continuously drives endless economic growth and accumulation by dispossession. If surplus value and the capitalization of the free gifts of nature are at the root of interest-bearing capital, they have coalesced into a form that stands in antagonism to Nature and workers and serves as a mechanism of discipline through debt in multiple forms or funding initiatives of neoliberal development.

The concentration of money capital into mammoth financial institutions with trillions of dollars in assets has created a situation in which international financial investors influence the fate of ecological conditions globally. Financial liberalization and the growth of global capital markets have enabled financiers to invest globally and corporations to borrow globally, regardless of their environmental or social records. This has opened a Pandora's box of financial capital that is difficult to regulate. Ultimately, this accumulated financial wealth mirrors the hierarchical international division of labor as it is largely located in the Global North, though emerging economies are increasingly important loci of accumulation. The entanglement of a wide variety of global financial actors with corporations, both domestic and multinational, in the natural resource sectors of the Global South is a channel of ecological imperialism, a direct funneling of profits to the hegemonic financial class. It represents another layer of inequality alongside the control of peripheral resources by TNCs and ecologically unequal exchange.

References

Act!onaid, Friends of the Earth, inclusive development international, & Rede Social de justiça e direitos humanus. (2017). *Invested in exploitation? TIAA's links to land grabbing and deforestation*. https://foe.org/resources/invested-exploitation-tiaas-ties-land-grabbing-deforestation/

BankTrack. (n.d.). *Dodgy deals map*. https://www.banktrack.org/dodgy_deals_map

Baran, P.A., & Sweezy, P.M. (1966). *Monopoly capital.* New York: Monthly Review Press.

Bello, W. (2006). The capitalist conjuncture: Over-accumulation, financial crises, and the retreat from globalisation source. *Third World Quarterly, 27*(8), 1345–1367. https://doi.org/10.1080/01436590601027222

Bracking, S. (2012). How do investors value environmental harm/care? Private equity funds, development finance institutions and the partial financialization of nature-based industries. *Development and Change, 43*(1), 271–293. https://doi.org/10.1111/j.1467-7660.2011.01756.x

Chesnais, F. (2017). *Finance capital today: Corporations and banks in the lasting global slump.* Chicago, IL: Haymarket Books.

Cypher, J. (2017). *The process of economic development.* (4th edition). London and New York: Routledge.

Daly, H.E., & Farley, J.C. (2011). *Ecological economics: Principles and applications.* Washington, DC: Island Press.

Data Deep Dive. (n.d.). Forests & Finance. Retrieved December 10, 2021, from https://forestsandfinance.org/data/

Davis, K.F., Rulli, M.C., & D'Odorico, P. (2015). The global land rush and climate change. *Earth's Future, 3*(8), 298–311. https://doi.org/10.1002/2014EF000281

Fichtner, J., Heemskerk, E.M., & Garcia-Bernardo, J. (2017). Hidden power of the Big Three? Passive index funds, re-concentration of corporate ownership, and new financial risk. *Business and Politics, 19*(2), 298–326. https://doi.org/10.1017/bap.2017.6

Fleming, S. (2020). What is green finance and why is it important? *World Economic Forum.* https://www.weforum.org/agenda/2020/11/what-is-green-finance/

Foster, J.B. (2007). The financialization of capitalism. *Monthly Review.* https://monthlyreview.org/2007/04/01/the-financialization-of-capitalism/

Foster, J.B., & Holleman, H. (2010). The financial power elite. *Monthly Review.* https://monthlyreview.org/2010/05/01/the-financial-power-elite/

Friends of the Earth. (2015). *Financialization of nature: Creating a new definition of nature.* https://www.foei.org/wp-content/uploads/2015/11/FoEI-financialization-of-nature-ENG.pdf

Galaz, V., Moberg, F., Gars, J., Repinski, C., & Nykvist, B. (2015). Why ecologists should care about financial markets. *Trends in Ecology & Evolution, 30*(10), 571–580. https://doi.org/10.1016/j.tree.2015.06.015

Goodwin, N.R., Harris, J.M., Nelson, J.A., Roach, B., & Torras, M. (Eds.). (2013). *Microeconomics in Context* (3rd edition). London: Routledge.

Harvey, D. (2005). *A brief history of neoliberalism.* Oxford: Oxford University Press. https://doi.org/10.1093/oso/9780199283262.001.0001

Heinrich, M. (2004). *An introduction to the three volumes of Karl Marx's capital.* New York: Monthly Review Press.

Hildyard, N. (2012). *More than bricks and mortar infrastructure as asset class: A critical look at private equity infrastructure funds.* The Corner House. http://www.thecornerhouse.org.uk/resource/more-bricks-and-mortar

Inequality.org. (n.d.). *Wealth inequality in the United States.* https://inequality.org/facts/wealth-inequality/

Jachnik, R., Mirabile, M., & Dobrinevski, A. (2019), Tracking finance flows towards assessing their consistency with climate objectives. *OECD Environment Working Papers,* 146. https://doi.org/10.1787/82cc3a4c-en

Klare, M. (2012). *The race for what's left: The global scramble for the world's last resources.* New York: Picador.

Konczal, M., & Abernathy, N. (2015, July 27). *Defining financialization: Society, savings, wealth, power.* Roosevelt Institute. https://rooseveltinstitute.org/wp-content/uploads/2020/07/RI-Defining-Financialization-201507.pdf

Krugman, P., Obstfeld, M., & Melitz, M. (2018). *International economics: Theory and policy.* (11th edition). Boston, MA: Pearson Addison Wesley.

Larsen, G., Smith, C., Krishnan, N., Weischer, L., Bartosch, S., & Fekete, H. (n.d.). *Toward Paris alignment: How the multilateral development banks can better support the Paris Agreement.* World Resources Institute. https://wriorg.s3.amazonaws.com/s3fs-public/toward-paris-alignment_1.pdf

Lohman, L. (n.d.). *Ecosystem service trading.* The Corner House.org. http://www.thecornerhouse.org.uk/sites/thecornerhouse.org.uk/files/ECOSYSTEM%20SERVICE%20TRADING.pdf

Marx, K. (1999). *Capital: A critique of political economy, volume III, The process of capitalist production as a whole* (F. Engels, Ed.). International Publishers. (Original work published 1894). https://www.marxists.org/archive/marx/works/download/pdf/Capital-Volume-III.pdf

Lapavitsas, C., & Mendieta-Muñoz, I. (2016). The profits of financialization. *Monthly Review.* https://monthlyreview.org/2016/07/01/the-profits-of-financialization/

Organisation for Economic Co-operation and Development (OECD). (2019). *Biodiversity: Finance and the economic and business case for action, Prepared by the OECD for the French G7 Environment Ministers' Meeting, 5–6 May 2019.* https://www.oecd.org/env/resources/biodiversity/biodiversity-finance-and-the-economic-and-business-case-for-action.htm

Palley, T. (2007). *Financialization: What it is and why it matters.* Levy Economics Institute of Bard College. https://www.levyinstitute.org/pubs/wp_525.pdf

Peet, R. (2011). Contradictions of finance capitalism. *Monthly Review.* https://monthlyreview.org/2011/12/01/contradictions-of-finance-capitalism/

Rainforest Action Network, BankTrack, Sierra Club, Oilchange International, Indigenous Environmental Network, Honor the Earth. (2019). *Banking on climate change: Fossil fuel finance report card 2019.* https://www.ran.org/wp-content/uploads/2019/03/Banking_on_Climate_Change_2019_vFINAL1.pdf

Sanders, D. (2018). Biggest banks in the world 2018. *Global Finance.* https://www.gfmag.com/magazine/november-2018/biggest-banks-world-2018

Sassen, S. (2014). *Expulsions: Brutality and complexity in the global economy.* Cambridge, MA: Belknap Press.

Segal, J. (2018). *The asset management industry is getting more concentrated.* Institutional Investor. https://www.institutionalinvestor.com/article/b1bk8n82qcc0kt/The-Asset-Management-Industry-Is-Getting-More-Concentrated

Shandra, J., Shor, E., Maynard, G., & London, B. (2008). Debt, structural adjustment and deforestation: A cross-national study. *Journal of World-Systems Research, 14*(1), 1–21. https://doi.org/10.5195/jwsr.2008.345

Shandra, J. M., Shircliff, E., & London, B. (2011). The International Finance Corporation and forest loss: A cross-national analysis. *Journal of World-Systems Research, 17*(2), 328–352. https://doi.org/10.5195/jwsr.2011.419

Sullivan, S. (2012). Banking nature? The spectacular financialization of environmental conservation. *Antipode, 45*(1), 198–217. https://doi.org/10.1111/j.1467-8330.2012.00989.x

Summerhayes, G., & Waterford, L. (2021). Biodiversity loss is a risk to the global financial system. *The Guardian*. https://www.theguardian.com/commentisfree/2021/jul/04/biodiversity-loss-could-wreck-the-global-financial-system-and-its-only-a-matter-of-time

SumofUS. (2019). *BlackRock: Stop financing the climate catastrophe!* SumofUs. https://actions.sumofus.org/a/blackrock-stop-financing-a-climate-catastrophe

Sweezy, P.M. (1994). The triumph of financial capital. *Monthly Review*. https://monthlyreview.org/1994/06/01/the-triumph-of-financial-capital/

Taskforce on Nature-related Financial Disclosure (TNFD). (n.d.a). *About*. https://tnfd.global/about/

TNFD. (n.d.b). *The TNFD Forum*. TNFD Taskforce on Nature-related Financial Disclosures. https://tnfd.global/about/the-tnfd-forum/

Tooze, A. (2019). Why central banks need to step up on global warming. *Foreign Policy*. https://foreignpolicy.com/2019/07/20/why-central-banks-need-to-step-up-on-global-warming/

UNFCCC. (2018). *Biennial assessment and overview of climate finance flows -2018*. UNFCCC. https://unfccc.int/BA-2018

United Nations Environment Programme (UNEP). (n.d.). *Principles for responsible banking*. https://www.unepfi.org/banking/bankingprinciples/

United Nations Framework Convention on Climate Change (UNFCCC). (2015). *Adoption of the Paris Agreement*. https://unfccc.int/sites/default/files/english_paris_agreement.pdf

Van Den Berg, H. (2017). *International economics: A heterodox approach* (3rd edition). London: Routledge.

Vasudevan, R. (2017). The significance of Marx's theory on money: Marx's analysis of monetary phenomena has remarkable resonance in today's world. *Monthly Review*. https://mronline.org/2017/09/18/the-significance-of-marxs-theory-on-money/

Vitali, S., Glattfelder, J., & Battiston, S. (2011). The network of global corporate control. *PLOS One, 6(10): e25995*. https://doi.org/10.1371/journal.pone.0025995

Wang, H. (2016). *A deeper look at China's "Going Out" policy*. Center for International Governance Innovation. https://www.cigionline.org/publications/deeper-look-chinas-going-out-policy/

World Rainforest Movement. (2012, August 30). *Growing speculation: From the appropriation and commodification to the financialization of nature*. https://wrm.org.uy/articles-from-the-wrm-bulletin/section1/growing-speculation-from-the-appropriation-and-commodification-to-the-financialization-of-nature/

Notes

1 Harvey (2005), for example, argues that capitalism has been experiencing a chronic difficulty of overaccumulation since 1973. He argues that accumulation by dispossession helped to solve the overaccumulation problem by releasing a set of assets, including labor-power, at very low cost. The answer to the overaccumulation of capital was the neoliberal project of privatization and the release of cheap raw materials into the system to reduce input cost. Bello (2006) argues that neoliberal globalization was the reaction to the underlying structural crisis of capitalism, its chronic crisis of overproduction, over-investment, and overcapacity, which in the 1970s and 1980s took the form of stagnation and disequilibria overtaking the global economy. But globalization has not brought about

an end to the crisis of overproduction. Instead, by 1997 profits in US industry had stopped growing. Financial globalization emerged as the response, and financial speculation, the squeezing of value from already created value, became the most dynamic source of profitability. Globalization and financialization were mechanisms designed to escape the inexorable pressures of overaccumulation and overproduction. However, these mechanisms have worsened it.

2 The Aichi Biodiversity Targets were established by the Convention on Biological Diversity (CBD), a multilateral treaty, in an effort to protect and conserve biodiversity.

3 See, for example, Forests and Finance Deforestation Free Funds, https://deforestationfreefunds.org/ and Fossil Fuel Free Funds https://fossilfreefunds.org/

4 According to the Forests and Finance Data Deep Dive, BNP Paribus extended $USD 6,777 million in credit and invested $USD 53 million in deforestation-risk sectors between 2013 and 2021 (*Data Deep Dive*, n.d.).

5 The nature of bonds and shares, Chesnais (2017) argues, is essentially drawing rights on previously produced surplus value, appropriated in the first case indirectly through the levying of taxes and the servicing of government debt, and in the second case, more directly, through the division of profit between retained profits and dividends.

6 The psychological disconnect that this creates is, in some instances, particularly striking—as for example when researchers directly involved in the criticism and analysis of global environmental degradation participate, often with no other option, in market-based retirement schemes. According to the report, *Invested in Exploitation? TIAA's Links to Land Grabbing and Deforestation* (Act!onaid et al., 2017), Teachers Insurance and Annuity Association (TIAA) is one of the largest pension funds in the United States, with $834 billion in assets under management for clients worldwide in academic, government, research, medical, and cultural fields. While TIAA has established certain investment portfolios that promote social and environmental responsibility, TIAA has at least $172 million exposed to the global palm oil sector, including shares in companies widely known to drive gross deforestation, species extinction, land grabbing, and human rights abuses. According to the report, TIAA has links through holdings in extractive industries to serious cases of forced eviction and displacement.

7 See https://www.banktrack.org/publications for publications and data.

8 As discussed in Chesnais (2017).

9 The international capital market is defined as a group of closely interconnected markets in which asset exchanges with some international dimension take place. The main actors in the international capital market are commercial banks, large corporations, non-bank financial institutions, central banks, and other government agencies. (Krugman & Obstfeld, 2006).

7 The Financing of Palm Oil

If the cultivation of any single crop were to represent the ecological destruction, socio-political conflict, and dispossession associated with cash crop monoculture, many would point to the contemporary cultivation of palm oil. The environmental and social costs of palm oil production have been copiously documented and include deforestation and biodiversity loss (Vijay et al., 2016), contribution to global carbon emissions (Carlson et al., 2016), displacement of peasants and indigenous peoples and violence against them,[1] associated political corruption and oligarchic power structures within palm oil producing countries (TuK INDONESIA, 2018), gross exploitation of palm oil workers (CNBC, 2020), and land grabbing by foreign palm oil companies in places like West and Central Africa (GRAIN, 2014). Palm oil is a crop with a long history of traditional use and there are arguably examples of small-scale, sustainable production. However, the palm oil sector at large is plagued by processes of accumulation by dispossession, backed by multinational corporations, domestic businesses, and oligarchic governmental elites (Gellert, 2015).

Yet behind these governmental and corporate elites stands an array of financiers often hidden from the public eye. More accurately, behind these elites stands an entire neoliberal system of globally liberalized international finance that operates in a manner that drives the expansion of palm oil and funnels profits to specific classes in specific countries. As is the case with many aspects of global ecological crises, the critical role of international finance in driving the expansion of palm oil production is frequently overlooked. More often, the unsustainable expansion of palm oil is attributed to the increase in consumer demand and the inevitable outcome of population growth and urbanization. Certainly, consumers drive the demand for palm oil and the products that use palm oil's derivatives. Yet the financing behind capital-intensive, industrial agricultural crops such as palm oil provides the necessary upfront seed capital without which expansion of production would be impossible. While major palm oil companies are largely Southeast Asian, the financing behind these companies is global and includes a wide consortium of financial actors representative of the contemporary era of global financialization.

DOI: 10.4324/9780429261305-7

This chapter is an analysis of the financing behind palm oil. It is, in other words, an analysis of the direct role of "interest-bearing capital" in enabling and driving the expansion of one of the most socio-ecologically problematic cash crops in the contemporary world. In the history of palm oil, we can categorize two primary sources of financial capital that have driven and enabled its expansion—international financial institutions in tandem with the state (under the auspices of development) and other investors including investment banks and institutional investors. The historical origins of palm oil production in Indonesia, currently the largest producer, are rooted in the funding from international financial institutions, specifically the World Bank and the IMF. Both organizations have provided the funding of palm oil as well as established the necessary development schemes for its success.

The second section of the chapter analyzes the current financing structure of the palm oil sector. It details the roles of a constellation of global financial actors, ranging from investment banks to state-owned banks to various institutional investors, in financing and expanding the palm oil sector in recent decades. It also examines the investment flows according to investor country/region, finding that financial capital in palm oil reflects the hierarchy of the world-system to an extent. Investors from core economies have historically played a significant role in financing palm oil, but Southeast Asian semi-peripheral economies are increasingly important. The final sector overviews the political economy of finance in Southeast Asia and how the availability of global financial capital has helped to foster an oligarchic elite connected to the palm oil industry.

The Origins of the Financing of Palm Oil: The Case of Indonesia

Throughout the periphery and semi-periphery, ecological imperialism hinges on continuing primitive accumulation, whereby previously existing socio-ecological relations are transformed through processes of enclosure, privatization, and marketization. As previous chapters have highlighted, international financial institutions, in particular the structural adjustments policies of the World Bank and the IMF, have played an outsized role in ecological imperialism. Primarily, they have act as catalysts for the transformation of the extractive and agricultural sectors of developing countries through development schemes in the second half of the 20th century that emphasized export-led development. In addition, these institutions, in particular the World Bank, have provided crucial funding for development projects. Palm oil production is the outcome of such development schemes and funding. Since 1965, the World Bank has committed nearly $1 billion to over 35 projects in the palm oil sector—12 countries in Africa, Latin America, and Southeast Asia. Additionally, the IFC since 1976 has invested $311 million in 26 palm oil-related projects and has funded plantations in Indonesia, Thailand, Ghana, and Nicaragua; palm oil refining in Indonesia and Ukraine; and palm oil trading in Indonesia and Singapore (Teoh, n.d.). The stated mission of the World Bank's International Finance Corporation is to deliver financing for businesses in developing countries in order to unlock private investment as well as create markets and opportunities. A strong private sector, according to the IFC website, is crucial to ending poverty (International Finance Corporation, n.d.b). Indonesia is the world's largest producer and exporter of palm oil, and palm oil has been considered a "development corp" that can assist in growth and poverty alleviation. Indonesia has been a central focus of World Bank lending for oil palm development projects and has accounted for slightly over half of the total lending for the sector (Teoh, n.d.).

Previous chapters have highlighted how the dynamics of economic crises, debt, and structural adjustments policies throughout the developing world in the 1980s were instrumental in forming the foundations of ecological imperialism in the neoliberal era. Yet in the byzantine era of economic nationalism and Cold War geopolitics, aid from Western powers to anti-communist, Third World dictatorships, which were often deeply corrupt, were also instrumental in establishing First World objectives in the Third World. In 1965, the Indonesian president, an economic nationalist, was overthrown in a violent coup led by General Suharto with clandestine support from Western powers. According to declassified documents, a 1964 British Foreign Office file called for the defense of Western interests in Southeast Asia because it was a "major producer of essential commodities." Western corporations also played an active role in determining the policies of Suharto; Time-Life, Inc. sponsored a 1967 meeting in Geneva between General Suharto, his economic advisers, and corporate leaders who represented major companies and banks, such as General Motors, Imperial Chemical Industries, British Leyland, British-American Tobacco, American Express, Siemens, Goodyear, the International Paper Corporation, and US steel. With Ford Foundation help, General Suharto reformulated a development partnership with foreign investment (McMichael, 2016).

Backed by military power, General Suharto established his "New Order" regime and installed technocrats to steer development and the massive aid flows from Western nations. Under Suharto's "interventionist government," Indonesia's central bank was reoriented to finance development programs directly through state-owned banks. Palm oil, originally developed as a colonial cash crop by the Dutch, was revived as a strategic commodity for earning foreign exchange, creating employment, accelerating growth in less developed areas, and securing a domestic supply of cooking oil. As executors of development programs, Suharto's regime arranged soft loans to state-owned companies (backed by World Bank credit), credit to smallholders linked with estate companies as buyers, and liquidity credit from Indonesia's central bank. Economic development and social equity as inclusion of palm oil smallholders were given priority, with limited attention to environmental protections (Pramudya et al., 2017).

Overall the Suharto dictatorship, a violent and corrupt military regime, received over $23.1 billion from the World Bank during its 30 years of dictatorship. During Suharto's military rule, Bank-supported economic policy reforms helped accomplish two of the primary currents that drove the ecological imperialism documented throughout this book—on the one hand, domestic regulations that centralized control in the hands of the government and liberalized foreign investment policies, which enabled well-connected elites, investors, and corporations to exploit the nation's natural resources, and on the other hand, the liberalization of trade necessary to create the markets for export. During Suharto's rule, the Forestry Law of 1967, for example, granted the central government's control over all forest areas, effectively legalizing the government's exclusive right to exploit nearly three-quarters of the nation's total land area. The Law on the Basic Provisions of Mining, also passed the same year, legitimized the state's control over all mineral resources and allowed foreign concessions. To the detriment of indigenous peoples and local communities who relied on common forest resources for their livelihoods, much of Indonesia's tropical forest was ceded to private forestry conglomerates with close ties to the government. During the 1970s, as Indonesia became the world's largest exporter of tropical timber, natural wealth and economic profits were plundered out of the country as multinational corporations heavily dominated the logging industry. According to the Bank, Indonesia's gross domestic product grew exponentially from $7.5 billion in 1968 to $242 billion in 1996. In turn, the World Bank considered the pro-growth and "politically stable" environment of Indonesia as a bastion of its neoliberal policies, calling it an "East Asian economic miracle" (Sonkin et al., 2018).

The administrations that followed Suharto's regime adhered to the same natural resource-intensive and pro-foreign investment economic development model. Between the end of military rule and the 1997 Asian economic crisis, the government embraced the Bank's SAPs, during the years known as the *Reformasi* (reform) period. In addition, the International Monetary Fund structural adjustments have played a key role in boosting palm oil production in Indonesia. Due to a prolonged economic crisis and the devaluation of the Indonesian rupiah in early 1997, Indonesia was forced to seek aid from the International Monetary Fund, and by the end of October, a first assistance package was agreed upon. As part of a $43 billion financial rescue package, reforms included stipulations on reducing export taxes on logs, sawn timber, and rattan as well as the removal of restrictions on foreign investment in palm oil plantations (Sonkin et al., 2018). According to one study, the IMF had recommended that Indonesia earn hard currency to repay its debt by restructuring its forest sector, which led to the harvesting of younger trees and more tree species. The IMF letter of intent to the Indonesian government also recommended removing all formal and informal barriers to investment in palm oil plantations. This led to increased forest fire burning in Kalimantan and Sumatra to clear forestland for palm oil plantations (Humphrey, 2006).

The Indonesian government also accepted IMF conditionality-attached loans aimed at making the country more attractive to foreign investors by abolishing its ban on foreign investments in palm oil plantations, liberalizing trade in the agriculture sector, reducing export taxes on timber and minerals, and accelerating the privatization of public enterprises. After 1998, the World Bank's projects and technical assistance loans soared, reaching approximately $4.5 billion by 2003 (Sonkin et al., 2018). As Gellert (2005) wrote,

> In Indonesia, following the crisis, the move toward neoliberalism translates into freer trade and foreign investment regimes and the "creative destruction" of overprotected national industries. Whereas the authoritarian state of Suharto's New Order attempted to bolster its legitimacy through job creation, poverty alleviation, and industrialization, neoliberal globalism implies fewer or no constraints on the plunder of resources, at least until market pressures signal the need for producing new supplies. In brief, neoliberalism implies no necessary "growing up" from primary commodity exports, or more generally no national "development"—at least not with state assistance. In this context, Indonesian timber, palm oil, and pulp and paper all present opportunities for global accumulation. Moreover, given the paucity of domestic capital during the crisis and reforms aimed to reduce barriers to foreign investment, these opportunities should be relatively more available to foreign capital.
>
> (p. 1347)

Both documentation and outcry over the extensive environmental and social damages due to the growth of the palm oil sector have been occurring for decades. Much of the criticism has been directed at the World Bank, and, in particular, at the IFC. The World Rainforest Movement argues that, according to an internal audit, the IFC knowingly allowed commercial interests to override its social and environmental standards by making major loans to the Indonesian oil palm sector despite being aware of the risks and in violation of its own standards (World Rainforest Movement, 2009). Specifically, the internal audit discusses four different investments made in the Wilmar Group, one of the world's largest processors and merchandisers of palm and lauric oils, as well as one of the largest plantation companies in Indonesia and Malaysia, between 2003 and 2008. The report states,

> For more than 20 years, IFC had information at its disposal on significant governance as well as environmental and social risks inherent in the Indonesian oil palm sector. Despite awareness of the significant issues facing it, IFC did not develop a strategy for engaging in the oil palm sector. With regard to its Wilmar Group investments, IFC applied a *de minimis* approach towards assessing each project's supply chain. For each investment, commercial pressures were allowed to prevail and overly influence the categorization and scope and scale of environmental social

> due diligence. Because commercial pressures dominated IFC's assessment process, the result was that environmental and social due diligence reviews did not occur as required.
>
> (Ombudsman, n.d., p. 2)

Problematically, many private banks look to the IFC for leadership in their lending procedures and use the IFC Performance Standards for guidance. According to World Rainforest Movement, complaints from NGOs included the following: failure to recognize the customary rights of local communities; land grabbing with the collusion of local and national state agencies; serious human rights abuses; extensive clearing of areas of forest and peat; illegal practices such as use of fire to clear lands; failure to comply with legal regulations and failure to carry out environmental impact assessments, among others. Over eight years, the Wilmar Group enjoyed IFC patronage as it grew into the world's largest trader of crude palm oil, worth an estimated $7 billion, with factories in Eastern Europe, ports and refineries in Sumatra, shipping facilities, a headquarter in Singapore (World Rainforest Movement, 2009).

By 2009, outcries from environmental groups and NGOs over the social and environmental harms associated with the production of palm oil forced the World Bank to suspend International Finance Corporation funding of the oil palm sector and order a review of existing projects, including the Wilmar Group, on social and environmental grounds (Mongabay, 2009). In 2011, the World Bank Group announced the adoption of a *World Bank Group Framework* and *IFC Strategy for Engagement in the Palm Oil Sector* to guide future engagement in the global palm oil sector. The new framework and strategy were developed following consultations with a wide range of stakeholders including environmental and social NGOs, farmers, indigenous communities, private sector companies, and governments. According to the Bank Group, the new framework would address "regulatory and governance reforms; responsible private investments; improved benefit sharing with smallholders and communities; and development and widespread adoption of environmentally and socially sustainable standards and codes of practice" (World Bank, 2011). *The World Bank Group Framework* and *IFC Strategy for Engagement in the Palm Oil Sector* also claimed it would give priority to institutional and market initiatives that support smallholders and foster benefit sharing with rural communities. To help protect forests and biodiversity and to move palm oil expansion from forested areas and peat lands, the Bank Group would give priority to initiatives that encouraged production on degraded lands and sought to improve productivity of existing plantations.

With the adoption of the new *Framework* and *Strategy*, it lifted the suspension in new investments in the palm oil sector (World Bank, 2011). According to the current IFC website on palm oil, the World Bank Group's approach in the palm oil sector now includes requirements for assessments that must be completed before embarking on a program or investment, particularly around the issues of land use and acquisition, governance, community concerns, and working conditions (IFC, 2021). However, according to the environmental group Rainforest Rescue (2014), the World Bank returned to business-as-usual in terms of funding after the suspension was lifted. Rainforest Rescue launched a campaign, calling the new World Bank Draft Framework for Palm Oil a "farce" and criticized the Roundtable on Sustainable Palm Oil (RSPO) certification. In a letter to the World Bank, Rainforest Rescue stated that 108 human rights and environmental organizations as well as 16,000 individuals worldwide wrote to the World Bank to demand no more funding for oil palm plantations (World Rainforest Rescue, 2014). Further, in 2018 an investigation by Greenpeace found that Wilmar International was still linked to forest destruction for palm oil almost five years after making a commitment to end deforestation (Greenpeace International, 2018).

The World Bank continues to play a significant role in boosting Indonesia's pro-business reforms to attract private investors today. Between 2009 and 2017, the Bank committed over $20.6 billion in loans and guarantees for Indonesia of which over 22% were loans aimed at enhancing the investment climate through policy and regulatory reforms, such as reducing tax burdens, facilitating licensing procedures, creating land administration reforms, and financing commercial infrastructure projects. Consequently, Indonesia has seen a sharp increase in foreign direct investments in recent years, with a net inflow of over $22 billion in 2017. Since taking office in October 2014, President Widodo has launched 16 economic reform packages to expedite business processes in various sectors. The boom of palm oil production in Indonesia—from 6.9 million tons in 2,000 to 32 million tons in 2016—can be attributed to policy reforms and the deregulation of foreign investment and trade (Sonkin et al., 2018).

The Global Investment Boom in Palm Oil: Trends and Implications for Ecological Imperialism

By the 21st century, the financing of palm oil has moved far beyond its originations of IFIs and state-led initiatives to include a wide consortium of global investors funneling billions into the highly lucrative palm oil sector as demand for the commodity grows. As discussed in the previous chapter, market economies around the world began liberalizing their financial sectors in the 1970s, which allowed banks and corporations to freely borrow money abroad while liberalized markets in stocks and other securities allowed foreigners to freely invest and repatriate profits. Through loans and underwriting, banks have continued to play an important role in financing palm oil. However, even more striking has been the growth of non-bank investors, such as pension funds, mutual funds, and insurance companies, in providing the bulk of the financing in this sector.

Under neoliberal globalization, the Natures of the Global South have become a site of accumulation for global financial capital through the entanglement of various financial actors, with corporations operating in natural resource sectors such as palm oil. The capacity for companies operating in natural resource sectors to obtain funding from sources globally creates a context in which—no matter their environmental and social record and as long as it is profitable—a company can find funding from somewhere. As the following section discusses, some European banks, wary over the environmental and social repercussions of palm oil production, are withdrawing their financing, but investors from Southeast Asia are filling the void. Financial liberalization and the tremendous growth of global capital markets have thus opened a Pandora's box. In this context, the Earth's manifold resources, ecosystems, and biodiversity, which have been enclosed, privatized, and marketized by the architecture and rules of international trade and foreign investment, are absorbed into the territory of international financial capital through global capital markets.

While IFIs and state interventionism were crucial in the origination of the palm oil sector in Indonesia, financial liberalization has brought the capacity for global financial capital, in all its multitudinous forms, to further finance its growth. The expansion of the palm oil sector is highly dependent on the availability of funding. The palm oil sector is capital intensive, requiring significant upfront financing for mills and refineries as well as land cleared for palm oil trees. The trees themselves take seven years to reach maximum production. As a result, most companies need to borrow money to establish their plantations. Investment banks generally provide two kinds of financial services to oil palm companies: syndicating loans[2] and underwriting initial public offerings. In both cases, banks provide oil palm growers with large amounts of capital that enable the expansion of land holdings and plantation acreage. Shareholders and institutional investors also directly support palm oil companies with capital investments, providing the seed capital necessary for commercial-scale palm oil agriculture. By abetting development and expansion, these financial actors directly finance the deforestation and biodiversity loss associated with palm oil production (Shibao, 2015b).

Some have argued that financial institutions can positively influence company action on deforestation through engagement by introducing loan criteria or even threatening divestment. This assertion is a central part of the movement to "green finance," a movement that is laudable, but as Chapter 6 discussed has had only limited success. As the previous chapter discussed, ultimately the stored-up funds in the financial sector are *capital* (in the Marxian sense) as commodity, whose primary objective is to yield M′. The fundamental conflict between finance-as-capital and the needs of Nature is reflected in reports such as the assessment by Forest 500 (2019), which finds that financial institutions at large are failing to recognize the risk of deforestation in their portfolios. Of the 150 financial institutions with the most influence on forest-risk supply chains, the 2019 report identified 102 that have no policies to address deforestation. Despite improvements by some, the sector as a whole has not made progress. The percentage of financial institutions with policies for timber and palm oil products was just 27% (Forest 500, 2019).

While individual financial actors may willingly comply with higher ESG standards, a company with a dubious ESG track record can obtain funding globally from a vast variety of financial sources and, in the end, what matters is how the financial sector operates as a whole. Further, research by Profundo and Indonesian NGO TuK indicates that, through placing pressure on companies to maximize dividends and returns on investment, banks create incentive for companies to clear land as rapidly as possible in order to get oil palm trees in the ground (Toumbourou, 2018). In their role as creditors and shareholders, financial institutions and investors exert direct pressure on palm oil companies to maximize dividends and returns, which incentivizes companies to adopt unsustainable practices (Shiboa, 2015a).

Palm Oil Investor Countries/Regions and the International Division of Labor

Along with the direction of the flow of resources, the direction of the flow of profits in the international division of labor is the critical question in the analysis of ecological imperialism. The portion of the profits from investments in sectors such as palm oil, which funnel into the global financial sector in the form of interest and dividends, represent, from a Marxian perspective, the appropriated surplus value of workers and the enclosure and exploitation of Global South Natures, an outcome of the many mechanisms of ecological imperialism described throughout this book. In many cases, this profit flows into core-based institutions, benefitting the financial class and the wealthier classes who hold the vast majority of financial assets. In terms of the hierarchy of the capitalist world-system, core regions benefit in a triple sense—from ecologically unequal exchange, as Global South resources end up as exports to consumers in the Global North; from the profits of transnational corporations that control many of the resource sectors in the Global South that get distributed to CEOs, managers, etc.; and from the financial profits associated with investments in those transnational corporations. In other words, core regions benefit from both ecologically unequal exchange, combined with, as Marx would call it, the highest form of commodity fetishism; the seemingly magical growth of financial profits from out of nowhere. For example, financial institutions such as the American investment management company Vanguard, the world's largest provider of mutual funds, holds shares and bonds from extractive and agricultural industries worldwide. Vanguard has invested some $1894 million in palm oil, rubber, timber, beef, pulp and paper, and soy from 2013 to 2021 in Southeast Asia, Brazil, and Central and West Africa. All of these industries are intimately connected with the heaviest rates of deforestation and destruction of highly biodiverse habitats (Forests & Finance, n.d.). Vanguard's case is a clear funneling of appropriated surplus value and ecological surplus from the periphery and semi-periphery to the core, though there may be non-core clients of Vanguard that also share in some of the surplus.

Yet as Chapter 5 emphasized, semi-peripheral emerging economies are increasingly important loci of accumulation in the capitalist world-system and this accumulation is being funneled into investments domestically as well as overseas. As this section shows, the flow of profits from sectors such as palm oil into the coffers of financial capital is not a one-way dynamic that solely benefits the core-based financial class. Rather, Southeast Asian investors comprise the majority of palm oil investors for companies based in Southeast Asia. As such, profits accrue to a Southeast Asian elite. However, unlike core economies that benefit from an ecological imperialism occurring somewhere else entirely and experience the seemingly magical growth of financial profits out of thin air, these countries must contend with the consequential environmental destruction and social unrest.

As large private enterprises dominate the palm oil sector and are overwhelmingly responsible for the deforestation,[3] this section takes a closer look at the financing of major palm oil companies through the Forests & Finance database. According to their database (which states that it likely contains conservative underestimates), almost $80 billion between 2013 and 2020 has been invested in the palm oil sector in Southeast Asia, Africa, and Latin America. As Figure 7.1 shows, investments within Southeast Asia strongly dominate the sector; a little over $78 billion was invested in Southeast Asia. Of the total $80 billion, Southeast Asian investors dominated the market and accounted for 61% of total palm oil investments, followed by East Asian investors at 15%, European investors (including EU27 and other European nations) at 13%, North American investors at 8%, and investors from other world regions accounting for the remaining 3%.

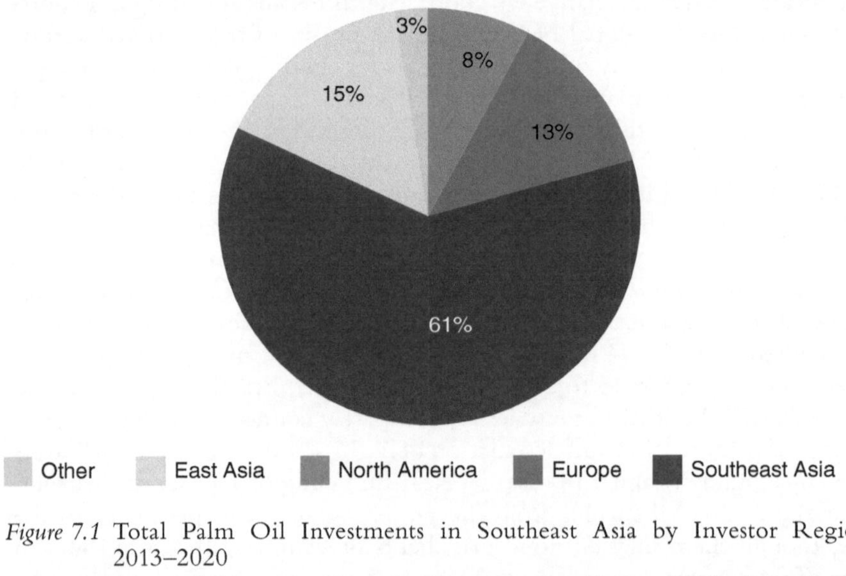

Figure 7.1 Total Palm Oil Investments in Southeast Asia by Investor Region, 2013–2020

Source: Graph compiled by author from data from Forests & Finance 2020 website, https://forestsandfinance.org/data/

Increasingly Southeast Asian banks and investors are providing financing in the palm oil sector. Southeast Asian banks, investors, and stock exchanges have not implemented the Environmental, Social, and Governance measures that are being adopted by other international financial institutions. A 2018 study by Profundo and TuK INDONESIA (2018) evaluated commercial banks to determine the strength of any publicly available policies relevant to tropical forest sector investment decision-making by ESG standards. The study found that in general European banks scored highest in terms of scope of commitments, environmental standards, and social standards followed by US and Japanese banks. Banks from China and Southeast Asia scored either very low, or, particularly in the case of Malaysian banks, had zero relevant publicly available ESG risk mitigation policies specific to the palm oil sector. A 2015 World Wildlife report (Stampe et al., 2015) found that among 18 domestic Southeast Asian banks with interests in forest commodities, only three had made statements on sustainable lending, and only four included ESG screening when extending credit to clients.

Besides commercial banks, the second major category of palm oil financiers is external equity investors. Several of the world's largest palm oil companies, such as Wilmar, Kuala Lumpur Kepong, and IOI Corporation, are publicly traded. Environmentalists often argue that because publicly traded companies are answerable to their shareholders and investors, institutional investors can influence the behavior of palm oil companies with enough activism on the part of the shareholders. Investors, so it goes, have the power to deny capital to environmentally destructive companies by divesting from them. In addition, publicly listed companies are subject to the ESG reporting the exchanges requirements where they are listed. However, the vast majority of Southeast Asian institutional investors lack a structured policy for managing ESG-related risks in their portfolios. Most of the publicly listed palm oil producers in Southeast Asia are listed on one of three exchanges: Bursa Malaysia (MYX) based in Kuala Lumpur, the Indonesia Stock Exchange (IDX) based in Jakarta, or the Singapore Exchange (SGX). Unfortunately, these exchanges also lag behind their foreign counterparts in terms of disclosure. Only one of the three exchanges, Bursa Malaysia, requires listed companies to report their sustainability activities (Shibao, 2015a). However, some Southeast Asian exchanges have begun to make efforts to improve their ESG standards.[4]

It is also worthwhile to mention that while Southeast Asian investors are clearly important in the palm oil sector, international financial capital is exceedingly complex in its variegated flows. This complexity can create a great deal of obfuscation that can make it difficult to trace and assign responsibility. In a typical large palm oil company, there may be a 100 or more investors from all across the globe, even if one or two investors hold substantially higher shares than others. Further, the variegated financial flows *between* financial institutions mask how other financial institutions outside of Southeast Asia have invested in some of Southeast Asia's largest financiers of palm oil. For example, the Malaysian bank Maybank has, over the years, been one of the prime financiers of the palm oil sector, financing a large number of controversial palm oil companies with known ESG issues. Yet, a 2018 report by Banktrack found a number of other financial institutions actively investing in Maybank—financial institutions from other countries that supposedly adhere to higher social and environmental standards. The report found that of the top 20 investors providing loans and underwriting services to Maybank from 2010 to 2016, three were from the UK, one from Switzerland, two from Singapore, two from France, two from Japan, one from the US, three from China, one from Taiwan, one from Australia, three from Indonesia, and one from Germany. The top 20 bondholders and shareholders were also from Europe, the US, and East Asia. In addition, several of the investors in Maybank are supposed adherents to a variety of environmental regulations and pledges. For example, three of the top five creditors of Maybank are members of Roundtable on Sustainable Palm Oil (RSPO)—HSBC, UBS, and Standard Chartered. These three RSPO ordinary member financial institutions accounted for approximately 38% of all loans and underwriting services to Maybank in the period from 2010 to 2016 (Profundo and TuK INDONESIA, n.d.).

Of final note, while Southeast Asian investors dominate in the palm oil sector in Southeast Asia, palm oil investments in Latin America and Africa are more diversified in terms of investor home region, as Figure 7.2 shows.

Overall, we can surmise that, in terms of financial profit flows from the palm oil sector, core economies still very much benefit simply by ownership of interest-bearing capital. However, the financial and wealthy classes of East Asia and Southeast Asia and Latin America are also major beneficiaries. As Chapter 5 discussed, the economic strength of the semi-periphery in the 21st century complicates the North/South dichotomy that was established

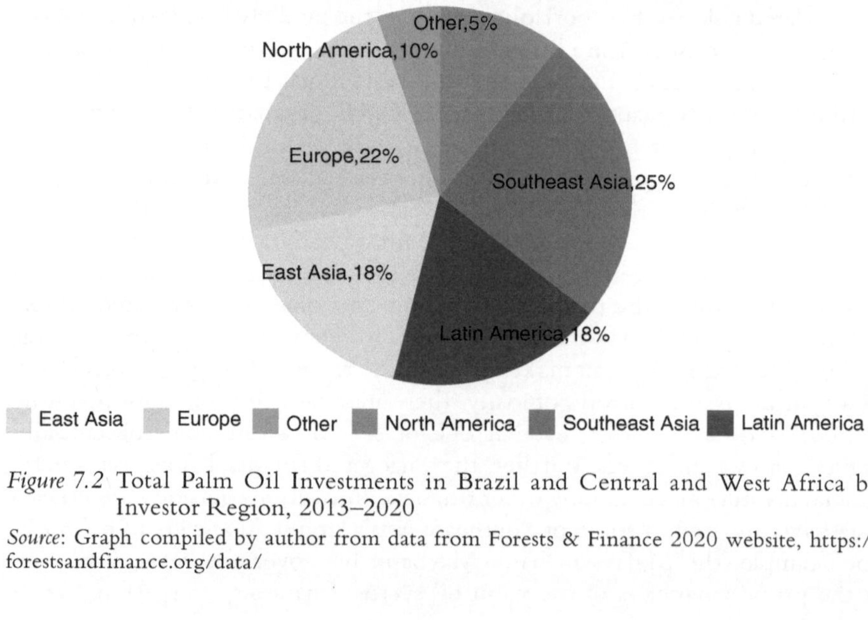

Figure 7.2 Total Palm Oil Investments in Brazil and Central and West Africa by Investor Region, 2013–2020

Source: Graph compiled by author from data from Forests & Finance 2020 website, https://forestsandfinance.org/data/

during the colonial era. However, it is noteworthy that North Africa and sub-Saharan Africa investors had negligible investments in the palm oil sector, even when analyzing the palm oil companies located within West and Central Africa. Once again, the pattern of profits and resources unilaterally flowing out of peripheral regions like sub-Saharan Africa holds, whether in the form of corporate or financial profits.

Top 12 Lenders and Underwriters in Palm Oil for 2020

Based on the Forests & Finance database, this section takes a closer look at the top 12 palm oil lenders and underwriters in 2020. In 2020, investors funneled a total of $19,983.08 million into the Southeast Asian palm oil sector. Of this, lenders and underwriters in palm oil invested $215.26 million in the form of corporate loans, revolving credit facilities, bond issuances, and share issuances.[5]

Table 7.1 shows the top 12 lenders and underwriters of palm oil in Southeast Asia 2020, who totaled about $176 million, or about 82% of the lending and underwriting of palm oil. In 2020, AmBank Group and Malaysian banking group invested the most at approximately $66 million in lending and underwriting, or nearly 31% of the total lending and underwriting.[6] With the exception of Indo Premier Securities, an Indonesian investment management company, all the other top 11 lenders and underwriters are banks, primarily investment banks. Of these top 12, Southeast Asian investors dominate, having invested a total of 119.6 million (68%), followed by China at $17.6 million (10%), US investors at $13.6 million (about 8%), UK investors at $9 million (5%), and investors from France at $7 million (4%).

Top Ten Bondholders and Shareholders of Palm Oil in Southeast Asia for 2020

On a much higher scale than lenders and underwriters, bondholders and shareholders in 2020 invested $19,767.82 million in the form of bond holding and shareholding, or nearly 99% of the total amount invested. Table 7.2 shows the top ten bondholders and shareholders in Southeast Asia in 2020. These top ten bondholders and shareholders invested a total of $14,072 million, or about 71% of the total invested in bond holding and shareholding in 2020.

In contrast to banks, which are the primary lenders and underwriters in the Southeast Asian palm oil sector, institutional investors, from investment management companies to pension funds, are the major financial actors involved in bond holding and shareholding. This essentially means that, as important as specific banks may be, non-bank entities, through the financial instruments of bond holding and shareholding, are financing the majority of the palm oil sector in Southeast Asia by 2020, some of which invested in dozens of different palm oil companies. For example, the Malaysian investment management company Permodalan Nasional Berhad alone invested

Table 7.1 Top 12 Lenders and Underwriters of Palm Oil in Southeast Asia 2020

Financial Institution	*Type of Financial Institution*	*Financial Institution's Country*	*Forest Risk Group*	*Amount USD Millions*
AmBank Group	Malaysian banking group	Malaysia	TDM	65.84
CSC Financial	Chinese investment bank and brokerage firm	China	COFCO and ZTE	17.61
Indo Premier Securities	Indonesian investment management company	Indonesia	Sampoerna Group	14.18
Bank Mandiri	Indonesian bank	Indonesia	Sampoerna Group	14.18
Standard Chartered	Multinational banking and financial services company	United Kingdom	POSCO and Olam International	8.98
Bank Negara Indonesia	Indonesian state-owned bank	Indonesia	Sungai Budi Group	8.49
CGS-CIMB Securities International	ASEAN investment bank	Singapore	Sungai Budi Group	8.49
Malayan Banking (Maybank)	Malaysian universal bank	Malaysia	Sungai Budi Group	8.49
Bank of America	American multinational bank and financial services holding company	United States	POSCO	6.81
BNP Paribas	French international banking group	France	COFCO and ZTE	6.81
Citigroup	American multinational investment bank and financial services corporation	United States	POSCO	6.81
HSBC	British multinational investment bank and financial services holding company	United Kingdom	POSCO	6.81

Source: *Ta*ble compiled from data from Forests & Finance 2020 website, https://forestsandfinance.org/data/

$6,442 million, or about 32% of total investments in the Southeast Asian palm oil sector in 2020. Yayasan Pelaburan Bumiputra is the parent company of Permodalan Nasional Berhad. The state-owned subsidiary is an investment company supporting share ownership within Malaysia's corporate sector. According to the Forest 500 report (2019), Yayasan Pelaburan Bumiputra scored zero in commitment strength and social considerations for investments in the palm oil sector.

The Comprador Bourgeoisie in the Semi-periphery: The Financing of Palm Oil and the Southeast Asian Palm Oil Tycoons

In theories of imperialism and dependency theories, the "comprador bourgeoisie" is typically defined as the part of the native exploiting class that

Table 7.2 Top Ten Bondholders and Shareholders in Southeast Asian Palm Oil 2020

Financial **Institution**	*Type of Financial Institution*	*Country of Financial Institution*	*Amount USD Millions*
Permodalan Nasional Berhad	Investment management company	Malaysia	6,442
Employees Provident Fund	Government-managed retirement saving	Malaysia	3,667.98
KWAP Retirement Fund	Malaysia's largest public services pension fund	Malaysia	1,084.34
Vanguard	Investment management company	United States	742.72
Public Bank	Bank	Malaysia	485.26
Lembaga Kemajuan Tanah Persekutuan (FELDA)	Malaysian development agency	Malaysia	478.66
BlackRock	American multinational investment management corporation based	United States	417.38
Oversea-Chinese Banking Corporation	Multinational bank and financial services corporation	Singapore	351.09
Prudential (UK)	British multinational life insurance and financial services company	United Kingdom	247.01
Malaysian Hajj Pilgrims Fund	Islamic savings and investment institution	Malaysia	155.97

Source: Table compiled from data from Forests & Finance 2020 website, https://forestsandfinance.org/data/

is allied with and subservient to foreign imperial powers and capital. The defining characteristic of the comprador bourgeoisie class is its *dependency*. The concept is so critical in the dynamics of imperialism that a fundamental political economic question must be, *what is the relation of foreign financial capital to the comprador bourgeoisie*? The case of palm oil demonstrates the nuances and complexities inherent in the study of imperialism, particularly in the semi-periphery. The typical definition of comprador bourgeoisie may only be partially applicable in some cases, particularly in the semi-periphery where domestic elites wield considerable economic power.

On the one hand, as discussed above, the profits of natural resource sectors like palm oil contribute to the accumulation of foreign financial capital. On the other hand, global financial capital also fosters the hegemony and economic power of the extractivist capitalist class in resource-intensive economies. In peripheral regions like sub-Saharan Africa where sectors like mining are almost wholly owned by foreign investors, the comprador class is more likely formed of government officials and elite who receive bribes and kick-backs from instituting policies that enable the exploitation of resources on terms amenable to foreign capital. The dependent nature of the comprador bourgeoisie class is imminently clear when the extractive technology, the mines themselves, as well as the management and skilled workers are primarily foreign. In other words, the elites in sub-Saharan Africa do not, in general, own the means of production, though there are instances where African elites or an African state owns shares in mining companies. As discussed, peripheral regions like sub-Saharan Africa generally suffer, relative to other regions, both ecologically unequal exchange and an immense outflow of profits overseas.

Yet in Southeast Asia's semi-peripheral and emerging economies such as Malaysia and Indonesia, many of the largest and most lucrative palm oil companies are primarily owned by Southeast Asians. In 2018, the top five leading palm oil companies worldwide, based on market capitalization, were listed as Wilmar International Limited, IOI, Kuala Lumpur Kepong, Sime Darby Bhd, and Golden Agri-Resources (Statista, 2020). All are Southeast Asian companies, primarily Malaysian or Singaporean. In the case of palm oil, both foreign and domestic financial capital have been critical in fostering a palm oil oligarchy *within* Southeast Asia. Interestingly in contrast to the orthodox notion of comprador bourgeoisie where economic and political policies are subordinated to the dictates of foreign capital, foreign financial capital has been utilized for the aims of a domestic extractive oligarchy.

In Malaysia, Robert Kuok is the richest man with a net worth of $11.3 billion and is one of the founders of the palm oil company Wilmar International (Forbes, 2021). Many of Indonesia's wealthiest citizens owe their fortunes at least in part to the production. In 2016, 14 of the 32 Indonesian billionaires identified by Forbes magazine were palm oil tycoons, having at least partially accumulated their wealth through palm oil production. Almost all of these men established themselves as members of the Southeast Asian nation's oligarchy during the 33-year reign of strongman President Suharto, who fell from power in 1998. During the palm oil boom of the 2000s, Indonesia surpassed Malaysia to become the world's top producer. So too did the number of Indonesia's billionaires rise during the decade from two to 11 (Mongabay, 2016). In Indonesia, environmentalists have criticized the deep connections between President Joko Widodo's cabinet, the Indonesian oligarchy, and the mining and palm oil industries. They have pointed out, for example, an environment minister with extensive business interests in the mining industry and a new energy minister with a record of championing fossil fuel and palm biodiesel projects (Gokkon, 2019a). Environmentalists have also leveled charges of corruption and the lack of regulation on companies with a track record of negative environmental and social impacts (Gokkon, 2019b).

TuK INDONESIA investigated the control of palm oil tycoons, how many land banks of undeveloped plantations remain under their control, and how financiers contributed to the concentration of power (TuK INDONESIA, 2018). The reports assess 25 of the most important tycoon-controlled business groups active in the Indonesian palm oil sector. The wealth of the 26 tycoon families who control the 25 palm oil groups is estimated at over $88 billion. Six of the 26 families controlling the 25 oil palm groups tycoons were from Malaysia, 17 from Indonesia, one was from South Korea, and one was from Scotland. According to the 2018 report, the 25 tycoon-controlled groups control at least 3.4 million hectares planted with oil palm as of the end of 2017, or at least 28% of the total area planted with oil palm in Indonesia in 2017 (12.3 million hectares). However, if the unplanted land banks controlled by these 25 tycoons were to be developed, the share of the total planted area controlled by the 25 tycoon-controlled groups would thereby increase from 28% to 40%.

As with the palm sector as a whole, the report by Tuk Indonesia (2018) points out how bank loans and investments in shares and bonds by institutional investors enable the tycoons to invest more capital than they would be able to otherwise, abetting in the expansion of their palm oil activities. Of the 25 palm oil holding companies, 20 are listed on a stock exchange, which means that they attract capital by issuing shares to private and institutional investors. Some companies also issued bonds, mainly to institutional investors. And all palm oil companies have attracted bank loans. The study analyzed the balance sheets of the 20 listed palm oil holding companies at the end of 2017 and two private holding companies. The authors looked at capital available for expansion and found that on average the tycoons financed 31% of the expansion capital available to the 22 analyzed palm oil holding companies themselves, while outside shareholders financed 18% and bondholders financed 5%. The study found that the most important institutional investors included Employees Provident Fund (Malaysia), Permodalan Nasional Berhad (Malaysia), Vanguard (United States), and BlackRock (United States).

In addition, the report pointed out how most tycoon-controlled oil palm groups attract bank loans to facilitate and accelerate their expansion process. Many of them regularly hire investment banks to help them sell new shares and bonds to investors in order to attract new capital for expansion. The investment banks then guarantee ("underwrite") that they will find investors for a certain volume of shares and bonds for a given price. On average, banks were the most important financial stakeholders for the 22 analyzed palm oil holding companies, financing 35% of their expansion capital. Joint ventures with other palm companies also bring in significant funds for some companies; on average, they contribute 11% to the expansion capital of the 22 analyzed oil palm holding companies. The most important banks providing the financing to 18 tycoon-controlled groups were Oversea-Chinese Banking Corporation (Singapore), CIMB Group (Malaysia), Malayan Banking (Malaysia), Bank Negara Indonesia (Indonesia), and Bank Mandiri (Indonesia). The most important European banks were Credit Suisse (Switzerland), Rabobank (Netherlands), and BNP Paribas (France). And the most important American bank was Citigroup (TuK INDONESIA and Profundo, 2018).

Conclusion

The case study of palm oil demonstrates some of the most significant interrelationships between global financial capital and ecological imperialism, and it is likely these interrelationships are a repeated pattern throughout the Global South for other resource sectors as well. Originating as a cash crop under colonialism, financial capital from IFIs such as the World Bank and the IMF has played both the part of carrot and stick in the production and expansion of palm oil. As a carrot, financing from the World Bank awarded a right-wing authoritarian government with the development capital necessary to expand palm oil production in exchange for geopolitical allyship. As a stick, financing from the IMF led to the usual export-oriented, extractivist policies common throughout the developing world in the wake of debt and structural adjustments. Common throughout the Global South, financing from the IFIs set the context for Global South resources to become the site of accumulation for global financial capital today. With international financial liberalization, the massive accumulation of capital in the financial sector, and the growth of a wide variety of financial actors, resource sectors like palm oil are wide open to funding from financial capital globally. At the hands of the financial class, the savings of workers, not just from the Global North but also from the Global South, are concentrated into a money power that circles the globe in search of the highest rates of return, providing the capital necessary for the expansion of environmentally destructive sectors such as palm oil.

While financial actors from the Global North are still important, the case of palm oil also demonstrates a major change in 21st-century ecological imperialism—the growth of semi-peripheral or emerging economies as loci of accumulation. At a regional level especially, financial capital from such emerging economies can play a significant role and can even dominate the influence of financial capital from traditional core economies. With this shift, financial capital is arguably even more difficult to regulate; no international law regulating financial capital for a uniform ESG standard exists; and Asian financial institutions on the whole lag behind financial institutions from other countries, particularly Europe. Ultimately, what matters for the planet is how the financial sector operates as a system at a global level. Finally, what is noteworthy about palm oil is the use of global financial capital to facilitate growth of oligarchic, financially powerful elite within the semi-periphery, complicating the orthodox notions of a wholly dependent comprador elite common in theories of imperialism and dependency. As palm oil production has resulted in the domestic destruction of Southeast Asian Natures as well as the accumulation of wealth of a powerful oligarchic elite, the palm oil production is now expanding outside of Malaysia and Indonesia into Africa, repeating patterns of environmental destruction and accumulation by dispossession.

References

Carlson, K.M., Curran, L.M., Asner, G.P., Pittman, A.M.D., Trigg, S.N., & Adeney, J.M. (2013). Carbon emissions from forest conversion by Kalimantan oil palm plantations. *Nature Climate Change, 3*(3), 283–287. https://doi.org/10.1038/nclimate1702

CNBC. (2020). *U.S. bans second Malaysian palm oil giant over forced labor findings.* CNBC: Asia-Pacific News. https://www.cnbc.com/2020/12/31/us-bans-second-malaysian-palm-oil-giant-over-forced-labor-findings.html

GRAIN. (2014). *Planet palm oil: Peasants pay the price for cheap vegetable oil.* https://www.grain.org/media/W1siZiIsIjIwMTQvMDkvMjUvMDdfMDBfNTRfNzE4X1BsYW5ldF9wYWxtX29pbC5wZGYiXV0

Forbes. (2021). *Profile #1 Robert Kuok.* https://www.forbes.com/profile/robert-kuok/?sh=137423a85eb5

Forest 500. (2019). *Forest 500 annual report 2019: The companies getting it wrong on deforestation.* https://forest500.org/publications/forest-500-annual-report-2019-companies-getting-it-wrong-deforestation

Forests & Finance. (n.d.). *Quick view: Explore links between financiers and deforestation-risk companies.* https://forestsandfinance.org/data/data-quick-view/

Gellert, P. (2005). The shifting natures of "development": Growth, crisis, and recovery in Indonesia's forests. *World Development, 33*(8), 1345–1364.

Gellert, P.K. (2015). Palm oil expansion in Indonesia: Land grabbing as accumulation by dispossession. In *States and citizens: Accommodation, facilitation and resistance to globalization (Current Perspectives in Social Theory, Vol. 34)* (pp. pp. 65–99). Bingley: Emerald Group Publishing Limited. https://doi.org/10.1108/S0278-120420150000034004

Gokkon, B. (2019a). Indonesia's new cabinet a 'marriage of oligarchs,' environmentalists say. *Mongabay.* https://news.mongabay.com/2019/10/indonesia-cabinet-jokowi-widodo-oligarchs-environment/

Gokkon, B. (2019b). Indonesian candidates find common ground in support for palm oil. *Mongabay.* https://news.mongabay.com/2019/02/indonesian-candidates-find-common-ground-in-support-for-palm-oil/

GRAIN. (n.d.). *Planet palm oil.* https://grain.org/article/categories/519-planet-palm-oil

Greenpeace International. (2018). *World's largest palm oil trader linked to rainforest destruction twice the size of Paris.* Greenpeace. https://www.greenpeace.org/international/press-release/17248/worlds-largest-palm-oil-trader-linked-to-rainforest-destruction-twice-the-size-of-paris/

Humphreys, D. (2006). *Logjam: Deforestation and the crisis of global governance.* London: Earthscan from Routledge.

IFC. (n.d.a). *Solutions.* International Finance Corporation World Bank Group. https://www.ifc.org/wps/wcm/connect/CORP_EXT_Content/IFC_External_Corporate_Site/Solutions/

IFC. (n.d.b). *Homepage.* International Finance Corporation World Bank Group. https://www.ifc.org/wps/wcm/connect/corp_ext_content/ifc_external_corporate_site/home

IFC. (2021). *IFC in the palm oil sector.* International Finance Corporation World Bank Group. https://www.ifc.org/wps/wcm/connect/industry_ext_content/ifc_external_corporate_site/agribusiness/resources/palmoil_landingpage

Lee, J.S.H., Abood, S., Ghazoul, J., Barus, B., Obidzinski, K., & Koh, L.P. (2013). Environmental impacts of large-scale oil palm enterprises exceed that of smallholdings in Indonesia. *Conservation Letters*, 7(1), 25–33. https://doi.org/10.1111/conl.12039

McMichael, P. (2017). *Development and social change: A global perspective* (6th edition). Thousand Oaks, CA: Sage Publications.

Mongabay. (2009). *World Bank's IFC suspends lending to palm oil companies*. Mongabay.com. https://news.mongabay.com/2009/09/world-banks-ifc-suspends-lending-to-palm-oil-companies/

Mongabay. (2016). *Indonesia's rich list stacked with palm oil billionaires*. Mongabay. https://news.mongabay.com/2016/12/indonesias-rich-list-stacked-with-palm-oil-billionaires/

Ombudsman. (n.d.). Home | Office of the Compliance Advisor Ombudsman. Retrieved July 15, 2018, from http://www.cao-ombudsman.org/uploads/case_documents/Combined%20Document%201_2_3_4_5_6_7.pdf

Pramudya, E.P., Hospes, O., & Termeer, C.J.A.M. (2017). Governing the palm-oil sector through finance: The changing roles of the Indonesian state. *Bulletin of Indonesian Economic Studies*, *53*(1), 57–82. https://doi.org/10.1080/00074918.2016.1228829

Rainforest Rescue. (2014). *No World Bank money for palm oil*. Rainforest Rescue. https://www.rainforest-rescue.org/petitions/587/no-world-bank-money-for-palm-oil

Segal, T. (2020). Syndicated loan. *Investopedia*. https://www.investopedia.com/terms/s/syndicatedloan.asp

Shibao, P. (2015a). Big palm oil's financiers. *Mongabay*. https://news.mongabay.com/2015/07/big-palm-oils-financiers/#_edn1

Shibao, P. (2015b). Who's funding palm oil? *Mongabay*. https://news.mongabay.com/2015/03/whos-funding-palm-oil/

Sonkin, F., Mousseau, F., Mittal, A., & Fraser, E. (2018). *Indonesia: The World Bank's Failed East Asian Miracle*. The Oakland Institute. https://www.oaklandinstitute.org/sites/oaklandinstitute.org/files/indonesia-world-bank-failed-east-asian-miracle.pdf

Stampe, J., McCarron, B., Harrison, A., Llavero, A., & Neyroumande, E. (2015). *Sustainable finance report. Sustainable finance in Singapore, Indonesia, and Malaysia: A review of financiers' ESG practices, disclosure standards and regulations*. World Wildlife Foundation. https://d2ouvy59p0dg6k.cloudfront.net/downloads/wwf_frc_forest_risk_commodities_report_2015_online.pdf

Statista. (2020). *Leading palm oil companies worldwide in 2020, based on market capitalization*. Statista. https://www.statista.com/statistics/477252/leading-global-plam-oil-companies-based-on-market-capitalization/#:~:text=Wilmar%20International%20Limited%2C%20a%20Singapore%20based%20agricultural%20business%2C,market%20capitalization%20amounted%20to%203.11%20b

Teoh, C.H. (n.d.). *Key sustainability issues in the palm oil sector: A discussion paper for multi-stakeholders consultations (commissioned by the World Bank Group)*. The World Bank & International Finance Corporation. http://www.biofuelobservatory.org/Documentos/Otros/Palm-Oil-Discussion-Paper-FINAL.pdf

Toumbourou, T. (2018). In funding palm oil giants, banks may share in 'sins of the companies'. *Mongabay*. https://news.mongabay.com/2018/11/in-funding-palm-oil-giants-banks-may-share-in-sins-of-the-companies/

TuK INDONESIA. (2018a). *Maybank: The single largest palm oil financier.* Banktrack. https://www.banktrack.org/download/maybank_the_single_largest_palm_oil_financier/maybankreportenglish210218.pdf

TuK INDONESIA. (2018b). *Tycoons in the Indonesian palm oil.* https://www.tuk.or.id/wp-content/uploads/2019/03/Tycoons-in-the-Indonesian-palm-oil-sector_compressed.pdf

Vijay V., Pimm S.L., Jenkins C.N., & Smith S.J. (2016). The impacts of oil palm on recent deforestation and biodiversity loss. *PLOS ONE, 11*(7). https://doi.org/10.1371/journal.pone.0159668

World Bank. (2011). *World Bank group adopts new approach for investment in palm oil sector.* https://www.worldbank.org/en/news/press-release/2011/04/03/world-bank-group-adopts-new-approach-investment-palm-oil-sector

World Rainforest Movement. (2009). *Indonesia: Call for suspension of World Bank (IFC) lending to oil palm.* https://wrm.org.uy/articles-from-the-wrm-bulletin/section3/indonesia-call-for-suspension-of-world-bank-ifc-lending-to-oil-palm/

Notes

1 See for example the series of reports by GRAIN on palm oil; https://www.grain.org/article/categories/519-planet-palm-oil

2 Loan syndication is the process of involving a group of lenders in funding various portions of a loan for a single borrower. Loan syndication most often occurs when a borrower requires an amount too large for a single lender to provide or when the loan is outside the scope of a lender's risk exposure levels (Segal, 2020).

3 For example, using data from Sumatra covering the period 2000–2010, researchers have found that smallholders were responsible for just 11% of the deforestation, even though their palm oil farms covered about 40% of the land. Large private enterprises, however, caused 88% of the deforestation. In terms of greenhouse gas emissions, the figures were almost identical: 9% attributable to smallholders and 90% to large private enterprises (Huay Lee, 2013).

4 For example, Bursa Malaysia is now a member of the Sustainable Stock Exchanges Initiative and offers a Corporate Disclosure Guide and has ESG reporting required as a listing rule. https://sseinitiative.org/stock-exchange/bursa-malaysia/

5 Revolving credit facilities are arrangements between banks and businesses where a credit line is extended with a maximum amount, and businesses can access funds when needed. Forests & Finance considers loans, revolving credit facilities, bond issuances, and share issuances as a type of credit, and thus these categories comprise the lenders and underwriters category (M. Van Der Mark, personal communication, June 30, 2020).

6 It should be noted that as a snapshot of 2020, this list does not fully capture the banks that have been instrumental in the preceding decade.

8 Climate Negotiations, UN Sustainable Development Goals, and Ecological Imperialism

Given the expanding scientific understanding, widespread media coverage, mounting grassroots activism, and daily incidences of environmental catastrophes globally, denialism of climate change and other environmental crises is no longer a realistic possibility for even the most trenchant forces that prefer the status quo. Rather, the challenges to addressing global ecological crises, with their attendant environmental injustices, will most likely arise from factions of the capitalist class, and closely aligned government elites, who will advocate for solutions that do not substantially interfere with the current structure of global wealth and power, and as a result perpetuate superficial and/or unjust responses. Business-as-usual solutions, greenwashing, policies and regulations that lack appropriate mechanisms of implementation and enforcement, all threaten to set humanity on a path of response largely inadequate to the scale and urgency of crises both ecological and social in nature. As long as we continue to follow historical trends, many major proposed solutions will continue to shift ecological burdens onto the most impoverished and marginalized.

How do the United Nations Climate Change Conference that occurred in Glasgow late Fall of 2021 (CoP26) and the United Nations Sustainable Development Goals developed in 2015 look when viewed from the perspective of ecological imperialism? Both international agreements put forward the most prominent climate and sustainable development solutions likely to be backed by governments, NGOs, development banks, and the private sector. Both international agreements shape the discourse and therefore the perceived solutions for climate change, other environmental crises, and sustainable development at-large. From a non-cynical perspective, both agreements deserve plaudits as important initial platforms for addressing our global socio-ecological crises, and both have overcome considerable obstacles in their creation, given the realities of international negotiations. Not too surprisingly, however, both largely overlook the deeply embedded structures of ecological imperialism in the global economy.

Through the investigation of the political economic workings of ecological imperialism, I hope that this book provides some analytical tools for

DOI: 10.4324/9780429261305-8

critically evaluating proposed solutions from a comprehensive, historically contextualized, systems-based approach that reflects the concerns being voiced by grassroots environmental and social movements globally. At the heart of ecological imperialism is a hierarchical international division of labor that allows wealthier countries and classes to shift socio-ecological burdens onto the poor and marginalized, and a global economy characterized by laissez faire economics and profit as the dominant logic of production. As a brief recap, the more specific aspects of ecological imperialism overviewed in this book that directly contribute to the global ecological crisis and/or environmental injustices include the following:

a Economies that have been structurally dependent upon resource extractivism in the Global South since colonialism, throughout all primary sectors, including the mining sectors, industrial agricultural sectors, timber and fishing, etc.
b Neoliberal development strategies concerning trade and foreign investment that encourage extractivism in the Global South
c Entrenched political structures within the Global South that foster a comprador elite whose interests overlap with resource extractivism and foreign investment and corruption
d Dynamics of debt that foster extractivism, vulnerability, and dependency on resource exports in Global South
e An international trade system that abets ecologically unequal exchange, shifting socio-ecological burdens from wealthier countries to more impoverished regions and hence allowing wealthier populations to consume beyond their sustainable means
f Relatedly, the current and historical extent of ecological debt across a wide variety of categories which remains largely unacknowledged by the Global North, including climate, resources, water, biodiversity loss, pollution, and land
g Rules and regulations in international investment through the WTO, international financial institutions like the World Bank and the IMF, multilateral treaties, and bilateral treaties that favor the corporate property rights of foreign investors and local elites. Such rules and regulation have allowed investors to crack open peripheral and semi-peripheral resources to unfettered foreign investment
h The activities of transnational corporations (TNCs) that result in processes of accumulation by dispossession (such as land grabbing) that arise from investment regimes that favor corporate property rights over the rights of local communities and indigenous peoples
i Simultaneously, international investment regimes that funnel the vast majority of profits from the capitalization of the free gifts of Global South Natures to TNCs, and their shareholders largely in the Global North
j Liberalized international finance that falls drastically short of adequate environmental and social governance (ESG) regulations

k Relatedly, the lack of an international ESG standard for financial sectors globally, meaning that environmentally degrading economic activities can always find funding from somewhere
l Relatedly, the entanglement of financial profits globally with extractive industries responsible for climate change, biodiversity loss, deforestation, and so on
m The expansion of manufacturing into areas of the Global South (emerging economies) and the consequent pollution and degradation of their environments and sink capacity
n Broadly, the growth of emerging economies and their ecological expansion into the periphery as they mimic the industrial capitalist path taken by the Global North

Realistically, it is unlikely that any set of top-down solutions such as the UN SDGs and UN Climate Conferences would tackle these components of ecological imperialism since to do so would require a major overhaul of global capitalism. As long as they work within the fundamental structures of global capitalism, we know the solutions will not do enough. The critical question, however, is to what extent do such solutions potentially exacerbate rather than mitigate the problems.

The United Nations Sustainable Development Goals

Neoliberal development policies have been, for decades, at the heart of ecological imperialism. They are responsible—post-colonialism—for encouraging and creating the socio-ecologically deleterious patterns of international trade, investment, and finance listed above and examined throughout this book. In 2015 all United Nations Member States adopted the 2030 Agenda for Sustainable Development, which consists of 17 Sustainable Development Goals (SDGs). These goals contain a blueprint for a variety of socio-economic development goals while simultaneously seeking to address the most significant environmental challenges. The question is, to what extent do the United Nations Sustainable Development Goals replicate the same patterns of neoliberal development?

Optimistically, the UN SDGs are the first set of development goals put forth by the UN that explicitly integrate sustainability considerations. Unfortunately, despite some attention to environmental objectives, the SDGs appear to embrace the export-led, unquestioning form of economic growth that has largely been the neoliberal development paradigm since the 1980s throughout the Global South. Economic growth, growth in international trade, financial services, and foreign investment are all broadly encouraged, with no acknowledgment of how these sectors are implicated in ecologically unequal exchange, accumulation by dispossession, the capture of profits by TNCs, or even the inevitable ecological costs of extractivism, which, for much of the Global South, would be the engine behind economic growth.

For example, SDG Goal 8 seeks to promote decent work and economic growth while reconciling the tensions between economic growth and sustainability by progressively improving, through 2030, global resource efficiency and decoupling economic growth from environmental degradation (United Nations, n.d.a). Despite acknowledging the need for green growth, it nonetheless presumes *endless economic growth as a primary goal of sustainable development.* As such, the SDGs make the same fatal assumption that has plagued modernization theory—that endless economic growth is somehow compatible with environmental objectives through the mechanism of technological advancement and decoupling. Yet, as shown in Chapter 1, *there is no empirical evidence of absolute, permanent, global, large, and fast enough decoupling of economic growth from all critical environmental pressures* (Parrique et al., 2019). In advocating for endless growth, the SDGs do not take into consideration the need for an optimal scale for national economies, nor for the global economy. All growth, even in "green" sectors such as renewable energy, has environmental costs that necessitate some sort of optimal scale. Instead, the SDGs cater to the fundamental drive of capitalism—that of the ceaseless accumulation of capital and constant expansion. Relatedly, the SDGs do not reflect the important reality that without major, structural changes such as degrowth and reduced consumption in the developed countries, development through increased economic growth in the developing world is not feasible from the standpoint of sustainability.

Specific details within the overall Goal 8 target are problematic as well. For example, Target 8.10 calls to strengthen the capacity of domestic financial institutions to encourage and expand access to banking, insurance, and financial services for all (United Nations, n.d.a). However, for all the reasons discussed in Chapters 6 and 7, the call to strengthen and expand domestic financial institutions and access to banking, insurance, and financial services for all without correspondingly explicit ESG regulations aligned with clear environmental and social goals is likely to exacerbate environmental degradation and attendant environmental injustices.

Goal 17 agglomerates a number of diverse targets with the overarching goal of strengthening global partnerships for sustainable development, which include calls for increased economic integration. Target 17.3, for example, seeks to mobilize additional financial resources for developing countries from multiple sources, which includes, according to its corresponding indicator 17.3.1, foreign direct investments (FDIs). Target 17.5 promotes adopting and implementing investment promotion regimes for least developed countries. Target 17.10 promotes a universal, rules-based, open, non-discriminatory, and equitable multilateral trading system under the World Trade Organization. Target 17.11 seeks to significantly increase the exports of developing countries, in particular with a view to doubling the least developed countries' share of global exports by 2020 (United Nations, n.d.b). However, such targets concerning foreign direct investment (FDI) and trade appear to replicate the neoliberal, export-driven development path critiqued throughout this book through encouraging increased international trade and foreign investment with no acknowledgment of ecologically unequal exchange nor the socio-ecological issues surrounding foreign investment.

Overall, a close reading of the above-mentioned SDGs reveals that while foreign investment and growth of the financial sector are strongly encouraged by the SDGs, increased environmental[1] and social regulations in these sectors are not. Without strongly and verifiably regulating the main economic actors driving growth, such as corporations, banks, and institutional investors, both environmental degradation and environmental injustices are likely to occur. Further, it is difficult to justify increased international trade when international trade accounts for a significant portion of environmental degradation, increased carbon emissions, and pollution and waste from shipping. Truly environmentally sustainable finance and transnational supply chains may well be impossible under capitalism, where profits are built on negative externalities and the capitalization of the free gifts of Nature. However, if the SDGs must encourage international trade, they should encourage fair trade practices built upon environmentally sustainable supply chains whose social and environmental practices can be regulated and verified.

The United Nations Conference on Climate Change CoP26 at Glasgow

The most recent United Nations Climate Change Conference, otherwise known as COP26, occurred in Glasgow in the late Fall of 2021. The Paris Agreement of 2015 marked the most significant international agreement on climate change with nearly every country in the world agreeing to limit global warming to below 2°C (while aiming for 1.5°C). Under the Paris Agreement, countries committed to national plans that detailed how they would reduce their emissions, known as Nationally Determined Contributions, or "NDCs." Countries agreed to meet every five years with updated plans that reflect their highest possible ambition at the time. COP26 Glasgow was the most recent set of negotiations (United Nations Climate Change, n.d.).

While such international diplomatic success is necessary, there are good reasons to question whether or not it is sufficient. Significantly, the accord is voluntary. There are repercussions neither for leaving the accord nor for missing one's targets. Tellingly, in the years since the agreement, the emissions that trap heat in Earth's atmosphere have continued to rise (Irfan, 2021a). By the end of COP26, 151 countries had submitted new climate plans (NDCs) to slash their emissions by 2030. To keep the goal of limiting temperature rise to 1.5°C within reach, global emissions must be cut in half by 2030. However, according to the World Resources Institute (Mountford et al., 2021), the actual commitments to deep cuts in GHG emissions necessary by 2030 are lacking.

Countries in the Global South, island nations, and grassroots activists have pushed for years to make climate justice a central issue addressed in the conferences. Climate debt is merely another ecological debt in the long list of debts, but one with perhaps the most alarming repercussions. The core issue of climate injustice is that wealthy countries have benefited from the production and consumption of fossil fuels while the poorest countries, which are the least responsible, are disproportionately likely to suffer the severest costs. The United States is by far the largest cumulative emitter of greenhouse gases since the Industrial Revolution, followed by China, the former Soviet Union, Germany, and the UK. Consequently, most of the warming that is witnessed today is due to wealthier countries (Irfan, 2019).

However, it is unlikely that climate injustices will be adequately addressed through UN Conferences on Climate Change. For one, despite promises, they have already accrued a poor record of being addressed. For example, in terms of climate finance, in 2009, rich nations committed to mobilize $100 billion a year by 2020 to support climate efforts in developing countries. However, developed countries failed to meet that goal in 2020; recent estimates showed total climate finance reached only $79.6 billion in 2019. Developed countries did agree to double funding for adaptation by 2025, which would amount to at least $40 billion. However, adaptation to climate is only part of the picture of climate injustice. The other issue is the loss and damage already done to lives, livelihoods, and environments caused by climate change. While a number of countries advocated for CoP26 to create a new finance facility dedicated to the loss and damage, they faced pushback by developed nations such as the United States (Mountford et al., 2021).

In addition, in CoP26, other issues plaguing the goal of climate justice emerged. To meet the goal of keeping global warming below 1.5°C by 2050, global emissions must be brought to zero by 2050. However, more than 130 countries will likely rely on *net-zero* emissions goals by 2050, including the United States, New Zealand, Costa Rica, Japan, the EU, Russia, Saudi Arabia, and Argentina (Irfan, 2021b). Central to meeting such goals, countries are pricing carbon dioxide emissions and creating accounting mechanisms for reducing them, such as through credits or offsets that are traded with other countries. Under Article 6 of the Paris Agreement, wealthier countries can compensate for their higher emissions by activities such as financing clean energy in developing countries or restoring carbon-absorbing ecosystems (Irfan, 2021a). CoP26 created a regulated and expanded global carbon trading market that allows countries to partially meet their climate targets by buying credits representing emission cuts by others (Lakhani, 2021). However, these developments continue historical patterns of shifting environmental burdens onto the poorest and most marginalized. For one, critics have noted that carbon trading was heavily promoted by big polluters at COP26, with more than 500 fossil fuel lobbyists, affiliated with some of the world's biggest oil and gas companies, granted access to COP26. Meanwhile, indigenous people and their traditional knowledge on sustainability practices were mostly excluded or sidelined (Lakhani, 2021). The central issue, according to critics, is that carbon markets incentivize countries and corporations to offset rather than actually cut emissions through investing in "green energy" projects. However, green energy projects, like biofuel monocrops and hydroelectric dams, are often linked to environmental destruction and accumulation by dispossession. Further, critics argue that carbon credit schemes threaten to appropriate the land, forests, and rivers relied upon by indigenous and local communities. An expanded carbon market, with more countries and industries participating, could further endanger indigenous lands and livelihoods (Lakhani, 2021). According to the Declaration of Members of the Indigenous Peoples' Biocultural Climate Change Assessment (IPCCA), such climate policies are *false solutions*, reflecting neoliberal mainstream policies pushed by a wealthy elite to allow extractive industries and agroindustrial activities to continue business-as-usual (IPCCA, n.d.).

The fears of indigenous and other local communities are not unfounded—previous schemes for conservation and carbon sequestration have led to forms of land grabbing. In fact, the land grabbing literature identifies the specific pattern of green grabbing. Green grabbing is defined as the appropriation of land and Nature for environmental ends (Vigil, 2018). For example, indigenous groups have strongly criticized REDD+, which stands for Reducing Emissions from Deforestation and Forest Degradation in developing countries (REDD) and includes conservation, sustainable forest management, and the enhancement of carbon stocks (the +). An international initiative negotiated under the United Nations Framework Convention on Climate Change (UNFCCC), REDD+ has been proposed as a central strategy for mitigating climate change in forests (Cabello & Gilbertson, n.d.).

However, as many remaining forests are found on indigenous lands (due to their stewardship) indigenous groups such as the IPCCA argue that REDD+ projects directly target indigenous peoples and their territories, violate indigenous governance systems, further concentrate control over forests into the hands of State institutions, block indigenous peoples' and local communities' customary use of their forests, and negatively impact traditional forest-related knowledge, food sovereignty and food security, and traditional healthcare systems. Further, the IPCCA argues that the drivers of forest loss and forest-land grabbing are not addressed by REDD+, noting that governments that are elaborating REDD+ policies are also promoting economic sectors such as cattle ranching, bio-energy, mining, oil exploration, and agro-industrial monocultures. In other words, extractivism, the main driver of forest loss in the Global South, continues unchecked (IPCCA, n.d.).

Chomba et al. (2015) found that, due to land tenure established by colonial and post-colonial land policies that left the majority of local people with little or no land entitlement, REDD+ initiatives concentrated benefits in the hands of elites and reinforced inequality. Kijazi (2015) found that climate initiatives for carbon capture in the Mount Kilimanjaro area were top-down, exclusionary and resulted in the centralization of forests and a renewed form of "fortress conservation." Another study found that out of 100 REDD pilot projects—almost all of them connected with carbon trading—many involved land grabs, evictions, human rights violations, fraud, and militarization (Cabello and Gilbertson, n.d.). Green grabs in general result in the eviction of peasant and indigenous communities while facilitating the entry of extractive industries, plantations, and industrial ecotourism in places like Chiapas, Mexico (Rocheleau, 2015).

Conclusion

The architecture of ecological imperialism is deeply embedded in the pillars of the global economy, the political and legal structures that support it, and in the cultural and ideological stances that define fundamental concepts such as sustainability, development, and progress. As a critical evaluation of the UN SDGs and most recent UN Conference on Climate Change (CoP26) demonstrates, ecological imperialism, having generated the problem, now infiltrates some of the most prominent, international solutions. Due to the global scale of such issues like climate change, international negotiations are vital but in the face of corporate influence and government commitment to economic growth above social and ecological concerns, only pressure from below can provide any real counternarrative. Ultimately, academics, grassroots environmental and social movements, indigenous communities, and voices from the Global South must continuously critique and actively resist proposed solutions that inadequately address scientifically established planetary boundaries, extractivism, ecological debt, an international trading system built on ecologically unequal exchange, the power of investors over local communities, the funneling of profits to the financial sector based upon the capitalization of free gifts of Nature, and the dispossession of land and destruction of livelihoods of the impoverished and marginalized.

As a final note, one that surely necessitates its own book, the voices that offer the sharpest critiques of top-down solutions also offer the most important and innovative solutions, alternatives, and resistances. Grassroots solutions arise from local communities directly affected, with a first-hand experience of their own needs and local realities of marginalization and dispossession. International peasant movements such as Via Campesina, the landless workers' movements such as Brazil's Landless Workers Movement (MST), and others bring to the forefront the environmental and social problems facing local communities, while pushing for food sovereignty, preservation of biodiversity and indigenous knowledge, climate and environmental justice, agrarian reform, agroecology, and peasants' rights. Local communities and indigenous communities, such as the Standing Rock Sioux Tribe resistance against the Dakota Access pipelines, are at the forefront of struggles against extractivism throughout the Global South and Global North. While fossil fuel interests still maintained heavy influence at negotiations like CoP26 at Glasgow, directly influencing government stances themselves (De La Garza, 2021), hundreds of environmental and land activists are murdered. The chasm between top-down initiatives and grassroots movements is wide.

References

Cabello, J., & Gilbertson, T. (n.d.). *NO REDD!* No REDD. Retrieved January 13, 2022, from http://no-redd.com/wp-content/uploads/2015/01/REDDreaderEN.pdf

Chomba, S., Kariuki, J., Lund, J.F., & Sinclair, F. (2015). Roots of inequity: How the implementation of REDD+ reinforces past injustices. *Land Use Policy, 50*, 202–213.

de la Garza, A. (2021, October 27). COP26's organizers can't get rid of big oil's influence. *Time Magazine*. https://time.com/6110667/fossil-fuel-companies-cop26-influence/

Frame, M.L., McDowell, W.G., & Fitzpatrick, E.T. (2021). Ecological contradictions of the UN Sustainable Development Goals in Malaysia. *The Journal of Environment and Development, 0*, 1–34. https://doi.org/10.1177/10704965211060296

IPCCA. (n.d.). *IPCCA. Indigenous peoples' biocultural climate change assessment initiative declaration of members of the indigenous peoples*. Global Forest Coalition. Retrieved January 13, 2022, from https://globalforestcoalition.org/wp-content/uploads/2011/12/IPCCA-Declaration-Durban-F.pdf

Irfan, U. (2019). Climate change: Animation shows US leading the world in carbon emissions. *Vox*. Retrieved December 30, 2021, from https://www.vox.com/energy-and-environment/2019/4/24/18512804/climate-change-united-states-china-emissions

Irfan, U. (2021a). COP26: Earth's fate is at stake at a UN climate conference in Glasgow. *Vox*. https://www.vox.com/22714800/cop26-un-climate-change-conference-glasgow-explained

Irfan, U. (2021b). COP26: The problem of targeting "net zero" greenhouse gas emissions. *Vox*. Retrieved January 11, 2022, from https://www.vox.com/22737140/un-cop26-climate-change-net-zero-emissions-carbon-offsets

Kijazi, M. (2015). Climate emergency, carbon capture and coercive conservation on Mt. Kilimanjaro. In M. Leach & I. Scoones (Eds.), *Carbon conflicts and forest landscapes in Africa* (pp. 58–78). London: Routledge.

Lakhani, N. (2021). 'A death sentence': Indigenous climate activists denounce Cop26 deal. *The Guardian*. https://www.theguardian.com/environment/2021/nov/16/indigenous-climate-activists-cop26-endangers-native-communities

Mountford, H., Hammond, T., Waskow, D., Gonzalez, L., Gajjar, C., Cogswell, N., Hold, M., Fransen, T., Bergen, M., & Gerholdt, R. (2021). COP26: Key outcomes from the UN Climate talks in Glasgow. World Resources Institute. Retrieved December 30, 2021, from https://www.wri.org/insights/cop26-key-outcomes-un-climate-talks-glasgow

Osborne, T., Bellante, L., & von Hedemann, N. (2014). Indigenous peoples and REDD+: A critical perspective. Indigenous People's Biocultural Climate Change Assessment Initiative.

Rocheleau, D.E. (2015). Networked, rooted and territorial: Green grabbing and resistance in Chiapas. *Journal of Peasant Studies, 42*(3–4), 695–723.

Sachs, J., & Ki-moon, B. (2015). *The age of sustainable development*. New York: Columbia University Press.

Vigil, S. (2018). Green grabbing-induced displacement. In R. McLeman & F. Gemenne, *Routledge handbook of environmental displacement and migration* (pp. 370–387). London: Routledge.

United Nations. (n.d.a). *Goal 8 | Department of Economic and Social Affairs*. Sustainable Development Goals. Retrieved January 13, 2022, from https://sdgs.un.org/goals/goal8

United Nations. (n.d.b). *Goal 17 | Department of Economic and Social Affairs*. Sustainable Development Goals. Retrieved January 13, 2022, from https://sdgs.un.org/goals/goal17

United Nations Climate Change. (n.d.). *What is a COP? – UN climate change conference*. COP26. Retrieved December 30, 2021, from https://ukcop26.org/uk-presidency/what-is-a-cop/

Note

1 In a paper written with colleagues on Malaysia and the ecological contradictions of the UN SDGs (Frame et al., 2021), we also found specific problems with the environmental targets themselves. While the indicators for the economic goals are well quantified, the environmental goals are not as precise, comprehensive, and verifiable. While economic goals promote growth and progress, ecological goals are largely about acceptable losses, rather than direct actions to improve the existing state of the environment, such as the need to increase populations and habitats. As such, the environment becomes a savings account that the SDGs allow to be steadily drawn down, one that is dwindling rapidly. Overall, we found a need for greater restorative environmental policies and strong, quantifiable environmental goals in the SDGs. Finally, we found that SDG environmental goals and economic goals do not reflect the precautionary principle. Given the high variability and uncertainty involved in ecosystem changes, climate changes, etc., the SDGs need to incorporate the possibility of tipping points and positive feedback loops. Environmental goals should be designed to be holistic and capture systemic losses. In contrast, the environmental indicators tend to be too narrowly focused to accurately benchmark environmental conditions, or so broadly defined that they are unquantifiable. As such, they run the risk of not systemically capturing environmental degradation, particularly with regard to uncertainty and risk, as well as long-term effects.

Index

Note: **Bold** page numbers refer to tables; *italic* page numbers refer to figures and page numbers followed by "n" denote endnotes.